Read over Christmas ... Dec 30th - ...17

dge

She was evidently a natural story-teller. She apparently disdained God & did not see the need for repentance or redemption. That's such a shame.

She was petulant, self-absorbed & duplicitous.

Some good info in here regarding writing & the daily life & even the business of writing.

Publishers really do get rich off of writers & don't seem to work as hard at it. Are they worth it? Do their connections, insights, suggestions & knowledge of the market validate them? Do they know the mkt. as well as they think?

Janice Holt Giles

Janice Holt Giles
A Writer's Life

Dianne Watkins Stuart

The University Press of Kentucky

Publication of this volume was made possible in part by a grant from the National Endowment for the Humanities.

Scholarly publisher for the Commonwealth, serving Bellarmine College, Berea College, Centre College of Kentucky, Eastern Kentucky University, The Filson Club Historical Society, Georgetown College, Kentucky Historical Society, Kentucky State University, Morehead State University, Murray State University, Northern Kentucky University, Transylvania University, University of Kentucky, University of Louisville, and Western Kentucky University.

Editorial and Sales Offices: The University Press of Kentucky
663 South Limestone Street, Lexington, Kentucky 40508-4008

99 00 01 02 5 4 3 2

Frontispiece: Janice Holt Giles, 1950

Library of Congress Cataloging-in-Publication Data

Stuart, Dianne Watkins.
Janet Holt Giles : a writer's life / Dianne Watkins Stuart.
p. cm.
Includes bibliographical references and index.
ISBN 0-8131-2095-0 (cloth : alk. paper)
1. Giles, Janice Holt. 2. Women novelists. Ameican—20th century—Biography. 3. Women novelists, American—Kentucrky—Biography. I. Title.
PS33513.I4628Z88 1988
813'.54—dc21
[b] 98-30125

This book is printed on acid-free recycled paper meeting the requirements of the American National Standard for Permanence of Paper for Printed Library Materials.

Manufactured in the United States of America

To Jim

Namaste

Contents

Preface

Kathy St. John, secretary and librarian of the First Baptist Church of Central City, Kentucky, had no idea she was directing a consequential adventure in my life when she handed me a book during my sophomore year of high school in 1956 and said, "Here, you'll like this." I *did* like the book, and the next and the next, written by Janice Holt Giles, whose first novel was published in 1950 and who, by 1956, had nine titles in print. I read them all and eagerly devoured each new book as it appeared in years to come.

I was fascinated with the strong, enduring character Hannah Fowler; the spirited, humorous Miss Willie; the courtship, marriage, and ridge life of Hod and Mary Pierce; the story of Giles's own experience moving from the city to a forty-acre farm in Kentucky; the strange religious sect called Shakers; and the adventurous tales of sturdy pioneers and their descendants in her historical fiction. I looked forward to Giles's books with great anticipation because I knew she would tell an excellent story in narrative filled with poetic imagery and always leave me with a happy ending. In spite of their trials, perils, and often tremendous difficulties, Giles's characters always endured—strengthened with faith and optimistic perseverance.

Years later, I began rereading Giles's novels and discussed *The Believers* with Penny Harrison at a Sunday afternoon tea in 1982. Neither Penny nor I suspected the events that would transpire after she told me that Janice Holt Giles had donated the greater part of her manuscript materials to Library Special Collections at Western Kentucky University in Bowling Green, where she had done much of her research.

After taking my five children to school, I visited the Kentucky Building, where Penny was archivist in the manuscripts division, and was captivated to hold in my hands the actual correspondence Giles had written and received from her editors and literary agency, as well as letters from her daughter and the courtship letters from Henry Giles.

I returned day after day and sat for hours mesmerized with Giles's personal papers until time to pick up my children. I will never forget the emotions I felt when I read the prophetic words in a letter from Henry Giles to Janice Moore three months after their meeting on a bus in Bowling Green. "Once I almost asked you if you ever tried writing poetry. Or at writing stories of any kind, but somehow I decided not to. *It seems you could write almost anything.*"

At the end of my second week of intrigue, Penny Harrison entered the room, discussing a graduate student assistantship with librarian Connie Mills; she casually mentioned that I should take some graduate courses and consider the assistantship. "Shh," I said, "let me read." But before I left, I inquired more about the job. By the next day, I was enrolled in the Folk Studies program and working in the building that housed the Giles manuscript collection. In June 1985 the faculty position of Education Curator of the Kentucky Museum, in the Kentucky Building, became available, and I was encouraged to apply. My employment in museum education for nearly a decade and my participation in the life study of Janice Holt Giles were serendipitous.

Elizabeth Hancock, Giles's daughter, and Pansy Phillips, illustrator of *A Little Better than Plumb,* visited the Kentucky Building in September 1988 to attend a Woman's Studies Conference during which a paper on Giles was presented. I was delighted to sit beside Libby Hancock at lunch and share with her my love of her mother's books and my appreciation for her manuscript materials. In talking to Libby about how interesting I found Henry Giles's correspondence and how apropos it was at that time, nearing the fiftieth year since the beginning of World War II, I said, "You should do something with your mother's letters." She replied, "*You* should do something with Mother's letters," and promised her support and assistance in every way. As a result, *Hello Janice: The Wartime Letters of Henry Giles* was published by the University Press of Kentucky in 1992.

During the reviewing and editing of the manuscript, I was introduced to Wade H. Hall, chairman of Humanities at Bellarmine College. Professor of English and avid collector of Kentucky books, Wade has great respect for Giles's writing. He had reviewed several of her novels for the *Louisville Courier-Journal* at the time of their appearance. His interest, encouragement, and suggestions for revisions were vital to the publication of *Hello Janice*.

In May 1991 I was invited to give a biographical presentation on Janice Holt Giles and also address sense of place in her writings at a symposium at Campbellsville College, Campbellsville, Kentucky, co-chaired by Wade Hall. During the two-day meeting, I spoke at length with Wade about Giles. He remarked, "*You* must write her biography. You know more about her than anybody."

In September 1991 I began traveling the state to present programs about Giles for the Kentucky Humanities Council Speakers Bureau.

During an evening in the Adair County Public Library I met Evelyn McCloud, a native of the region who had at one time lived with her seven children in a house belonging to Miss Piney, located at the foot of the Ray Williams Road where Henry Giles grew to manhood. Since Evelyn was "of the ridge," her friendship and introductions to people who knew the Gileses gained me acceptance and established immediate trust. Countless hours of interviews with ridge folks in Evelyn's company helped provide me with an intimate understanding of a talented author.

Five years after her death, Janice Holt Giles's story began to unfold before me not only through her written words in the manuscript collection but also through numerous personal interviews I conducted with family and friends using skills I had gained in the Folk Studies curriculum.

A fascinating part of pursuing the path of Giles's past was a journey westward to the region of her birth. I stood in front of Grandmother McGraw's house in Altus, Arkansas; walked around the small home in Kinta, Oklahoma, where John Albert Holt Jr. was born and *The Kinta Years* had its origin; visited her sister in Fort Smith; wandered through the yard where *The Plum Thicket* grew; knelt beside the graves of ancestors; gazed down the street in Charleston where Grandpa Holt led the annual Confederate parade; and sat in her daughter's home in Santa Fe surrounded by her grandsons. As I drove to Santa Fe, I was keenly empathetic to the many times Janice and Henry had traversed that great distance before the advent of air-conditioned cars and long, smooth stretches of interstate highways. I also made countless trips to Adair County to trace the trails of the Piney Ridge trilogy and seek out the day-to-day lifestyle where Giles lived in her middle and late years.

Although meticulous in using historical fact in her fiction, Giles sometimes stretched the truth in writing about herself. She created a self-image through sketches that presented a portrait often more rosy than realistic. The dramatic ups and downs of her life through some very difficult years are carefully concealed in skillfully chosen words. She later admitted that one of her autobiographical books "did not tell the whole truth, after all. It couldn't. It wouldn't do to read," but she allowed the truth to remain in her manuscript materials. In *Around Our House*, she vowed, "If I ever do write a family history, it is certain I shall be honest and that the ugly things in our background will have their place alongside the fine and honorable things."

Janice Holt Giles lived a quiet, somewhat reclusive life nestled in the ridges of Kentucky. Privacy was essential for the time she devoted to writing. She relished life surrounded by the beauty of the hills that gave her "a certain amount of peace, a certain quietude of spirit." The knolls and "sweet swelling valleys" provided her with a "stillness of soul" that enabled her to "gather" her "forces." That strength sustained her in later years when her health began to fail before the ridge became her final resting place.

On May 16, 1997, I sat on the porch of the log house at Spout Springs talking about Janice Holt Giles in an interview by Kelli Summers for Byron Crawford's "Kentucky Life," which is produced by Kentucky Educational Television. Responses to questions about Giles's life and her work flowed easily, but when I was asked, "Why are you writing the biography?" I made three attempts to answer and each time faltered. I did not have the answer. There were no words to explain something that has directed its own course since 1956. Through the years, Janice Holt Giles's inspiring words and enduring spirit have spoken to me so profoundly that I simply want to tell her story through the memories she left behind, in the pages of her letters and books and in the hearts of her family and friends.

Chronology

1905 March 28	Janice Meredith Holt was born in Altus, Arkansas, at the home of her maternal grandparents.
1909	The Holt family moved to Kinta, Oklahoma.
1917	The Holt family moved to Fort Smith, Arkansas.
1922	Janice graduated from Fort Smith High School.
1923 November 27	Janice married Otto Jackson Moore of Fort Smith, Arkansas.
1924 September 30	Birth of Janice's only child, Elizabeth Ann (Libby).
1933	Janice moved to Little Rock, Arkansas. Served as secretary and director of religious education for the Pulaski Heights Christian Church.
1936	Janice became director of children's work for the Arkansas-Louisiana Board of Missions.
1939 September 19	Janice divorced Otto J. Moore. Accepted position in Kentucky as director of religious education, First Christian Church in Frankfort.
1940 April 6	Death of John Albert Holt.
1941 August	Janice began work as secretary to the Dean of the Presbyterian Theological Seminary, Dr. Lewis J. Sherrill, Louisville, Kentucky.
1943 July 12	Janice departed Louisville around 2 P.M. on a Greyhound bus to visit an aunt in Texas. In Bowling Green, Henry Giles, of Adair County, became her seatmate for the remainder of her forty-eight-hour journey.
1943 July 19	Henry wrote his first letter to Janice in response to one he had received from her.
1944 July 30	Libby married Nash Hancock, a native of Finchville, Kentucky.
1945 October 11	Janice Moore married Henry Giles.
1946	Janice, at age forty-one, began writing her first novel at night while continuing to work at the seminary.

1947	Henry completed requirements for his high school diploma under the G.I. Bill and worked in Louisville as a machinist for International Harvester.
1948 April 10	Birth of Janice's first grandchild, Bartlett Neal Hancock.
1949	Westminster Press accepted and published Janice's first novel, *The Enduring Hills*.
1949 May 3	Birth of Janice's second grandchild, John Graham (Mike).
1949 May 30	Janice and Henry left Louisville for a forty-acre farm in Adair County, located within two miles of the area where Henry's ancestors settled in 1803.
1950 September 1	Birth of Janice's third grandchild, James Scott.
1951	Houghton Mifflin began publishing Giles's books.
1953	The Gileses moved to the 106-acre farm known as the Felix Price place.
1954	Pyramid Books published *Hill Man* under the pseudonym John Garth.
1954-57	In August 1954, Janice began writing a column for the *Campbellsville News-Journal,* "The Bookshelf." She changed the title of the column to "Around Our House" in January 1956. During this time Henry worked for the *News-Journal* three days a week. From 1957 to 1970, he also wrote "Spout Springs Splashes" for the *Adair County News.*
1957-58	Janice and Henry purchased four old log structures to use in building a house on their seventy-six acres in Spout Springs Hollow. They moved into the house in August 1958.
1961	North Adair County received telephone service.
1963 August 7	Death of Lucy McGraw Holt.
1967	The log house had to be moved 1,200 feet "up the creek and across the field" because of the construction of a flood control dam on the Upper Green River.
1979 June 1	Janice Holt Giles died of congestive heart failure at dawn in the Taylor County Hospital.
1986 October 1	Death of Henry Earl Giles. He was buried next to Janice in the Caldwell Chapel Separate Baptist Church cemetery, Knifley, Kentucky.

1
Words and Music
1899-1901

In the fall of 1960, Janice Holt Giles, successful author of twelve books, was invited to return to her native state of Arkansas to address the Library Association. When asked "How did you become a writer?" she began her remarks with a simplified "recipe": "Take one girl child, let her be born to schoolteacher parents; endow her with great curiosity and imagination and a love of words; provide her with freedom to read and express herself; give her enough hard knocks to make her tough; let every major job she ever has provide her with challenging associations and unbelievable opportunities for developing her own latent abilities; and finally let her marry Henry Giles and through him be introduced to her perfect writing environment. Mix and stir well, bake at high heat and you have this novelist."

Through the years, family members fondly told and retold the tale of Janice's parents' courtship. The story began when John Holt rode away from his childhood home in Charleston, Arkansas, on a late October day in 1899 and directed his spirited bay mare toward the hills of Altus. The small hamlet, fifteen miles to the northeast and across the Arkansas River in Franklin County, had originally been settled by a small cluster of German immigrants and had grown to nearly five hundred residents.

At age twenty-eight John had received his first teaching assignment. When he arrived in Altus, he inquired about a place to board and was directed to a large, white clapboard house. Satisfied with the arrangements, he carried his clothing and personal items up the stairs and down a wide corridor to his room, then hurried back downstairs to locate a livery stable for his mare.

The next day John was invited by his landlady to join a group of youths who were planning a musical evening in her home. Soon after he arrived with his fiddle in hand, a young woman struck a series of chords on the piano and the music began. Strains of "Soldier's Joy," "Annie Laurie," "Sallie Stuck a Needle in Her Heel, by Joe," "The Rose of Tralee," "Kathleen Mavoureen," and other favorites were played in rapid succession.

John's attention was repeatedly drawn to one of the young ladies in the center of the room. Her ivory shirtwaist with narrow emerald stripes billowed gracefully about her tiny frame and shimmered in the light. A satin ribbon of the same rich green wound around the high neckline of her dress and looped into a small bow. When she glanced his way, John looked into the most intriguing eyes he had ever seen, laughing eyes as clear and blue as unclouded sky. Her thick, brown hair, highlighted with hints of red, was swept away from her face and swirled on top of her head. Each time John looked at her, she was laughing and talking to a cluster of gentlemen surrounding her. She was clearly the most popular girl in the room.

The music stopped and a tap on his shoulder returned John's attention to the group around the piano. A young man extended his hand. "My name is Fred McGraw," he said. "I sure do like the way you handle that violin!" Declaring himself "a fiddler of sorts," Fred had tried all evening to match the skill of the newcomer. John Holt warmed to Fred McGraw immediately and listened intently as he explained how his family often gathered in their parlor for musical entertainment. Two of his sisters played the piano and one the mandolin and guitar. All of the McGraws loved to sing.

Fred inquired where John was staying and asked if he would consider sharing a room at his house. At age twenty-five, Fred, the fifth of ten children, was working as a bookkeeper for the Western Coal and Mining Company, living at home and paying board. "I could have my mother put another bed in my room for you," he said.

The McGraw's two-story steamboat Gothic house with a wraparound porch was already crowded with eight children still at home, but Fred knew his request to include one more person would not addle his proficient mother. He was right. Catherine McGraw did not hesitate a moment and warmly welcomed the new teacher into her home.

At dusk on the first evening, daughter Mamie went into the parlor and began to play hymns at the piano. Catherine slipped into the room and started singing "There is a Fountain Filled with Blood." Hearing the music, Fred told John to grab his violin. Together they bolted down the steps and into the parlor, where John could not conceal his profound surprise and delight. Seated at the piano was the young woman who had played the night he met Fred, and beside her stood the beautiful girl who had attracted and held his absolute attention.

Fred introduced John to each of his brothers and sisters. When he heard, "And this is Lucy," John could only see her teasing, azure eyes.

Taking her hand, he smiled and whispered, "I'm very pleased to meet you, Miss Lucy." Completely smitten, he meant it.

John and Fred often joined his sisters to fill the McGraw house with music. During the lively tunes, Catherine sometimes lifted her skirts slightly above her ankles, threw back her head, and gracefully danced a polka or schottische around the room. Swirling and laughing, she whirled until shortness of breath propelled her one-hundred-and-seventy-pound frame in the direction of an overstuffed chair.

Catherine had kept a diary since the day she married Dan McGraw. On November 6, 1899, a few days after the arrival of Fred's new friend, she recorded: "Mr. John Holt came to board with us last Thursday the 2nd. He commences teaching school today." It was the first mention of John Holt, but it would not be the last.

Catherine Ophelia Babb had met Daniel Murdock McGraw in the summer of 1871 at a party in the home of mutual friends. After a brief courtship, the young couple married in the parlor of her home on Dan's twenty-second birthday, January 22, 1872. At the time of their wedding, Catherine was seventeen years old, stood barely over five feet tall, and weighed ninety pounds.

The second eldest of five daughters and one son, Catherine had enjoyed life in a large, two-story antebellum home in Byhalia, Mississippi, where lavish house parties and balls were catered by numerous servants. Those memories were mixed with the horror her family experienced and the losses they suffered as Yankee soldiers swarmed and fought through their land during the Civil War. Dan's family had a small landholding in northern Mississippi, not far from Byhalia, which also had been ravaged by the cruelty of Yankee soldiers.

In the early years of their marriage, Catherine and Dan moved from one tenant farm to another as Dan hired out as a farm laborer and Catherine taught in the district school. In 1878, with three children to support, Dan wrote to a friend describing their struggle: "It is the hardest time down here that you ever saw. The merchants are closing out everybody that can't pay but what the people are to do I don't know. I was strongly in the notion of going West, either to Texas or Arkansas but I hear of as much or more complaint of hard times there so I concluded to remain here awhile longer. I think with Catherine's assistance teaching we will make something next year."

In spite of his conflicting thoughts concerning a venture west, Dan soon succumbed to the lure of homesteaders and traveled to western Arkansas to examine prospects. In 1879 he filed a claim in Cass, Arkansas, located at the foothills of the Ozark Mountains, built a log cabin, and sent for his wife and children.

At age twenty-four, traveling alone with three small children and expecting a fourth, Catherine boarded a train bound for Arkansas. When she arrived, she settled her family into the cabin with a pounded dirt floor and a window and door covered with deerskin. She carried water from the mountain stream that flowed behind her house and prepared meals over an open-hearth fire. The young housewife made and mended the clothing she washed over steaming kettles of hand-carried water, milked the cow, churned butter, preserved food, baked bread, and tended chickens as well as children.

Dan McGraw planted and harvested corn crops, raised vegetable gardens, and supplied the table with wild game from the forest and fish from the stream. He also hired out as a farm laborer, sowing wheat, hoeing corn, or picking cotton to earn extra cash.

In the cabin, assisted by her husband, Catherine gave birth to their fourth child. In addition to the domestic demands of her primitive household, she taught basic subjects to her children and ten additional students whose parents paid her one dollar per month. A strong woman imbued with a happy spirit, Catherine's hands were never idle and her voice seldom quiet. She was known to sing while she worked during the day as well as when she rocked her babies at night. Dan vowed his wife even sang hymns to ease the pain of childbirth.

Following three years of exhausting work on their homestead, Dan became deputy sheriff of Franklin County, Arkansas, and moved his family into a rental house in town, where their fifth child, Lucy Elizabeth, was born October 6, 1882.

In the fall of 1885, Dan and Catherine became house parents to twenty-five girls at the Central Collegiate Institute in Altus, Arkansas, a boarding school established by the Reverend Isham L. Burrow, a Methodist minister from Tennessee. Soon after their move into the rambling, seventeen-room dormitory, Catherine gave birth to a fourth daughter.

Dan decided one school term was enough to parent twenty-nine girls and sought the office of surveyor of Franklin County. After his election, he spent his tenure riding horseback over the county trails with surveying instruments in his saddlebags. Catherine soon bore their eighth child, a son, and resumed teaching in the small district schools.

Since age twelve Catherine and Dan's oldest child, Percy Pinckney, affectionately called "Brother," had been working after school and on Saturdays as a printer's devil for the weekly newspaper, the *Ozark Democrat*. At fifteen he purchased a newspaper hand press and began publishing his own weekly, the *Altus Albion*. Catherine's diary reveals that, in addition to teaching school, she wrote articles for the *Altus Albion* and traveled around town taking catalog orders for corsets.

During the 1890s, Dan McGraw was employed by the Western Coal and Mining Company and eventually became superintendent. Catherine continued to teach and, in 1893, was named principal of the school in Altus. Four years later, at age forty-three, she gave birth to her thirteenth child; ten of her children survived to maturity. A diligent worker and devoted mother, Catherine was possessed with a positive spirit and an abiding faith. It was said that her "every thought was governed by her efforts to be a good Christian." Each of the McGraw children was labeled a "bull-headed individualist" with Lucy receiving an additional dubbing as "a little imp of Satan."

Lucy Elizabeth McGraw was captivated by John Holt from the moment she first saw him, as was every other available maiden in Altus. A dashing dresser with a pleasant sense of humor and a roguish twinkle, the new schoolteacher danced in all their dreams. Lucy was determined to be the first one in the buggy seat by his side.

In early June, John invited Lucy's sister, Sallie, to ride with him to a picnic to be held at nearby Horsehead Creek. Lucy couldn't stand it. Shortly after everyone arrived at the picnic site, she and several other girls wandered away from the group. They followed a narrow path to the edge of a cliff and entered a cave. As soon as they were missed, John set out in search of them.

As their teacher neared the path, one of the girls called out, "Come quick, Lucy's got her foot hung in a crack at the back of the cave. We can't get her loose!" John raced to the opening of the cave and entered it. Within minutes, he reappeared at the path, carrying Lucy.

Lucy's long skirt and layers of petticoats trailed gracefully over her tiny feet and ankles. Her light brown hair, sparkling with red glints in the sunlight, was coming loose from the pins on top of her head, and her translucent cheeks were slightly flushed. The young professor gently placed Lucy on a quilt that had been spread out on the grass. Looking up into the faces of the other students who gathered around, he explained, "She fainted when I had to free her foot. She must have been suffering greatly."

John Holt gathered Lucy in his arms and carried her down the hillside. He placed her in his buggy with the promise, "I'll have you home in no time, Miss Lucy."

Of course, Lucy was pretending just to get John Holt's attention—and John knew it. He later admitted to her, "You were the prettiest girl I ever saw, Lucy McGraw, and the most popular. I fell in love with you the first time I saw you, but I didn't think an old bachelor like me would have a chance with you!" To Lucy, John Albert Holt was the most fascinating man she had ever encountered, and she had intended from their first meeting to have him for her own.

At the end of the school term, John returned to his family's home in Charleston. On Thursday, October 11, 1900, Catherine entered in her diary, "Mr. Holt & his sister spent from last Friday till Monday with us." What she omitted was that Lucy's eighteenth birthday had been Saturday, October 6.

John returned to Altus the first of November to begin his second school term. His name, always "Mr. Holt," persistently appeared in Catherine's diary as he and Lucy attended musicals and theatricals at the college, sat in the parlor on Sunday evenings talking and eating chocolates, and provided "good music" with Fred, which Catherine "enjoyed very much."

John left for Charleston when the spring term ended in April. When he returned to see Lucy on May 4, 1901, an excited Catherine posted: "Mr. Holt came over—*bro't Lucy a ring!* Oh, dear! The only encouraging tho't about it is that since she has discarded two or three others *this* may not be the one she wants either." Lucy had broken a previous engagement to an eminently suitable young man, of whom Catherine and Dan approved. Her parents were unaware that she had broken it because of her feelings for John Holt.

Catherine made no comment explaining her opposition to "Mr. Holt." Perhaps it was because John was eleven years older than Lucy or that the McGraws, who had come from old, established families of culture in the Deep South, felt they were superior to the families they found in the new frontier, including the Holts of Charleston. Whatever the reason for her parents' reluctance, Lucy proudly wore an opal engagement ring with tiny diamonds on either side and spoke excitedly of September wedding plans. The change in those plans is best expressed in her mother's diary entry for Saturday night, August 31, 1901.

"Well, old Journal, how the unexpected transpires. I am alone tonight with only five children left. Papa went to Mississippi last Sunday night, having a telegram that day (25th) that his father was dying. Yesterday Lucy & Mr. Holt married. She had told us they would marry the last of September & I had her some nice dresses made. Florence just sent one the day before, but she disappointed us all. He walked in suddenly yesterday morning, wanted to marry her in a few minutes. Bro. Burrow was over in his room then. Well, of course, I was powerless, tho' Mamie & I said everything we could to persuade them to wait at least until Papa came home, but no. Well, I did not *consent* to their marriage but couldn't help myself & pray God to help them."

Many years later, John and Lucy's daughter, Janice Holt Giles, would write about her mother and give this description of Lucy: "At eighteen she was lovely to look at, with Grandmother's soft, fine, brown hair, clear blue eyes and delicate white skin. But Lordy, what a fiery, unpredictable young thing she was! Like mercury, rolling free! Like a prairie fire, fast burning and swift! Like river rapids, boxed in a narrow stream bed! Volatile, quick, high-tempered, merry, gay, nervous, quick-silvery, and courageous beyond all ordinary meaning of the word. She loved every minute of life, ate it down greedily, burped with indigestion, and went on to swallow whole the next bite! Lucy Elizabeth! My mother!"

2
Prairie Winds
1901-1917

Immediately following their wedding, John and Lucy left for Charleston to visit his parents, Mary Tolleson and James Knox Polk Holt, who, like the McGraws, had raised a family of ten children. The young couple's visit was brief as John had contracted to teach school in Ozark, Arkansas, a small town five miles west of Altus.

After teaching one year in Ozark, John received a better offer in a new system. In 1901 the Department of the Interior made systematic provisions for the education of white children in the Indian Territory and established public schools in the incorporated towns. The superintendent at Ozark, whom John admired very much, was one of the first appointed teachers. He, in turn, recruited John to teach the second year of the newly created public school in Dow. After considering the increase in salary and greater opportunities for advancement, John and Lucy made the decision to leave Arkansas.

Catherine's diary ended August 20, 1902, with the brief words, "Mr. Holt is going to Indian Territory to teach—$60 a month." The effervescent, oft mischievous Lucy Elizabeth would be moving seventy-five miles away, across the Sans Bois Mountains, to an area her parents referred to as "wild and lawless country." In the pioneering spirit of her mother, Lucy McGraw Holt, age nineteen, left the security of her parents' nearby home and followed her husband into the rough frontier.

When the couple moved into a three-room rental house, Lucy was beginning to show her first pregnancy. In January 1903, she almost lost her life when she delivered a stillborn son. Critically ill, Lucy remained in bed for a week with her mother at her side. Before Catherine left, she made her daughter promise that before the birth of the next baby she would travel home to Altus.

Soon after the move to Dow, John Holt met John Snodgrass, manager of Seoman's Department Store. When John Snodgrass learned the professor's wife had lost a baby, he sent his wife, Annabelle, to visit her. Annabelle took a freshly baked pie to the Holts' house and offered to help Lucy in any way she could. Having herself given birth to a son six months previously, Annabelle had great empathy for Lucy. The act of kindness was the beginning of a lifelong friendship.

John Holt taught one school term in Dow and was again offered an increase in salary if he would accept a different position in the same school district. Without hesitation, he and Lucy moved the short distance to Haileyville. Lucy was soon expecting another child and, heeding her mother's advice, traveled home to Altus for the last six weeks of her pregnancy where she delivered a nine-pound baby girl on the morning of March 28, 1905.

The baby received her name from the title of a book her mother had been reading as she whiled away the waiting time preceding birth. The book, published in 1899, was Paul Leicester Ford's popular, romantic Revolutionary War novel, *Janice Meredith*. The infant was to have been named Mary Catherine, after her two grandmothers; however, the sound of the words and the beautifully scrolled letters on the book's cover so impressed young Lucy that she changed the baby's intended name to that of the impetuous heroine in the novel.

After two years in Haileyville, John Holt moved his family to Howe, a small mining town. During that tenure, Lucy gave birth to a second baby girl, Mary Catherine, on July 9, 1907, at her parents' recently purchased summer home in Paris, Arkansas.

In 1909, John was named principal of the new school in Kinta, Oklahoma. With their two young daughters, John and Lucy left Howe and moved to Kinta, a town of about three hundred residents situated in the middle of the prairie. The first settlers of Kinta had built a string of small log cabins along Beaver Creek, habitat to the animals for which it was named. When the Holts arrived in 1909, the town contained several stores, a blacksmith shop, two churches, and the new red brick schoolhouse where John would be principal.

Oklahoma, previously unorganized western territory, had become the forty-sixth state of the Union in 1907. The Five Civilized Tribes of the area—Cherokee, Choctaw, Chickasaw, Creek, and Seminole—were designated into nations, each of which established its own legislature and elected a principal chief or governor. Kinta, meaning *beaver* in Choctaw, was the capital of the Choctaw Nation.

On Saturdays in Kinta, farmers, Indians, and cowhands loitered along the main street and shopped for supplies. Occasionally throughout the year, peddlers appeared in their wagons loaded with goods. In the springtime, large, brightly painted wagons teeming with bands of gypsies halted at the edge of town where the wanderers camped in the sparse thickets. The gypsy men were tinkers who went from house to house offering to sharpen knives and scissors and to sell and repair tinware. The dark-skinned women in their tawdry clothing were fortune tellers and spun tales of fate by reading cards and palms.

Fort Smith, Arkansas, was about one hundred miles northeast of Kinta and across the Arkansas River, which divided the state from Oklahoma. The Fort Smith and Western Railroad connected Kinta with the outside world by supplying the daily paper, the *Southwest American*, as well as ice in the summer and coal in the winter. Twice a week the train delivered bakery bread and other commodities to the small community.

Lucy was four months pregnant when she and John traveled with their two small daughters from Fort Smith to Kinta on the morning train in August 1909. John hired a hack from the Beaver Hotel to transport them from the depot along the narrow dirt road to the home they would know for the next six years.

The four-room white frame house with red trim around the windows and doors had a sitting room and a bedroom across the front and a dining room and kitchen in an ell at the rear. A porch extended across the front of the house, and a back porch filled the corner of the ell. The house did not have electricity, plumbing, or closets. Lucy strung a curtain to conceal their clothing in a corner of the bedroom that contained two iron beds. She cooked on a large black woodstove and kneaded bread dough on a cabinet John fashioned from furniture crates. Water was drawn from an unhoused well, kerosene lamps provided light, and necessary trips were made to an outhouse, which they called "the closet."

The yard around the house was bare and baked hard by the sun. There were no trees to buffer the wind or to offer shade from the blistering heat that beat down on the flat prairie. Beyond the backyard, a fenced lot contained a stock barn, a corncrib, a chicken house, and a smokehouse. John acquired chickens, a pig, and a cow that Lucy milked. Each year they lived in Kinta, John raised a large vegetable garden.

About their house, Janice later wrote: "My father and mother never did put too much emphasis on home furnishings. Our home was always a little skimpily and raggedly put together. The essentials were comfortable beds and chairs, a good lamp or two, a stove that would cook the meals, and rugs and curtains and fancy doodads just didn't matter. Lucy McGraw never had a complete set of dishes but couldn't have cared less. Money, all her life, was better spent on books and music, travel and having fun than in any other way. . . . Housekeeping bored her. She was the world's best homemaker, for it was warm and radiant with love, but she was the world's poorest housekeeper. How she loved for my father to come in from school and say, 'Lucy, let's go for a ride.' How quickly she could shove a kettle of preserves to the back of the stove, step into her riding habit, and go for a long gallop over the prairie. And how little it bothered her to leave beds unmade, dishes unwashed, clothes unironed, and gather at a moment's notice all the things needed for an overnight camp to fish. 'Pooh,' she'd say, 'they'll wait. This chance to fish won't.'"

The daughter of Green McCurtain, a full-blood Choctaw and the governor of his nation, lived across the road from the Holts. Lena McCurtain and her husband, Herbert Moore, had three children who became inseparable playmates to the Holt children: Corinne Moore was five; Janice, four; Inez Moore was three; Mary Catherine, two; their son, Green McCurtain Moore, was less than a year old.

Five months after the move to Kinta, Lucy gave birth to John Albert Holt Jr. on January 11, 1910, only thirty minutes past his father's thirty-ninth birthday. Long known for her determination, Lucy tried her best to bring the baby on the tenth, but John Jr. had his own way, perhaps already exhibiting a trait inherited from his mother. The ten-pound infant was Lucy's first delivery without the assistance of her mother, but she was attended by the local physician, Dr. Johnson. The Moores' second son, Herbert M. Moore Jr., was born soon after John. Perfectly matched playmates, the Holt and Moore children were together constantly.

Since her teen years, Lucy had suffered migraine headaches that often forced her to bed for several days. During those intense times of pain and nausea, the children were instructed to be extremely quiet and not cause any disturbance. A favorite "quiet play" was paper dolls. When the new issues of *Sears and Roebuck*, the *National Cloak and Suit*, and the *Bellas, Hess* arrived, the outdated copies were given to the girls. Instead of having different costumes to put on a single paper doll like the manufactured ones, Janice and Corinne cut out numerous women to represent the same person. To change a dress, a different cutout would be selected. If the play character was going out on a winter day, a cutout was chosen wearing a winter coat. They did the same for paper doll children, because the women *always* had children.

Janice was the one invariably appointed to make up the stories. She determined the size of the fantasy families, the places they lived, where they traveled, and when they shopped, went to church, attended weddings, or had weddings. Gifted with a vivid imagination, Janice created dramas with interesting family names set in distant, romantic places. "They all went to Paris," Mary Catherine said. "I suppose Janice had read something about Paris, France, but I don't suppose we knew it was across the ocean because I don't remember us ever having them on boats!"

When John was five years old, Lucy began teaching school and assigned her children house chores. Janice and Mary Catherine took turns doing the dishes. Without indoor plumbing, water was drawn from the well, carried to the kitchen, and heated on the stove. Whoever washed the dishes had to also sweep the floor while the other finished drying the dishes and put them away. When Janice washed, she would stubbornly hold back a fork and call out, "Mama, make Mary Catherine come back and dry this fork. She's left a fork!" Lucy had to intervene so both girls could leave the kitchen at the same time to go play.

To Janice, Mary was a "truly good child with a loving heart and an amiable disposition." She described herself as "strong willed and stubborn, defiant and rebellious to the point of folly." Janice defined the Holt genes as "even-tempered, rather easy-going," and the McGraw traits as "volatile, high-tempered, and easily angered." "From the day I was born," Janice wrote, "there was a clashing of wills between Lucy McGraw and me because we are as much alike in temperament as two peas in a pod. We had the same flaring tempers, the same stubbornness, the same strong wills, the same toughness and resiliency and determination. . . . I even had her same way of sticking my chin out."

The Holt household centered around music, books, newspapers, and magazines. Christmas and birthday gifts always included books. Janice Meredith Holt taught herself to read by age four by constantly asking her parents what the words were in the newspapers and books that surrounded her. The first book she received for Christmas was *The Sunbonnet Twins*, a picture book with short sentences. Her father pulled her into his lap and read it to her. Janice in turn, to her father's delight and surprise, read it to him. By the time she was eight, she had read David Copperfield from her Grandmother McGraw's library. "No book was ever forbidden to me," Janice wrote, "except the big 'doctor book' in Mother's dresser drawer. With my insatiable appetite for reading, I read everything. Dickens and Shakespeare, Kipling and the John L. Stoddard lecture series, by the time I was ten years old. From other youngsters I got hold of the Horatio Alger books, Mary J. Holmes, Bertha M. Clay, but I hid them from Mama because she thought they were trash. I read Hawthorne, Washington Irving, James Fenimore Cooper, Dostoevsky, Tolstoi, Schopenhauer, *Little Women, Rebecca of Sunnybrook Farm,* Robert Ingersoll, Tom Paine, Thoreau, Emerson and even slipped out the doctor book, but horrified by the pictures, returned it."

Before his children were born, John had assembled camping gear and equipment. He acquired a sizable tent, bedrolls, and a grub box that he cleverly crafted into a kitchen cabinet. Provisions for cooking included a Dutch oven for baking, a spider-legged skillet for frying, a black kettle for stewing, and a big enamel coffeepot.

As often as they could, John and Lucy took their children to Charleston, Arkansas, for the annual family reunion. All ten of the Holt sons and daughters tried to make it home with their families during the first week of August for the gathering that was held in conjunction with the annual Confederate reunion in Franklin County.

One summer John decided to make the journey in a covered wagon. He rented a large wagon and a team of horses, filled the bed with straw, and stretched a tarpaulin over the frame. John and Lucy rode in the spring-seat; the three children rode in the back, peeking out and pretending to watch for "wild Indians."

At night a campfire was lit and Lucy cooked over the open flames. The straw-filled wagon became the children's bed. During one night, wolves formed a distant ring around the wagon and filled the air with their eerie, persistent howls. John stayed awake with his gun nearby and kept the campfire going to hold the frightening creatures at bay. After a week of camping along the way, they arrived in Charleston.

The two-day picnic reunion was held at the fairgrounds two miles from town and opened with a parade through Charleston's main street. Promptly at ten o'clock, a bugle blew and drum rolls began. Grandpa Holt, who had fought in the Battle of Pea Ridge, at Challah, and at Chickamauga, always led the parade. Proudly he bore the Confederate flag and marched down the street in his old, tattered gray uniform. The dusty road was stirred and scattered by the cadence of shuffling feet as about sixty uniformed veterans followed Grandpa Holt through the town as a band continuously played the Confederate rallying song, *Dixie,* with great gusto.

Grandpa Holt loved all the activities of the Confederate reunion. His grandchildren crowded around him to hear again the old stories of his battle years. In the early evening hours, Grandma Holt unbraided her long dark hair and her granddaughters brushed it. Before the children bedded down to sleep on thick pallets of quilts in the wide hallways, Grandma Holt would sit in her rocker and gather them in her lap and all around her while she read her favorite Bible stories.

From Altus to Kinta to Charleston, John and Lucy provided a rich heritage for Janice, Mary Catherine, and John. The years on the prairie of Kinta, Oklahoma, imbued them with poignant images of Indians, gypsies, farmers, and cowboys. Other reflections included childhood friends, paper doll dramas, prairie winds, music, books, picnics, camping trips, reunions, and innumerable experiences that welded their family into meaningful, loving unity.

For two years, Lucy discussed with John her desire for their children to have more than just the eight grades of instruction available in the Kinta school. John preferred to live and teach in small towns, but Lucy aspired for her offspring to have the advantages offered in more advanced schools where there were also greater cultural opportunities. Lucy's strong will and persistence usually prevailed. Janice wrote of her mother: "Whatever he thought he was getting in the way of a wife when he married Lucy, I never heard my father say. But I know one thing as sure as sin. It took that imp of Satan, that fiery, quick-tempered, fearless, indomitable woman to make life what it was for him and for her children out there in the middle of the Choctaw Indians and cowboys! If she had been what her pictures look like, she wouldn't have lasted a year, for there was no room for frailty, for femininity, for demure innocence, for girlish need of protection. There was just room for nerve and guts and backbone, and she had them. Had them and to spare. Had them to such an extent that our life, which could so easily have been drab, bitter, harsh and terrible, was instead rich and gay and full and sweet.

"And it was Lucy McGraw who did it. For my father, who was quiet and distinguished looking, scholarly and reserved, was also a dreamer. A man who made big plans but who rarely got around to doing anything about them. A man who was not greatly pricked by ambition. Tomorrow was always soon enough for him to tackle anything. He was a man who was so terribly proud and at the same time so awkwardly shy and timid that he could never, even in the face of direst need, bring himself to ask for a job. Perhaps that's why he took up teaching. There was a dignified approach to obtaining work! It was the iron in Lucy's soul that stiffened his, the ramrod in her backbone that propped him up, the raw, quivering nerve of her courage that kept him from being afraid."

Was it an idealized, romanticized childhood? "If it ever had any romance to it," Janice surmised, "I strongly suspect it wore off very soon, under the constant dust storms blown by high winds off the prairies, the struggle to maintain even the common decencies of life and to provide some semblance of culture, the isolation from people of mutual interests and background, the drab unloveliness of daily life, for when life is pushed down to its barest necessities it can become mean and ugly. It is only redeemed from that by courage."

The superintendent John admired in Howe had relocated to Cowlington, thirty-five miles northeast of Kinta. John and Lucy accepted his offers to teach in the farm and ranch town because it was closer to Fort Smith, Lucy's eventual goal.

The move in August 1915 was almost six years to the day after their arrival in Kinta and was made by horse-drawn wagons. It took three wagonloads to transport their domestic goods, which now included an upright piano.

John and Lucy taught two years in Cowlington, Oklahoma, before Lucy's ultimate dream was fulfilled. In 1917 they crossed the Arkansas River and moved to Fort Smith, Arkansas.

3
The City
1917-1924

To Janice Meredith Holt, the years her family lived on the western prairie in Kinta, Oklahoma, represented the most memorable and stable period of her childhood. Willa Cather, whose work Janice admired and respected, believed "the years from eight to fifteen are the formative period in a writer's life, when he unconsciously gathers basic material. He may acquire a great many interesting impressions in his mature years but his thematic materials he acquires under fifteen years of age." Not only did Kinta provide images of Indians, gypsies, cowboys, and farmers, but special friendships and happy familial relationships. For six years, the pattern of Janice's everyday life was a steady pulse of existence in the intimacy of a small town where one knew and cared about everyone else. A sense of shared experiences endowed her with social acceptance and emotional security. The love and nurture of family and the constancy of playmates provided an unequaled sense of value and stability.

The announcement of a move away from Kinta when she was ten years old had a profound effect on Janice. At the time, she felt her mother's desire to leave Kinta was very cruel, and she resented the familiar things she loved being snatched away from her. On the day of departure, Janice was so heartsick she was nauseated. When she embraced Corinne for the last time, she wept inconsolably. Years later, Janice wrote, "I knew, in my heart, that there would never again be anybody who meant as much to me as a friend, with whom I would share so much, who would know so instinctively from such long association what I was thinking, feeling and knowing, for she had thought and felt and known with me for so long. I knew I would never find anybody else who knew just how to play as we did; sometimes without even having to say words, the same idea would come to us. And I knew I would never love another friend as much again. And I never did—not in my childhood. I left my childhood behind me with those precious Kinta years.

"I know my mother was right about moving to the city where our high school education was concerned, but she was wrong about what it did to our family life. I am not at all sure that the four years of high school education was worth breaking up the close unity of the family. Small towns are beautiful places for families."

When the Holts relocated in the summer of 1917 to the southern outskirts of Fort Smith, Arkansas, the city had a population of around thirty-three thousand. Before that time, they had not lived where the population exceeded one thousand. Always before the entire family had attended or taught in the same school. After the move to Fort Smith, they began to go in separate directions. Janice, in the seventh grade, rode the streetcar five miles into the city to attend Weaver Junior High. In 1919 Mary Catherine attended Weaver Junior High, and Janice attended Fort Smith High School.

While in Oklahoma Lucy received her bachelor of arts degree from the former Cherokee college at Tahlequah, which eventually became Northeastern State College. John and Lucy continued to advance to larger schools and higher salaries. With varied interests in different schools, Janice felt her family members "did not need each other as much." That feeling caused her to experience an anguishing alienation, as revealed in her own words: "Coming from a small school into a large city high school, being an unusually sensitive, introverted girl with a questioning, never-satisfied mind, I did not make an easy adjustment. Perhaps it was the very closeness of our family life which had made me so.

"I was not a pretty girl, and I had none of the easy grace and winsomeness that makes for popularity. I desperately wanted to be liked and I went through untold agonies of mind when I thought I was disliked. I probably was liked enough at school, and it may be that I was just used to being a big frog in a little pond which made me so unhappy."

The emotional shift in the transition from Kinta to Fort Smith created an awareness in Janice of her differentness, her individuality. She felt diminished as her personality was diluted by the large numbers of students in each class at Fort Smith High School. She had become a tiny frog in a big pond at the sensitive age when young girls began to dream of handsome princes.

It was necessary for Janice to work during her high school years to help as much as possible with clothing and personal expenses. With an unquenchable passion for reading, particularly now that she had more time alone and fewer close friendships, Janice spent many hours perusing shelves and checking out books in the Carnegie Library and soon became a familiar face to the staff. Miss Ethel Keeler, head librarian, asked Janice if she would like to work at the library.

Janice happily accepted the job and worked until nine o'clock in the evenings during the week and all day on Saturdays. Her parents would drive from the suburban area of Hendricks Hills to pick her up after work. Invariably Janice had an armful of books. Some were school textbooks, as she often completed her homework at the library desk. Others were library books for pleasure reading at home. According to Mary Catherine, Janice was always reading and was acutely interested in discovering how books were "put together with characters, plots, and solutions."

During her second year of high school, Janice determined that, if she could not be noticed for her physical beauty, she would focus her energies in other directions. Describing herself as possessing a "quick, facile mind," she set goals to achieve a scholastic record "that would be hard to ignore." An honor student, Janice sought every prize and medal offered in literary contests and achieved most of them.

Fort Smith High School sponsored the Athenians and Columbians for young women who labeled themselves as the "intellectual Athenians" and the "social Columbians." Janice, an Athenian, opposed Gladys Mae Davidson of the Columbian society in her senior year. The subject of her oration was Florence Nightingale, of which Mary Catherine remarked, "I do swear every member of the family learned that *long* oration by the time it was presented!" Janice received the individual medal and her team won the gold cup.

In Janice's senior yearbook, *The Sounder*, her classmates prophetically chose the words to place beneath her name, "We expect great things of you, Janice." The adjustments to a new environment may have been difficult, but like her mother and grandmothers before her, Janice Meredith Holt not only succeeded but excelled. She graduated salutatorian of the class of 1922. Beginning with Catherine, a favorite adage of the McGraw women was, "Where there's a will, there's a way." Janice acknowledged: "Seeds of desire all through my grandmother to Lucy and her fiery flame, fused with the shy, quiet scholar that was my father, passed on and embedded in me, making of me a bookish, quiet, unbearably sensitive person, so quickly and so easily hurt as hardly to be able to live, and yet giving me at the same time an armor of some sort, to set goals, to live through hurt, to harden and strengthen and above all to keep fanned alive some flame, some mood, some passion for expression!"

After graduating from high school Janice began working in the ticket booth at the Palace theater on Garrison Avenue, with plans to enter Park College in Parkville, Missouri, in the fall. Her parents were eagerly anticipating her enrollment at Park but during the summer learned that her father had a borderline case of tuberculosis. Even though he was not visibly ill, their alarm was magnified as the disease had been the cause of the early deaths of one of his brothers and two sisters.

The more recent death of John's father from tuberculosis was very much on the hearts and minds of his family. On February 5, 1918, the Charleston, Arkansas, newspaper headlined, "J.K.P. Holt Called Beyond," and narrated, "The spirit of one of the best, most highly respected and beloved men with which this community has ever been blessed, passed into the presence of its maker." Grandpa Holt had asked to be buried in his tattered gray uniform and to have his casket draped with the Confederate flag. Friends and family viewed his body in the parlor of his home before the old soldier was carried for burial in the Nixon Cemetery, which was very near the Confederate Park and picnic grounds.

During the summer after her graduation, Janice began working as a laboratory technician at the Holt-Krock Clinic and continued to work nights at the theater. Because of her father's health, Janice decided to delay attending Park College for a year. "I was needed at home," she stated simply. "As a result, that year of delay allowed me time, at seventeen as my mother and grandmother had before me, to fall in love and marry."

Mae Moore, a high school classmate, introduced Janice to her brother, Otto. Janice was infatuated with Otto Moore from the first moment of their meeting. She described herself as fifteen pounds overweight with a thin veil of freckles across her rounded face. A "bookworm," her previous boyfriends had been "bookish," too. Otto Moore was different. He was older, more mature, wonderfully tall and thin. Otto was as dashing as any movie star on the silver screen.

In late summer Janice persuaded her parents to let her remain in Fort Smith to continue working at the clinic and theater while Lucy enrolled in a six-week course at the University of Colorado in Boulder. When her parents returned to Fort Smith, they found Janice totally enamored with Otto Moore, the second son of Jack and Henrietta Crabtree Moore.

Jack Moore, born in Smith County, Virginia, in 1864, was an engineer for the Missouri Pacific Railroad Company. He frequently traveled to Huntington, Arkansas, a coal mining rail center about twenty-five miles south of Fort Smith, where he spent the night in a boarding house owned by John B. and Nancy Crabtree and met their tall, slender daughter Henrietta. Whenever he was in town, he spent as much time with Henrietta, whom he affectionately called "Retta," as he could. He accompanied her to church functions, took her for buggy rides, and taught her how to shoot a pistol.

Henrietta Crabtree, born in Tazewell County, Virginia, March 13, 1868, married Jack Moore on January 3, 1893. Soon after their wedding, they moved to Argenta, Arkansas, now North Little Rock. Jack continued to work for the railroad and also purchased and operated a dairy farm.

Henrietta and Jack's first child, a son, Oren, was born in December 1893. Ora, the second baby, died soon after her birth in 1895. Their third child, Otto, was born October 20, 1897. Three more daughters, Erie (1899), Lenore (1901), and Mae (1905) were born before 1907.

On January 6, 1907, Jack Moore was swinging his lantern as he crossed the tracks in the railroad switchyard at the end of an exhausting day. The noise of the steam engines in the yard muffled the sound of a runaway boxcar that sped toward him. Jack was knocked down by the enormous freight car and his legs were severed. His agonizing screams for help were lost in the resonant sounds of numerous engines as he bled to death beside the railroad track. Henrietta Moore was two months pregnant.

The Missouri Pacific Railroad Company provided passage for Henrietta and her five children to accompany Jack's body to Fort Smith for burial in the Oak Cemetery. The young widow gave birth to Annie on August 25, 1907. Unfortunately, no further assistance was received from the railroad company.

In 1914 Henrietta purchased a house at 1119 South Nineteenth Street and moved her family to Fort Smith. When Janice met Otto, he was twenty-seven years old and living in his mother's home. Otto managed the office and drove a delivery truck for the Majestic Laundry, a job he began following his graduation from Draughn's Business College in Fort Smith.

Lucy and John very much wanted their oldest child to go to college, but, during the summer she willfully chose to remain at home and work, Janice became intent on marrying Otto Moore. Lucy recognized that it would be impossible to discourage her determined daughter from marrying at the same young age as she had married.

In September Lucy and Janice put a dress for the wedding on layaway at Mark's Dress Store. Lucy paid the balance of the $24.95 bill during the three months before the appointed date. On Wednesday, November 27, 1923, Janice Meredith Holt married Otto Moore in the living room of her parents' home on Hendricks Road. The young bride's flat crepe dress of dark beige had a high scoop neck and was accentuated above the hem with a row of large square designs stitched in blue wool flannel threads. The long full sleeves, buttoned at the wrists, were made of crepe de chine.

The Holt house was filled with relatives for the wedding. Lucy's youngest sister, Babb McGraw Beltrand, age twenty-six, played the piano for the ceremony, and Mary Catherine sang the sentimental "O Promise Me." Mary enjoyed singing and was active in the high school chorus but was so nervous when she started to sing at her sister's wedding that she had to begin the song a second time.

After their marriage Otto and Janice lived in a three-room apartment of his mother's home, and Otto continued to work at the laundry. Henrietta had not given any of her children middle names at birth. During that time Janice playfully added Jackson to his name because she liked the sound of it.

Three months after the wedding, Janice Holt Moore made an appointment with a doctor to confirm a suspicion. "Well, you're definitely going to have a baby!" the doctor told her. "And I remember that for the next seven months," Janice wrote, "I lived on a cloud, terribly thrilled and excited because *David* was coming! Somewhere I had heard that the name David meant beloved. It fitted my baby perfectly. For beloved he was from that moment in the doctor's office."

4
Distance
1924-1939

It was not "David" who arrived on a "rather chilly night at 12:45 A.M., September 30, 1924," but a nine-pound baby girl, delivered in a tall, four-poster bed in her Grandmother Moore's home. The young mother was assisted by Dr. E.H. Havenor, "an old-fashioned doctor who did not believe in "*even* an aspirin for an anesthetic." The infant was named Elizabeth for Janice's mother and Ann "for good measure."

Rocking Elizabeth became a nightly ritual that Janice described as "the richest hour of the day," and added, "Before a week was out I knew what I had been missing, and I knew that I was making a selfish hour of close communion which I was deliberately cultivating because it held such sweetness for me. Those were precious twilight hours we had together, as still and as sweet as the dusk itself." Later she wrote, "Mothers should have lots of children, of course. Lots of boys and lots of girls to know the complete fullness of motherhood. But if fate decrees otherwise, and gives to a woman only one child . . . then let it be kind and give her a woman-child! A small being like herself, one with whom she is at home. Whose body and whose emotions and whose spirit are akin to her own, a sister under the skin!"

Elizabeth was still a baby when Janice and Otto moved from his mother's home into two bedrooms of the Holts' house at 712 South Twentieth Street. They used one of the bedrooms for a kitchen, and carried water to do kitchen chores from the bathroom they all shared at the end of the hall.

A couple of months after Elizabeth's second birthday, word came on November 17, 1926, that Catherine and Dan McGraw were both seriously ill in Orlando, Florida, where they were visiting two of their sons. It was reported that the couple had contracted malaria while en route by automobile. When Lucy received the news about her parents, she left immediately by train, not knowing before she arrived in Florida that her mother's death had occurred the morning of November 18. Lucy's brother, Tom Dan McGraw, was a passenger on the train that returned their mother's body to Fort Smith. Lucy stayed at his home in Orlando to care for her father, who remained gravely ill.

On December 1 the *Fort Smith Times Record* announced the tragic news: "Double Funeral Held for Prominent Couple." An account of their deaths explained that Dan McGraw followed his wife of almost fifty-five years in death on the eighth day after her demise. Although he had not been told, he knew his wife was deceased. Catherine's funeral was delayed because of the impending death of her husband. The joint service of Catherine Ophelia Babb McGraw, seventy-two, and Daniel Murdock McGraw, seventy-six, was held at 2:30 P.M., November 30. They were buried in the Oak Cemetery on top of a hill overlooking Fort Smith. Of them, Janice wrote: "That he adored my grandmother I am certain. But I always had the feeling that she was all he needed. That she filled his heart to the exclusion of either his children or his grandchildren. Kate, he called her. 'When I die, Kate,' he said, 'I want you to sing *Lead Kindly Light.*' But Kate died first. He followed within a week and they were buried side by side. To me it was inevitable that he should die with her. He wouldn't have wanted to live without her."

In 1927 Otto Moore and a friend entered a dry cleaning partnership. The two quickly established a profitable business, which allowed Otto to move his family out of the Holts' house. Their elation ended abruptly when the business partner appropriated their earnings and some of the clothing and fled Fort Smith. Otto was left with nothing and had great difficulty dealing with his losses.

In a short time Otto began working as a door-to-door salesman. Without a steady income, he and Janice soon used all their meager savings and had to move into a cheaper apartment. One week later, at age twenty-three, Janice began experiencing bouts of nausea, vomiting, and mild diarrhea. The local physician diagnosed food poisoning and treated it as such. Her symptoms persisted, then improved somewhat. Over the next couple of years Janice's digestive system would be constantly aggravated by the ups and downs of financial insecurity.

In 1930 Otto lost his sales job and moved his family to Little Rock, where he was employed by Glick's Cleaners. The couple rented a one-room efficiency apartment that Janice described as being "quite literally in the slums." Of the effect of it, she wrote, "We had a young daughter just starting to school. I worried very much about her surroundings and the children she had to associate with, and once again, the nausea and vomiting started."

Soon after their relocation, Elizabeth entered first grade. When she came home from school on the very first day, Elizabeth proudly announced to her parents, "My name is Libby now." When questioned as to why, she quickly responded, "That's what the kids call me!"

After a year in Little Rock, Otto moved his family to Tulsa, Oklahoma, where he worked as a salesman for the Jewell Tea Company. Libby attended two different schools for second and third grades as her parents moved from one low-cost apartment to another. They returned to Little Rock in 1933 and rented an upstairs room in Janice's Aunt Florence McRaven's home. When the rent was due, Aunt Florence would sit on the bottom stair step and wait for it.

Still extremely disheartened since the absconding of his business partner, Otto had difficulty finding any work except that of door-to-door sales. By 1933 not only was Otto suffering, the whole country was in the throes of economic depression. Many people were without work. When jobs were lost, the search for new ones was often in vain.

Unemployment created anxiety and increased tension in families. The identity bestowed on married women by society of that era was that "a woman's place is in the home." Most men did not want their wives to work outside the home. Working wives were testament to a family's poverty and implied that husbands were unable to provide. For a woman in an unhappy marriage, the work experience helped her establish an independence that often became a prelude to separation or divorce.

In 1934 Janice was twenty-nine years old; her daughter, ten. Unquestionably, her feelings toward Otto were influenced by the trying times brought about by the Depression. Individuals often lost control of their own destiny and, as a result, family life suffered. The Moore family was no exception. Almost twenty years later, in a lengthy letter written to Libby in 1953, Janice described her innermost feelings and frustrations during that difficult period. "We lived on Valmar Street. We were very poor. It may be that poverty acts as a challenge to some people. I rather doubt it except to instill the determination to overcome it. My own reactions were that it was inescapably dull, limiting, even binding. I found nothing exhilarating in pinching pennies, in buying hamburger instead of sirloin, in dyeing and making over old dresses and coats, in buying Baker's $3.95 shoes instead of the slim, expensively narrow lasts my feet were made for. I did not even feel any great satisfaction in being able to do these things rather well. Anyone, I felt, with sense at all could take a certain amount of money and make it do. There was neither achievement or strengthening of character in being able to do it. The day by day routine of cooking cheap meals, washing dishes, making beds, and listening to neighborhood gossip had become almost unendurable to me. Each morning (and I do remember exactly how hopeless they were) when I woke up, the same, dull, futile day waited.

"Worse though than the poverty, worse even than the dull routine, was the gray desert that my marriage had become. None of the things Otto is commonly supposed to have made me suffer were terribly important. He drank too much of course, but if he had had a sparkling mind when he was sober, if there had been any wit and fun in him, one might have regretted the drinking, but it would not have mattered too much. He gambled away much of his salary, it's true, but he never had enough to lose, or ever won enough, to make any great difference. If we had wanted the same things from life, if we had ever shared even an ideal, the gambling wouldn't have been too important. He was not unfaithful in those days, and when, later, he was, it was a half-hearted sort of thing because for some reason (and I know this too well to rationalize about it) he never quit loving me. It was as if he hopelessly grabbed at some last straw.

"The thing that made a grayness of my life was the gradually growing knowledge that I was in a trap of my own making—that I was married to a man who bored me almost, literally to death, who chattered ceaselessly and never said anything, whose mind was like an empty box rattling with purposeless pebbles. The future stretched ahead of me so dry and gray that I remember standing one morning, with my hand on the foot of the bed I had just made, thinking—'If this is what life is going to be, why live it?'

"Being an idealist and believing that marriage was sacred, I was shocked to find myself probing and judging my own. I shrank from examining it with clear vision. I believed what society believed—what I read and heard and was told on every side—that marriage, per se, is worth holding onto. I believed it and yet I felt like someone condemned to prison. With the vision of a good many more years I know now that a marriage should survive only if it is good enough; only if beneath the surface irritations and problems there is a deep accord and purpose; only if the two people involved, even though each to some extent follows an individual bent, have something wonderfully fine to bring to each other and to the mutual life. If I had had such wisdom then I could have spared myself, and perhaps you, some long, dragged-out years of false hope and wasted emotions. For whatever gifts I had to bring were lost on Otto, and with all the fairness in the world to him, plain common sense makes me have to admit that he had nothing to bring me. In his favor were his industry—he worked and worked very hard. He was meticulously clean and neat and he had a winsome public personality. Many people liked him, for he was courteous, thoughtful of his customers, and he was a loyal servant of his employers. He stayed busy with a thousand small details, and I sometimes think he came home only when he could find nothing else to do. Not because he didn't love us, for he loved us in the only way he knew how to love; but because when he came home life closed in on him and he had nothing to give it. Life for him began when he drove off in the morning, his mind already full of the day ahead; it ended when he drove back as late as possible that evening. I am not sure, no matter what kind of man he had been, that it would have been enough for me to be so  tightly pigeon-holed. I am not sure any man could bring enough to the kind of woman I was to make it interesting and challenging and vital. At any rate, being the kind of person he was, eventually it didn't matter to me when he came or went, or whether he came or went at all.

"It isn't to my credit that I did nothing positive about the situation, but it is an excuse that I didn't know what to do. I did not know I could write. It never entered my head to try anything like that. I was not trained for any kind of work. To myself I seemed to have very meager talents for assuming the responsibility for you. I could cook and sew and keep house. I had a little experience working in a library, and even less experience working in a doctor's office. But it was the height of the depression and even skilled and experienced workers were without jobs. I couldn't see one chance in a thousand of finding any kind of paying work.

"That was my 29th year."

Janice had been married eleven of her twenty-nine years. The first year of her marriage was spent in her mother-in-law's home, the next six were in or near her own parents' house. A series of moves to nondescript apartments plagued the remaining four years—from Fort Smith to Little Rock to Tulsa and back to Little Rock—constantly uprooting, constantly changing jobs. In menial household tasks in characterless apartments, Janice's creativity was stifled as she perceived her limited horizons.

When Janice and Otto returned to Little Rock in 1933, Janice wanted Libby to attend Sunday School. Otto would not go with them to the Pulaski Heights Christian Church where Dr. Joseph Boone Hunter was minister. Janice took great interest in the church activities and was soon teaching Sunday School. Dr. Hunter quickly recognized her eagerness and willingness to be of service in the church. A former missionary to Japan, Dr. Hunter made plans to return there during the summer of 1934 to do research for an international relations course he would be teaching at the University of Arkansas. He approached Janice to see if she would be interested in becoming his part-time secretary during his absence and directing the education programs of the church.

Janice felt that her later work in the field of religious education began "entirely by accident . . . by accident, and the grace of God working in a good man's heart." Not only did she accept Dr. Hunter's challenge, but when he returned from Japan, she had mapped out a comprehensive religious education program for all the youth groups.

In his depressed state of mind, Otto's self-esteem took an even greater plunge when his wife went to work. The words of Dorothy Thompson, in a September 1939 article in *Ladies Home Journal,* best express his behavior: "Men demand and need in marriage the full emotional power of the women they love. If that power is dissipated in demanding intellectual or creative work they feel they are being cheated." Because of his own frustration, Otto belittled Janice for taking Libby to Sunday School and intensified his criticism of her when she began working in the church.

With tremendous energy and creative interest, Janice consistently tried new projects and ideas in her work. Her accomplishments were soon noticed outside her own church and led to an offer to serve as director of children's work for the Arkansas-Louisiana Board of Missions. When she accepted the full-time position, it involved more hours away from home and some travel. Janice employed a housekeeper named Ada, who also took care of Libby during the next six years they lived in Little Rock.

As director of children's work for the Board, Janice worked with Paul Kennedy, a former missionary to the Philippines who directed conferences and workshops in the field of religious educational programming. She later described her personal growth during the two years she was associated with Kennedy: "I learned to think on my feet and to speak before groups with some confidence. The experiences I had teaching in young people's camps and conferences, in local church training schools, in district conferences, taught me a measure of poise and helped me to believe in myself. And little by little a new door was opened to me. That of writing. For now I began to be called on to write various materials in children's work, and increasingly in young people's work, and it was discovered that I had a flair for dramatization which resulted in many short playlets for use with children and young people."

The continuing success of work and consequential growth of self-esteem created an increasing friction in Janice's marriage. Otto felt more and more excluded from his wife's priorities and continued to seek psychological refuge in alcohol. The more he drank the more he belittled Janice. The tension between her parents spilled over to Libby, who was becoming increasingly aware of her mother's unhappiness. She became a nervous child and was extremely underweight.

Dr. Hunter, who was still Janice's pastor, recognized that she needed help. On several occasions, he had counseled Otto, who would say that he would try to change, but no change occurred. The minister realized Otto was not going to improve his behavior or his attitude toward Janice. His drinking and gambling were habitual, and he contributed little money for food or rent.

Extremely stressed in her marriage and worried about its effect on Libby, Janice began contemplating divorce. By 1937, she was bearing the total financial responsibility of their living expenses. Aware of Janice's situation and need of assistance, Paul Kennedy and another minister friend, Myron Hopper, informed her of a position in the First Christian Church located on Ann Street in Frankfort, Kentucky, with a membership of over twelve hundred. Myron Hopper wrote a letter in Janice's behalf to the minister, A. Cleon Brooks.

Once Janice learned she had been accepted for the job in Kentucky, Dr. Hunter, Paul Kennedy, and Myron Hopper helped her prepare for the move and make her departure from Little Rock. She needed distance from Otto Moore. Of her sixteen-year marriage, Janice wrote: "In the years we were married I never once found anything within him I could reach. I don't know what sort of man he was, for we couldn't even talk to one another. If we had been persons of different nationalities, unable to communicate through a common language, we could not have been further apart. We never meant the same things when we talked. We could never get through to one another. I had the constantly frustrated feeling of ramming my head against a stone wall, and doubtless he had much the same feeling."

When the marriage dissolved, Janice felt she had spent those years with a stranger. She knew what foods Otto preferred, how he liked to dress, and what his creature comforts were, "but that," she admitted, "literally, is all."

"Not once did I ever have a clue to what his deepest emotions and thoughts were. He didn't read, he didn't like music, he didn't like the outdoors. Those things wouldn't have mattered if I could have discovered one thing at all he did like, except liquor too much and too frequently, and penny-ante poker. He worked hard all day, came home to eat and sleep, and lived in a world of his own which was entirely closed to me. We produced Elizabeth, and she was the only thing we had in common."

Janice felt there were marriages that carried the seeds of separation in them from the beginning and that hers was one of them. "What those years of waste and futility cost are buried deep within me," she bemoaned. "If Elizabeth's father has scars from them, I hope they have healed with time. I think the kindest thing I ever did for him was to set him free early enough that he might make another and happier life for himself with a woman more in tune with him."

A divorce petition was filed by Janice Moore in Sebastian Chancery Court on Monday, July 31, 1939. The alleged cause was cruel treatment. During the proceedings, the anxieties that Janice previously experienced in the form of nausea, vomiting, and diarrhea were manifesting themselves in a different way. She felt a constant compulsion to swallow and at the same time feared swallowing. She consulted a physician who gave her vitamin B, which did little to relieve her anxiety. Only when an uncontested divorce decree was granted seven weeks later and she knew she could support herself and Libby with the new job in Kentucky did her condition begin to improve.

5
The Move to Kentucky
1939-1941

In late August 1939, Janice and Libby packed their bags and, with less than a hundred dollars, traveled a thousand miles from everything that was familiar to begin a new life in Frankfort, Kentucky. "It was hard going those first few months," Janice wrote. "We forgot, and set the table for three. We forgot, and tuned in radio programs for a man who was no longer there to hear them. We forgot, and made chocolate cakes for a man who was no longer there to eat them. We forgot, and waited for a familiar step at the door at night. We forgot, and missed the smell of a pipe, and shaving things in the bathroom, and a long, lean figure in the easy chair. But we held tight to each other, and by sheer force we kept hammering at our fears and our loneliness."

Janice rented an apartment at 412 Murray Street. She described Frankfort as "a small town, set like a jewel in the hills." At first she felt smothered by the hills, having been accustomed to "the wideness of the southwest, to long looks toward the horizon, to more spacious skies." In addition to adjustments to the topography, Janice had to adjust to opposing regional traditions. "In the southwest we were a brisk, pioneering people," she wrote, "breezy, friendly, forward-moving, each generation standing on its own feet, content to make its own way without looking back, determined to send down its own roots." She viewed Kentuckians as "a people rooted in history, proud of their traditions, complacent in their dignity, certain in their awareness of their own culture," and she found Frankfort "a little stiff, a little smug, a little creaky in the heaviness of its own superstructure, a little root-bound and more than a little unyielding!" With humor she realized that most of the people she came in contact with honestly believed she had come "gratefully and breathlessly, out of the wilderness and into Paradise!"

The Christmas holiday of 1939 was the first Janice and Libby had ever spent away from family members in Arkansas. Saddened they could not be there for the celebration, Janice was extremely distressed in early spring when she learned that her father was ill. She and Libby left for Arkansas immediately and arrived in time for Janice to be with him before his death April 6, 1940, which "occurred suddenly, unexpectedly, tragically."

"He wasn't even very ill," Janice wrote. "A storm blew up late one afternoon and he ran out to huddle my mother's little chickens under shelter, and he fell, a hemorrhage from a perforated stomach ulcer pouring out his life." Janice described her father as "a sweet and gallant gentleman," whom a young friend once dubbed "Sir John."

"Sir John the gentle knight! Sir John of the schoolroom who taught two generations of boys and girls the Golden Rule, not by precept but by example! Sir John of the clear streams and lakes, who wore the summer hours away fishing and philosophizing! Sir John of the back-lot garden, who sifted the warm earth through his fingers lovingly and carefully! Sir John of the fireside, who drew his family close about him on winter nights and fiddled, and told tall tales, and popped corn and parched peanuts! Sir John, my father!"

Janice said she did not hear the words of the funeral service for thinking, "If Sir John could see this how he would hoot! He should have been wrapped in an old blanket and laid to sleep by the side of the creek, with a fishing pole at his feet!" John Albert Holt was buried in the Rose Lawn Cemetery in Fort Smith.

Honored to be a child of her parents, Janice felt that, when she was conceived, "Fate was kind" to her, "unbelievably kind when one thinks not only of Professor John Holt and Lucy McGraw Holt, but of all the parents behind parents and all the genes of all the generations possible to draw on for those particular genes which made Janice Holt. Which gave her good health, vitality, humor, resiliency, a capacity for joy, a reasonably good mind, the ability to learn and a forgiving disposition."

Returning to Kentucky, Janice busied herself in her work using resources from the rich experiences of working with the Arkansas-Louisiana Board of Missions. While she dedicated herself to giving her best, some of the members began to shun Janice upon learning she was a divorced woman. The positive characteristics she described in the lineage of her birth were being called forth for their strength to help her endure the year of inordinate demands on her emotions—the divorce, the new job a thousand miles away from the region she had always known and loved, the death of her father, and the increasing problems of discontent within the church.

Janice later wrote of her experience in Frankfort, "We were there less than a year. We were not congenial. I take my own share of blame by admitting I was spoiled and untested by criticism. I had never worked except with people who loved me personally, people who gave me perfect freedom in my work, people who trusted my motives, people who thought anything I did was fine. My work had been nurtured in fellowship so completely Christian that it had never occurred to me that there could be relationships within the church which were not Christian. Now I learned that there could be, and I was both bewildered and confused."

The minister and his wife had been with the congregation only a year when Janice was hired. There were "personality conflicts" and professional jealousy among the staff, as well as the "politics of the church." Some of the members resented the fact that one of their leaders was divorced. In time a couple of ladies in the church asked Janice to resign.

Frankfort, Kentucky, was rooted in southern traditions. In 1939, social acceptance of divorced persons remained "a cool aloofness—a cold shoulder rejection." Divorced people were often made to feel that they were disqualified as human beings as well as members of the church by reason of the failure of their marriages. Nowhere was the widespread disapproval of divorced persons more evident than in the church, particularly in the Bible belt of the South where traditionalists were strictly opposed to divorce on biblical grounds. Divorce was unthinkable in the ministry, which in most churches was restricted to the married.

The Frankfort congregation knew only that Janice was a divorced woman but had no knowledge or understanding of the circumstances. Even though they witnessed an attractive, vivacious woman with a beautiful young daughter giving unselfish devotion to her work, it was not enough for them to overcome their prejudices. Janice's father's death occurred at the height of her disillusionment. "My mother's world crumpled about her," Janice wrote, "for by this time my sister and my brother were both married, with families. It seemed logical that I should be the one to stay with her until she could become adjusted to life without my father. I came to this conclusion slowly, for it seemed presumptuous to assume she needed anyone at all. I investigated other work, one place in the far north, another in Florida, but I could not bring myself to take either. Finally, for my mother would not ask me, I decided Libby and I could be helpful to her, so we went back to Arkansas for a brief time."

In June the church bulletin contained Janice's tongue-in-cheek goodbye: "Libby and I wish to express our appreciation for the love and friendliness which has made our stay with you happy. Many of you have come to be dear friends and we shall miss you. We terminate these months in your midst with only sorrow and regret that it must be so. Thank you for everything, and know that we shall always remember you with love and affection."

The July bulletin printed the church's rather hypocritical response: "Mrs. Janice Moore, our secretary-director, and Libby will be leaving us this week and we deeply regret that we must give them up for we have grown to appreciate both of them. Mrs. Moore has rendered significant service to our church which will be greatly missed. We wish for them the best of life's riches and pray God's blessings upon them always."

In Fort Smith, Janice worked as a stenographer for Jennings Stein, of Stein Wholesale Dry Goods Company, whom she had known since high school. Each time Stein entered the office, he would "swing the little gate behind him, start ripping his coat off, and begin spouting words at the rate of about 200 per minute before he even reached his desk." Janice had secretarial experience in each of her jobs, but none had required the dictation skills that Stein commanded. "I guess he slowed up for me in the beginning," she wrote, "but it is a matter of pride with me that he didn't have to very long! But it wasn't my kind of work. I was out of pocket and naturally I was anxious for that not to become permanent."

After ten months with Stein Wholesale, there came what Janice described as "the opportunity of a lifetime." Again, her old friend Myron Hopper informed her of another position in Kentucky. Dr. Lewis Joseph Sherrill, Dean of the Louisville Presbyterian Seminary, was looking for a secretary with a background in religious education. Combining her experience in that field with a honing of her secretarial skills while working for Stein, Janice was primed for the job.

Dr. Sherrill had been on sabbatical leave during the academic year of 1939-40. In his absence, his secretary, Maxine Post Strain, moved to the office of the seminary president, Dr. Frank H. Caldwell. When Dr. Sherrill returned, he found that Dr. Caldwell consumed most of Maxine's time. He realized he needed to hire another person and sent out word about the position. Upon receipt of a letter of recommendation from Myron Hopper, Dr. Sherrill invited Janice for an interview in June 1941.

Janice felt the conference with Dr. Sherrill was "mutually satisfying," but the salary was "disappointingly small," and she realized more than a third of the eighty-five dollars a month would have to go for a place to live. Renting an upstairs apartment at 1437 Hepburn Avenue, the "Moore girls" returned to Kentucky in August 1941. Their three rooms in the "tall, thin house," owned by Basil D. Burch and his wife, Ollie, were a living room with a black cane-frame divan with dark cushions (which Janice covered as soon as she could afford bright, flowery chintz), a small bedroom, and a tiny kitchen. Janice and Libby shared the single upstairs bathroom with occupants of the other two apartments, two working girls and a young man.

Janice began her job at the seminary in September, and Libby entered her senior year at Atherton High School. Janice committed an additional $2.50 a month for telephone service, considering it a necessity for an attractive high school senior enrolled in a girls' school.

Maxine Strain described Janice as "very direct, very formal, nice mannered, and someone who always knew her subject." She remarked that Janice "dressed very plain, sedate, and wore medium sized heels." The two women worked each weekday as well as a half day on Saturdays but still found time to enroll in evening classes at the seminary, and later Janice took courses at Transylvania College and the College of the Bible. Soon best of friends, Janice and Maxine often lunched together and occasionally went to the Canary Cottage for a drink after work. Getting paid monthly and both having to "pinch pennies," they sometimes borrowed from each other until the next paycheck.

When Janice began working for Dr. Lewis J. Sherrill, born April 18, 1892, in Haskell, Texas, he was very much involved in the writing of his seventh book, *The Rise of Christian Education*. In the preface, dated August 1943, he noted, "Janice H. Moore has placed me under lasting obligation by her assistance in the preparation of the manuscript, and still more so, if that is possible, by her collaboration as the book was passing through the press."

With the publication in 1944 of *The Rise of Christian Education*, Dr. Sherrill reached preeminence as a scholar of Christian education. His writings were considered of utmost significance, and he was invited to present the Sprunt Lectures at Union Theological Seminary, Richmond, Virginia, in February 1945. When he received the invitation, his eyesight had been impaired to the point he could no longer read the printed page. It became necessary for his family, friends, and colleagues to read to him. Handicapped by his vision, the intensive research for the lectures was exhausting.

In 1945 John Knox Press published the substance of the Sprunt Lectures under the title, *Guilt and Redemption*. Again, Dr. Sherrill acknowledged his secretary, Janice H. Moore, who "rendered invaluable assistance by reading, gathering material, making digests, investigating special topics, preparing the material both for delivery and for publication, and seeing the book through the press. I cannot thank her sufficiently for help in finding ways of surmounting obstacles."

Of Dr. Sherrill, Janice wrote, "He had the best mind, barring none, I have ever known. The soundest, the surest, the most careful, and the quickest. It was a thrill to work with him. He exacted a meticulous type of work from me that was good discipline. We were the best of friends, mutually respectful of each other's abilities, and companions in quick-flashing insights which needed no words. Because he shared his thinking and his work so wholly with me, I can describe his association as an adventure. For me it was like doing research on a graduate level. My mind bloomed and flowered under his tutelage, and I have never felt the food of mental and spiritual nourishment to such a degree as I did during those years with him."

When Janice began working for Dr. Sherrill at age thirty-six, she had little time for socializing. She defined that period of her life quite simply as being too busy with the practical business of making certain she and Libby had a roof over their heads and "bread and butter in the pantry," to have much time for fun. She was so engrossed in Libby and her work that she felt no lack of companionship in her life.

6
Journeys
1941-1943

In the fall of 1941, Libby's "Prince Charming" came "zooming out of the wild blue yonder in a Cub training plane." At age twenty-one, Nash Hancock, who had grown up on his family's farm in Finchville, Kentucky, and attended two years of college, decided he would rather take flight instruction to become a pilot than complete a degree. After obtaining his private license in Louisville, he made application to the Army Air Corps.

The young pilot was staying with relatives who lived near Hepburn Avenue and was introduced to Libby Moore by his cousin. The first date Libby had with Nash Hancock was on a Sunday morning when he called and asked her mother for permission to take her flying.

Janice did not know until later that her seventeen-year-old daughter was his first passenger, but she was much impressed with the young pilot. "There was something special about Nash. It may have been because he was reared on a farm that something steady, quiet and assured was in his bearing. It may have been because he was a little older and more poised and mature. It may simply have been an inherent dignity in him which pleased my own sense of niceness. But whatever it was, I liked him."

In March 1942, Nash was accepted by the Army Air Corps and left Louisville for training in Tucson, Arizona. Libby did not see him again for two years, but he kept in touch with her.

Libby graduated from Atherton High School in June 1942 and enrolled in the fall at the University of Louisville. She also worked at the YWCA in the afternoons and on Saturdays. At the end of her freshman year, Libby decided to spend the summer with her grandmother Lucy in Fort Smith and left for Arkansas in late June.

Janice's vacation was scheduled to begin in July. She made train reservations for a trip west to visit her Aunt Sally McGraw Greenwood in Texas and planned to join Libby later in Arkansas. A shift in office personnel delayed Janice's vacation for two weeks. She canceled her train reservations and almost postponed the trip as the United States was at war in Europe and the mobility of soldiers to bases and camps across the country crowded all forms of transportation.

Janice decided to chance her travel by bus and left Louisville around 2:00 P.M., Monday, July 12. She sat "directly behind the driver and had for a seat mate a very nice young girl." When the bus "nosed into the dock" at Bowling Green, Janice noticed, "a very neat, trim, nice-looking soldier" standing at the corner of the station.

Janice got off the bus and went inside the station to get a newspaper. Moments after she returned to her seat on the bus, the "nice-looking soldier" stepped up into the coach. The soldier was Henry Giles, who was nearing the end of a ten-day furlough spent visiting his family in Adair County, Kentucky. Many years later in an unpublished autobiography, he recalled his chance meeting with Janice Moore: "All I remember about the furlough home is that I started back to Camp Swift, Texas, three or four days earlier than I needed to. I can't recall how I got back into Columbia, the county seat, but from Columbia I hitchhiked to Bowling Green, Kentucky. I meant to catch a bus there, ride the rest of the day and that night, then thumb my way on to Swift.

"At Bowling Green I fooled around the bus station, maybe had a sandwich, and waited for the next coach to Nashville. I had my ticket ready, but had to wait until all the incoming passengers had loaded back onto the bus before I could enter. When I finally stepped up and surveyed the situation inside the bus, there was room left for two more passengers to sit down. One space was on that long seat in the back, the other was half of the seat behind the driver. The passengers on the back seat were male and dull looking. The lone occupant in the seat behind the driver was female and not dull-looking. So, after the proper 'do you mind?' to the girl, I chose the seat up front. Nashville was sixty-some miles to the south.

"During most of the sixty-some miles the girl in the seat beside me read a newspaper; apparently unmindful of all that surrounded her—me in particular. Eventually, though, she memorized the contents of the newspaper and put it away. Then there was some small talk between her, the driver, and me. Only small talk but one little item was established before the bus reached the Nashville terminal: The girl was going to El Paso, Texas, and I was going to Camp Swift, near Austin.

"The bus arrived in Nashville at about the right time for supper. I asked the girl if she would eat with me if we could find a place. She agreed to eat with me, if there was time between buses; and there was time.

"When we finally found an eating place that would hold two more hungry people, the only table left was in front of the cookstove and exhaust pipe. Over the roar of the exhaust fan we finally got it across to the waitress that we would have fried chicken—since they were out of steaks and almost everything else, anyhow. Then, because a hot stove and a roaring exhaust fan are not conducive to normal conversation, the girl and I ate without trying to talk to each other. Across the table from each other, we communicated with hand signals.

"Shortly after the meal the bus was to leave Nashville for Memphis. I bought a ticket to Memphis and the girl and I fell in at the end of a line of passengers; a line that seemed a little shorter than the others. (There appeared to be plenty of buses, but there also appeared to be more than plenty of passengers to get on the buses.) We took turns standing by our bags (her luggage, my musette) while each went to restrooms to freshen up for the trip to Memphis. When she returned from the powder room she was saying, 'We'll *never* get out of this place, and I know it. I should go straight back to Louisville on the next bus.'

"I reminded her that *never* was a long time, and that she might as well go along with the crowd; it might be fun.

"Nashville must have been where and when I found out that the girl's name was Janice. By the time we reached the driver and the door of the bus, the vehicle was loaded. The driver told us so. Janice was bewildered. I still had hopes. 'Driver,' I said, 'my wife and I are going to Dallas. I'm due in Camp Swift day after tomorrow, and my wife is going on to El Paso to wait for me. We *have* to leave here now.'

"The 'wife' business seemed to upset Janice a bit, but she didn't blink an eyelid for the driver. The driver intoned, 'Standing room only,' and punched our tickets. Then, after three or four more couples of standees had boarded the bus, we were off.

"We hadn't cleared the city limits of Nashville before the girl, Janice, asked, 'Why on earth did you tell the driver that I am your wife?'

"'Well,' I said, fumbling for a good un-obvious answer, 'I thought it would be better than walking from here to Texas.'

"Janice shook her head; not in anger, but more in disbelief. I didn't know what else to say at the moment, but then a GI behind us spoke. 'Listen to the Corporal, Girl. Alma and I here, are to be married tomorrow in Memphis, but the driver had to think we were man and wife already if he let us on the bus to Memphis.'

"Janice brightened, looked at me, then back at the man who had spoken. It was a game. She liked to play games.

"We had not gone far down the road toward Memphis before everybody on the bus—all GIs, most of them traveling alone, some with a wife, and others like me with a 'wife'—had settled down to make the best of a long trip on an overcrowded bus. We stood facing the front of the bus, I with my right hand holding onto the back of a seat, Janice standing in the crook of my elbow.

"As we laughed and talked—about what, I don't remember—Janice would look around at me ever so often. That brought us face to face close up. It gave me an idea, so after a while when she turned her face to me, I kissed her. 'Now, what brought that on?' she asked, not too seriously.

"'You don't know, now do you?' I said.

"She laughed, and didn't seem too disturbed, so the performance was repeated two or three more times before we reached Dallas about thirty-six hours later.

"We reached Dallas, our point of departure, early in the morning. By then we had become good friends, and were sorry to be at the end of the line but that was it. Some place around the bus station we said goodbye to each other while we waited for the bus to leave for El Paso. I believe we agreed to write to each other, and I suggested that on her way back to Louisville she should stop at Camp Swift for a weekend. I could make arrangements for a room for her at the post guest house.

"I had left home with enough money for hitchhiking to Camp Swift, but not enough to ride buses that far. So, after the tickets and eats at all the bus stops, I ended up broke in Dallas. Somehow Janice found it out, so she insisted that she loan me money for the rest of my trip. I accepted it—about three dollars, I think it was. Then she was off for El Paso, and I headed for Swift.

"That's how it started."

The friendship that began on a bus was continued through correspondence. A letter written by Henry Giles to Janice Moore on October 19, 1943, one week from the date of their meeting, reveals that she wrote to him first. Henry responded: "Hello Janice, It was nice of you to write to me. I was glad to hear from you and will now try to answer by first saying that I'm not much at writing letters. (Which you will soon find out.)" Henry ended his first letter with an invitation: "I know it would possibly be out of your way to come by Camp Swift, and some trouble to you, but I'm asking with a prayer in heart that you will try to, for (please believe me), I do want to see you again."

Janice answered that she would indeed stop at Camp Swift on her way back to Louisville. In the meantime, Henry learned his company was leaving for maneuvers in Louisiana, and their plans had to be canceled. When his unit returned to Camp Swift, all their equipment had been marked BPOE—Boston Port of Embarkation.

Janice Moore did not see Henry Giles again before he boarded the *Santa Elena* on October 8, 1943, and with his battalion began a two-year struggle throughout England, France, Belgium, Luxembourg, and Germany. It would be two years from the day the ship slipped out to sea before he stepped again on American soil.

Born June 23, 1916, Henry Earl Giles was the first child of Bessie Hazel Bottoms and Thomas Franklin Giles of Knifley, Kentucky, where, in 1803, his great-great-grandfather "swapped a rifle for two ridges and a hollow" in a rugged, rural region of northern Adair County. When he was five years old, Henry had typhoid fever and had to learn to walk again by using crutches his father fashioned from an oak tree. He started school on the first Monday in July 1922 and daily walked a mile and a half along the wooded path of an old church road to the Spout Springs schoolhouse, where four generations of Gileses had attended before him.

When Henry enrolled at Spout Springs School, nineteen of the forty-seven children from fourteen families were Giles kin. His first teacher in the one-room schoolhouse was Julius Hatfield, followed by Hazel Williams, Annie Sanders, and Lorena Grant. Annie Sanders recalled Henry as one of her brightest pupils and said he was always eager to help the younger children with their schoolwork.

At age thirteen, Henry completed the eighth grade. For young boys raised on the ridge in the 1920s, schooling ended at Spout Springs. Ridge families prided themselves on self-sufficiency, and further studies in a high school elsewhere in the county would take them away from the ridge where they were needed to help raise a garden patch, corn and tobacco crops, and tend a few head of livestock.

The Gileses attended the Caldwell Chapel Church on the ridge where circuit ministers from the Church of God, Baptist, and other faiths took their turn behind the pulpit of the nondenominational church and expounded the gospel of Jesus Christ. Before the fiery preaching began, the congregation lifted their voices in songs of Zion from shape-note hymnbooks, usually to the accompaniment of a guitar, often played by Henry. At one time, friends and family thought Henry would become a minister. Joe Spires said he and others often heard him praying aloud while he was out in the woods. There were several ministers among the numerous members of the Giles and Bottoms clans.

Life on the ridge offered little opportunity; jobs were rare in the best of times. When Henry was growing up, the Depression years produced even greater hardships. Cornmeal was more easily obtained than flour as most families grew enough corn to have ground for a year's supply of meal, but flour had to be purchased. With a sense of humor Henry wrote, "The first sign of hard times was when there was cornbread for breakfast."

Henry Giles was sixteen years old in 1932 when Franklin Delano Roosevelt ran for the presidency. Henry recalled a slogan used in Adair

County during that election: "Vote for a damn dog if you have to, but vote against Hoover." The first public relief to reach Adair countians following Roosevelt's election was the food commodity. Henry walked the four miles to Knifley to pick up the foodstuffs for his family, consisting of grapefruit, canned pork, government flour, and butter. He later said he would "rather have spent the same amount of time waiting for a firing squad to pull the triggers. The wheels of poverty grind slowly, but they grind exceedingly fine—extinguish the soul."

Henry's first job in the federal relief programs was with the National Youth Administration (NYA). His assignment placed him behind a crosscut saw, supplying firewood for the area county schools. His next employment was with the Works Progress Administration (WPA) county road project for which he obtained his Social Security card, dated June 29, 1937. Using a pick, a shovel, and a wheelbarrow, Henry spread gravel on the narrow passageways that threaded the countryside. At age twenty-one, Henry worked with the Civilian Conservation Corps (CCC) and for the first time in his life rode on a train and left the state of Kentucky. Following a physical examination in Stearns, Kentucky, Henry continued the train journey to Lebanon, Indiana, where the workers dug drainage ditches for several weeks. When questioned after a month and a half of work if he would like to remain on the job or return home, Henry chose to return. He was homesick for the hills of Adair County.

During the next two summers Henry worked, or intended to work, in Indiana. The first season he picked tomatoes; the second, he got a job in a canning factory in Edinburg. His assignment at the cannery was, in his words, "to catch big steel buckets full of canned corn as they rolled down an overhead track from the cooling vat, and land the big buckets on a hand truck to be taken someplace else in the factory." Henry recalled his first day on the job: "Somehow the first tub to land at my station hit the truck without any difficulty. I made out all right up to then. Then ten feet behind that one came the next big bucket. Then, something went wrong. I was out of time; un-synchronized. That big tub missed the truck, turned over, and about nine thousand cans rolled in all directions, all over hell and back. And by the time I realized what had happened, another nine thousand cans were upon me. I hadn't been told what to do in such an emergency as that, so I just calmly walked away from the whole damn mess. Before I was out of the cannery yard I heard the next big tub strike, turn over, and the cans of corn rolling around, but I didn't look back.

"My guess is that that debacle closed the factory down, and threw a lot of innocent people out of work for the rest of the season. In fact, they may still be picking up canned corn at the place, and wondering whatever happened to me. With less than fifty cents to live on, I hitchhiked back to Knifley."

By 1940, the economy had improved but there were still few opportunities for work in Adair County. In March of that year, Henry and a cousin hitchhiked to Louisville, Kentucky, in an effort to join the Army. Henry did not pass the physical examination because of six bad teeth, which he had extracted three months later.

Needing a few extra dollars before returning to Louisville for a second attempt to enlist, Henry cradled three acres of wheat on a stumpy hillside and was paid $2.50 for the job. Cradling wheat was his last job on the ridge. At Fort Knox, Kentucky, on July 16, 1940, he "fell in line with all other civilians wishing to join the Army." After removing his clothing for the physical and being ushered through lines where he received "shots in both arms at the same time," Henry asked an assisting soldier if he had passed. The soldier replied, "Yes sir, Buddy. You never would have been this far along in the line if you hadn't passed everything else." That was the response Henry had been waiting to hear.

"At *last,* by God."

"Each of us had joined the Army because we wanted something better than we had had during the past decade," Henry said. "Some had waited for that day because they were too young before; others, like me, had waited for circumstances that would permit them to leave home."

Henry's circumstances involved a southern rural belief and practice that a son owed his working time to his father until he was twenty-one. Henry was twenty-four in 1940. He had never complained of carrying the burden of responsibility in his father's stead. However, upon learning that his mother, just past forty, was expecting yet another child, which meant increased dependency on him, he decided to join the Army. Always a devoted son, he made sure an allotment was sent from each of his paychecks to his mother and father.

On Wednesday morning, July 17, 1940, Henry was sworn in and, two days later, boarded a Pullman car for a long train ride to March Field, California. At March Field, the recruits were assigned to the 28th (Air Force) Engineers and got their first tastes of soldiering, for which they were paid twenty-one dollars a month.

"Our days were often long, our nights short," Henry wrote, "and the training tiring; but all this was easier on an Appalachian boy than pulling a crosscut saw, sawmilling, or cradling wheat on a stumpy hillside. The Army pay was better, too. A big rain didn't mean a loss of time and pay, and there was no food to buy, no clothing, no lodging problems. So for me, anyhow, this was the best life I had ever known. And it has never embarrassed me to admit it."

When Henry Giles left Knifley on July 12, 1943, he knew he would soon be going to Europe—to war. He had no idea when he boarded a bus in Bowling Green for his journey back to Camp Swift that he would meet a woman whose strength would help sustain him through his many months of military service during World War II.

7
Newlyweds
1943-1945

There were 822 days between the date Henry and Janice met on a bus in Bowling Green, Kentucky, and the time they saw each other again in Louisville on October 11, 1945. In the meantime, Henry wrote Janice 634 letters, which she carefully saved and stored. It is impossible to know how many times she wrote him, but it is easy to assume she wrote as many letters as she received. A foot soldier had no place to keep his mail from home. As Weapons Sergeant for the 291st Engineer Combat Battalion, Henry was involved in continuous mobility during the Normandy invasion, the Battle of the Bulge, and the crossing of the Rhine at Remagen. Throughout the European Theater, his unit dug foxholes, slept in pup tents, and worked under extreme conditions and artillery fire. They repaired roads, built bypasses, reconstructed bridges and culverts, cleaned up debris, and opened bombed-out roads. In those surroundings, a soldier's letters were lost, scattered, or burned across the battlefields of war.

To the soldier "across," letters were a life support. They provided a touch of home, a boost to morale, a will to live. In addition, the letters written by Janice and Henry represented their entire courtship—a courtship that transcended two continents and, as she described, "the spread of sea between them and the dark night of war." Through almost daily correspondence, their friendly greetings soon turned to expressions of love. On September 10, 1943, Henry wrote: "Wonder what could be wrong? Do you believe a guy could meet a girl, say—on a bus and ride with her a few hours, then find out he loves her? Do you think that could be possible? Well anyhow, it seems like you are always on my mind."

To Henry, a twenty-seven-year-old soldier who, before enlisting in the army, had not traveled more than a few miles from the simple home where he was born in the Cumberland foothills, letters from Janice were a mainstay. To Janice, a divorced woman far from her childhood home who was working to support herself and her young daughter, Henry's letters offered encouragement. In a time of war, she had a soldier; he had a girl. The emptiness in each of their lives was quietly dispelled day by day through letters that bore endearing words that instilled hope for a brighter, happier future.

Three letters were written September 19, 1943, the last one containing the words that took Henry Giles over two months to put to paper: "I don't know why Darling, but when I try to write you, it seems that something wells up inside and words fail me when I try to tell you what you do mean to me.

"Perhaps it should be strange that I write you like this since we have seen each other only once, but somehow it seems only natural. Oh! Darling, it seems that there is only one thing I can think of to write now, which is only three words, I love you." Somewhat apologetically, Henry then sought to learn more about Janice: "Darling, *please* don't be offended at this very rude question, but I would like to know your age. Not that it would matter if you were two, or two hundred, I would still love you more than I can ever tell you. *Please* don't be angry at that question. *I love you Baby.*" It is not known if Janice admitted her actual age of thirty-eight, but Henry's response two weeks later revealed he at least learned that she was older than he. "My age is 27," he responded. "I know our ages won't matter. My Grandmother was ten years older than my Grandfather. She died at ninety-one years of age. My Grandfather was eighty years old when he died. They had almost sixty years of married life."

The letters between Henry and Janice were newsy notes of discovery, a continuance of the things they had learned on the bus trip to Texas. Henry's constant praise of her letters revealed that Janice was a wordsmith, capable of writing beautiful, descriptive letters. In his thirty-first letter to her, dated October 26, 1943, he did not realize what prophetic words he penned when he wrote, "You know, once I almost asked you if you ever tried writing poetry. Or at writing stories of any kind, but somehow I decided not to. It seems you could write almost anything."

Henry replied honestly but evasively to Janice's questions of what he planned to do when he was discharged. "After being in the Army this long, it's actually hard to state one certain thing. One thing I'm sure of, is I want *you* no matter what I decide to do. I know Darling that we want the same things as far as a home is concerned, peace and quiet and above all, love and faithfulness. I've known for a long time that I don't want to go back as far in the 'sticks' as I came from. It's *too* quiet. I trust you will understand that it *is* difficult to be exact."

Whether Janice understood the depth of his uncertainty or not, an announcement appeared two weeks later in the Sunday edition of the *Fort Smith Southwest American:* "The engagement of Janice Holt Moore to Sergeant Henry E. Giles of Knifley, Kentucky, has been announced by her mother, Mrs. John Albert Holt, 501 North Thirty-ninth Street. The wedding will take place when Sergeant Giles returns from foreign service where he is with an engineers unit in England. The bride-elect is secretary to Dean Sherrill of the Louisville Presbyterian Theological Seminary at Louisville, Kentucky."

When Janice prepared her first Christmas box to Henry, she included a different form of communication. She read a letter she had written into an RCA transcription machine and carefully tucked the recording in between his presents. On December 21, Henry responded: "Not only did I have a letter from you today,—but I heard you talk!! Yes, I played the record you sent at a little cafe in a town where I was working. Darling, how my heart cried for you as I heard you talking, bringing back memories, happy memories, of the few hours we were together. The hours that have since meant so much to me.

"Several of the fellows heard it, and while they were making remarks as to how good it was, and how well you talked etc., it had a far greater meaning to me. It was hearing you speak, the one I love. The voice I remember so well.

"While the record was being played, one fellow asked if you were a college professor. Others wondered why a woman like that would have anything to do with me. Of course, I didn't know the answer to that one."

Henry's gift to Janice was a locket with a mother-of-pearl inset on which was attached a tiny silver castle, the insignia of the Engineers. She described it to him as "quite perfect," and added, "Now that I have put it on, I shall not take it off again."

Letter by letter, the couple shared their ideas and dreams concerning marriage and family life. Henry wrote, "I could never see a wife of mine working. I believe it's a man's responsibility to do the earning and providing. Don't you, really? I would be ashamed to be seen if my wife had to earn or even help earn a living for us. I mean so far as working for wages is concerned. A wife, to me, would be a lot more than just a woman to live with. She's something very precious, to love, and cherish and care for. I trust you see it the same way." Even though Henry was unsure of *what* he might do "to earn a living," to a woman married sixteen years to a husband who never held a steady job, his acknowledgment of "a man's responsibility" and his ensuing promises to provide must have touched Janice deeply.

The letters had been flowing for six months when Henry wrote that he "told Mama about the difference in our age," and added, "I'll tell her in time that you have been married. There's always the best time for everything, not that it would matter with me if it did with her. After all that's a very small thing, as far as I'm concerned."

Henry's hesitancy to tell his mother that Janice was a divorced woman was indicative of the continuing social attitudes toward divorce through the 1940s. Of the 8 percent of marriages that ended in dissolution prior to World War II, a greater percent took place in urban areas as opposed to rural. The strict religious beliefs of the Kentucky hills did not allow for divorce under any circumstance. "What God hath joined together, let no man put asunder," were the biblical words adhered to by God-fearing folks.

To the letter Henry received from "Mama, in answer to the one I told her about your age," he remarked, "she seemed a little surprised, because your picture doesn't look it." Assuring Janice it did not matter to him that she was divorced, Henry continually wrote about marriage and commitment: "Unfaithfulness is one thing I wouldn't dream of. I am now and shall continue to be just what you expect of the one you are going to marry and to be your husband. Believe me Darling, I *will never* do anything to hurt you or cross you. I love you too much.

"As for drinking, I've always drank what I wanted (which is nothing to be proud of) and have been a few places but have never been 'called down' by any law officer. Military or civilian.

"Gambling, in almost any degree, is in excess. Basically, I mean. I do sometimes play poker or blackjack if there's a low limit. I mean low. It's usually done for want of pastime." Henry's brief replies to drinking and gambling were most likely in response to questions asked by a woman who was married to a man who abused both. To add a lighter note to his seriousness, Henry postscripted: "Flash: We had chicken for dinner today. And I had a leg besides the usual neck. G.I. chickens are usually made of wings and necks."

Frequently Henry reminisced about their meeting and informed Janice her letters written on the twelfth of the month were "always aces." He consistently expressed his feelings on the anniversary date: "Today, it has been eight months since we met and learned to love each other! These eight months have been the happiest part of my life."

Henry always tried not to sound "too gloomy" when he wrote to his mother or Janice. In a letter to Janice on June 25, 1944, he humorously tried to assuage her burdensome fear since the invasion: "I'm in France now, but don't worry honey, for I don't think the bullet has been made with my name on it, and I'm not worried about those addressed 'to whom it may concern,' and since my name isn't Smith or Jones, there shouldn't be any mix-up there. So, just take it easy. I'll be back and I'll be thinking of you every day and loving you with all my heart, until the day we can be together again."

As Henry wrote Janice far more often than he did to his parents, Janice began corresponding with them to share the news she received. Henry was delighted and told Janice that he hoped "you and Mama are doing a good job cheering each other up." Each wanting to meet the other, Frank and Bessie Giles invited Janice to visit their home in Knifley during her summer vacation, one year from the time she had met their son.

Janice accepted their invitation and traveled by bus from Louisville to Campbellsville, where she was greeted by Henry's oldest sister, Irene. As the Gileses did not own an automobile, they paid an acquaintance one dollar to transport Janice the remaining twenty miles to Knifley. Henry eagerly awaited the letter describing Janice's first visit to his homeland. He was also glad to receive the words from his Mama, "We sure do like her."

Nothing had prepared Henry for the surprising information he received from Janice shortly after her visit with his parents, as is clearly indicated by his August 15 response: "Received your letter yesterday, written August 1st, and I've waited until today to answer so as to be sure of what I wanted to write. I am going to tell you *frankly* what I think of your not telling me of Libby.

"In the first place, there was no earthly reason for you not to, and you caused yourself a lot of 'sweating,' (pardon the slang) there was no use of. Trying as you did, you failed miserably to present one good excuse for your silence. And evidently, you wouldn't have said anything about her until we were married, had she not married first, causing you to feel so alone. Darling, I too wish I could have been with you to tell you everything *is* alright.

"I love you darling and nothing that has been can keep me from wanting you for my own. Don't let the way I started this letter mislead you. I knew what I wanted to write but wanted to use what I thought was the proper sequence. This is the only letter there will ever be anything in about your not telling me about Libby. And there will never (and I mean *never*) be a 'flare up.'"

On Sunday, July 30, 1944, Elizabeth Ann Moore had married 1st Lt. James Nash Hancock in Tucson, Arizona, where Nash was stationed at the Davis-Monthon Air Base. Her mother later wrote about their courtship and wedding: "It was March of 1942 when Nash left Louisville, and it was January of 1944 when he returned. When he left again, Libby had one of his lieutenant's bars and the letters started flowing, and the phone started ringing, from Albuquerque, from Lincoln, from Tucson.

"He called one hot July night and he and Libby talked with their usual leisure. I was in the bedroom and when Libby wandered in after hanging up, she shared, 'Mom, Nash wants me to come to Tucson, and I want to go.'

"I knew then. 'When?'

"'Now. He can't get another leave, and there's just a few weeks left.'

"'O.K.'

"In all the whirl of Libby's hurried packing and getting away, in the mad confusion of that last morning when she scrambled out of her shorts and old blouse and left the pins from her hair scattered over the top of her dressing table, in all of that and in all of our excited, laughing talk, I knew the time had come. Not that there was a word said about it. But I knew just the same.

"I said goodbye carelessly and gaily enough. Like it was just another trip. Like it was an everyday occurrence for her to take off so suddenly for Tucson. Like my heart wasn't tied in a tight knot. 'I'll be back in ten days,' she said, waving to me as she went down the ramp. But I knew better. I knew she would never be back! Not the way she had always been. I knew she was getting out of our life forever. I said goodbye to nineteen beautiful years with her, said goodbye to my daughter and let her go to become a wife.

"For she did, of course. They like to remind me that they themselves didn't know they were going to be married then. I don't argue with them about it. Maybe they didn't know it. But I did. And when I went back to the lonely, solitary emptiness of the apartment and saw her faded, worn little shorts, and the ragged, discarded old blouse, and the scattered pins and the old, unwanted hair ribbons on top of her dressing table, it was like seeing the still warm, still shaped garments of someone who has just died. For a way of life had died . . . a beautiful, precious way of life.

"But even as I went completely to pieces and clutched the shorts and the blouse to me, and sobbed my heart out, I knew I wouldn't have had it any other way. For if our way of life was dying, Libby was starting a new way, her own way, and it was right that she should. The currents of life are forward, and I would not have kept Libby from going with them!

"Her letters came every day, full of the things they were doing, places they were going, people they were seeing, fun they were having. And as the end of the visit drew near there was no mention of its being prolonged. 'I'm flying home,' Libby wrote, 'and I leave Thursday evening. Will be home early Friday.'

"But Friday morning came without Libby. I hadn't expected her. But I did expect the call that came that night. 'Do you mind if I marry your daughter Sunday evening?' Nash said.

"As ready as I thought I was for it, it stopped the very beat of my heart. But I like to think my voice was quiet and steady as I talked to first one of them, then the other. 'Mom, we didn't decide until I was ready to leave last night! Mom, is it all right?'

"'It's perfect!

"'Oh gee, mom! Gee, we've been going in circles! We've already got the license, and we're going to be married in the little church in the hills, and we've already talked to the minister, and I'm going to wear a suit! I bought it today. Mom, it's pale blue, and I'm going to have white things with it, and just a little veil on the hat.'

"Just a little veil! She was always going to be married in the seminary chapel, with white satin, and a long veil! And Dr. Sherrill was going to marry her! And there would be six bridesmaids, and a flower girl and a ring bearer. All the trimmings. That's what Libby was going to have!

"'It sounds lovely, darling. What time Sunday evening?'

"'Oh! Oh, of course! Seven-thirty. And we made it Sunday because Nash can't get off Saturday. But he has Sunday and Monday off. Mom, we've got seven weeks before he has to go.'

"Seven weeks! But what a great pride I took in them both. A pride in their daring and their courage in facing the grim, hard facts which lay before them. A pride in their hope and in their faith, not only in themselves, but in life. I also took pride in the fact that they expected me to have as much courage as they!

"How could you bear to have Libby married so far from home? people asked me. How could you bear not seeing her married? How could you bear not being there? How could I bear it? Why, I was there. I was there the whole three years they were being married, for that little ceremony in the little church in the hills was only the final ceremony. Libby and Nash were being married when they quarreled and bickered that first winter in our little apartment. They were being married through all the letters that came and went during the two years he was gone. They were being married each time he phoned. And I was there.

"But I was there, too, at that final ceremony. That Sunday afternoon Dr. and Mrs. Caldwell, the seminary president and his wife, drove by. 'We've come to take you home with us for dinner,' they said. But they understood when I said I'd rather be alone. Dr. Benfield, the vice-president, also understood when he called to ask if I would like to spend the evening with them. And Dr. and Mrs. Sherrill understood when I borrowed his book containing the marriage service. I didn't know about the fly that settled on Nash's nose and almost spoiled the dignity of the occasion, but, keeping my place in the marriage service, I followed them through their responses. Oh, yes, I was there."

Libby and Nash chose St. Phillips Episcopal Church for their wedding, following the suggestion of her great-aunt Ophelia McGraw Romero. At that time, "the little church in the hills" was in the desert; now, it is a part of the city of Tucson. Janice was comforted in the knowledge that her Aunt Phele and cousin Lorraine could be with Libby. Seven weeks later, Nash was sent to Taranto, Italy, where he served as a bomber pilot with the 15th Air Corps. His young bride returned to the Hepburn Avenue apartment and her mother.

Now Henry knew it all. The facts were laid out before him. He knew that Janice was older than he, that she had been married before, and she had a daughter. But he was not shaken. His letters of endearment continued to be written. "I got a letter from Mom," Henry wrote two days after his response to Janice's letter informing him of Libby, "and she was telling me again how everyone liked you. She also told me how you left on the truck with the goats, etc." Janice had ridden back to the bus station in Campbellsville with "six goats, a cow, and two pigs."

In April 1945 Janice mailed Henry a copy of an eighty-eight page manuscript she had completed December 14, 1943, and titled, "Elizabeth-Libby." The pages related anecdotes of her daughter from birth to high school graduation. On April 27, Henry acknowledged receipt of it: "Darling, if there was ever a time when I didn't know where or how to begin a letter, it is now. The mail came through and I had one letter and the story of Libby's life. I've already read it and there's no words that will express the pleasure I had in doing so. I've never read anything that held my attention as much, or anything as interesting and full of life. For some reason, I feel closer to you and if possible, love you more. You already know that I love you more than words can tell."

At long last, the news the world waited anxiously to hear spread throughout the country and were included in Henry's letter May 7, 1945: "The war is over! Thank God." Finally the words Janice had waited two years to read were scrawled September 4, 1945: "Hello Honey, In a few more hours I'll be on my way home to you. You be ready and maybe soon I'll be there."

The war was over; the weary soldier was on his way home. Henry sailed from Marseilles, France, on September 15, 1945, aboard an old *Liberty* ship that was three weeks in reaching the New York harbor. He received his discharge from the army at Camp Atterbury, Indiana, on

October 10, and arrived in Louisville at 2:00 A.M. on Thursday, October 11. Janice Holt Moore and Henry Earl Giles were married in the small living room of the 1437 Hepburn Avenue apartment at 9:00 P.M. the same day.

The wedding was performed by Rev. James M. Gilbert Jr. in the presence of Janice's friends, Dorothy and Lloyd Naveaux. Immediately following the ceremony, Mrs. Janice Holt Giles telephoned her daughter, Mrs. Elizabeth Hancock, in Santa Fe, New Mexico. The newlyweds left soon after the wedding to spend a few days with Henry's family in Adair County and then traveled on to Arkansas so Janice could introduce her husband to her family.

8
Inbetweenst the Work
1945-1949

When Janice and Henry returned to the Hepburn Avenue apartment, they quickly discovered a whole lot more about each other than they could possibly have learned through a forty-eight-hour bus ride and 822 days of letter writing. Henry sandwiched his few items of clothing in their one closet and stashed his shaving gear in the bathroom he and Janice shared with a bachelor and two working girls.

Settled into the apartment, Henry began to contemplate what he was going to do as a civilian and as a new husband, how he could fulfill his promise to support a wife. "It's actually hard to state one certain thing," he had written Janice. Now he was faced with the decision of finding that "one certain thing"—and it was not easy. He later wrote: "I had adjusted well enough into the military life from an Appalachian, but I could not un-adjust from the Army into the middle class society of which Janice was a part. It wasn't her fault, and in a sense not mine. And, though it was necessary at the time, choosing to live in the city—Louisville—didn't help matters any. If I had gone immediately back to Appalachia—Adair County—I might have re-adjusted better. But what about Janice? We were in it together, and one doesn't just arbitrarily force one's will upon another so abruptly.

"I didn't have a job, and there was nothing I could do except manual labor. If I had been a technician of some sort I might have made it better. But I was a warrior. And nobody needed a squad leader or a platoon sergeant, and certainly not a good machine-gunner. So there I was—alone in the masses."

After two months of marriage and confinement in an apartment without a job, Henry slipped out one morning without telling Janice he was leaving and traveled by bus to Adair County. With no telephone service on the ridge, he wrote her a letter a few days later telling her where he was and that he planned to spend an indefinite time with his family.

The adjustments to civilian and married life did not come easily for Henry Giles, nor were they easy on his wife. When he returned to Louisville, Janice soon realized "the country boy" would not be satisfied without some land of his own. She went along patiently when they began to search for a place, hoping to find a small acreage tract near Louisville where Henry would be happy and she could continue working at the seminary—which she was beginning to view as a necessity. It is no surprise that the symptoms of anxiety Janice experienced before in times of financial insecurity were aggravating her nervous system again.

By spring 1946 Henry and Janice had purchased two acres with an old log structure in Bullitt County, twenty miles south of Louisville. In sublime contentment, Henry busily set about dismantling the V-notched logs and reconstructing a cabin to provide a weekend retreat in the country. By the end of summer he had completed most of the work of tearing down the old building and reworking the logs. New windows were purchased, new doors were made, rafters were raised, and a roof put on to secure the small structure. Henry chinked and filled the spaces between the logs in the same tradition his ancestors had done half a century before him.

In the fall of 1946 Henry considered attending high school but could not see himself sitting in a classroom with students half his age. He learned that a veterans' school was being organized in Louisville under President Franklin D. Roosevelt's Servicemen's Readjustment Act. Veterans who had not graduated from high school were required to take the GED (General Education Development) examination before enrollment. After testing, Henry was informed that he had scored high enough to qualify for a high school diploma and could enter college, but he felt that, since it had been sixteen years and a world war since he completed eighth grade at Spout Springs School, he needed basic high school courses—*and* the ninety-dollar allowance a month he would be paid while he attended the veterans' school.

Janice gave an insightful description of Henry's dilemma and frustrations during the first year of their marriage: "Few men getting out of the army could have had a more difficult time of adjustment than Henry Giles. After five and a half years in the army, the last two of them overseas with a very closeknit outfit, it was hard for him to become a civilian. I have vivid memories of his discomfort with civilian clothing. It didn't fit. It was too loose. The trousers flapped around the ankles; the shirts were baggy. And I recall his lost feeling that he didn't understand civilians, the way they thought and lived, their aspirations, or even their conversations. 'I have nothing in common with anybody,' he used to say. 'Nobody talks my language.'

"A country boy, he had also to live in the city, which he loathed. A bachelor for a good many years, he had to learn to be a husband. And he added a final difficulty in returning to school and having to learn to study again. Twice in the first year he was on the verge of re-enlisting in the army, feeling almost desperately that he was so conditioned to 'soldiering' he would never be happy doing anything else. To this day I am not sure it was wise of me to counsel patience. Perhaps a career soldier was precisely what Henry Giles was best cut out to be."

While Henry attended the veterans' school during the winter of 1946, an announcement from Westminster Press, the Presbyterian publishing house, appeared in the mail that crossed Janice's desk at the seminary. The Press was opening a fiction department and offering a prize of eight thousand dollars and publication for the best manuscript submitted. Since the beginning of her work in 1934 in religious education, Janice had written Sunday School lesson materials, articles for denominational magazines, poetry, and worship services. Her worship service, "Glory to God in the Highest"; a poem, "Out of the Darkness"; and an Easter drama, "Publish Glad Tidings," had been published in Westminster Press literature.

When Janice completed the autobiographical sketch of Libby's life in 1943 and mailed a copy to Henry, she also submitted a copy to a publisher, but it was returned unaccepted. In 1948 she researched and wrote a centennial history for the Warren Memorial Presbyterian Church in Louisville, but she had never given thought to writing fiction.

But apparently Henry had. And he had admitted to Janice that he had even gone so far as to develop a synopsis of a novel but had thrown it aside in discouragement. Janice showed her husband the announcement from Westminster Press and pleaded with him to write his book. Instead, Henry encouraged his wife to write it. After numerous trips to Adair County, it occurred to both Henry and Janice that a good book could be written about life on the ridge. Janice recognized that the traditional culture of Henry's people had changed little from the time his ancestors settled there in 1803. Having grown up in the intimacy of the society, Henry's esoteric understanding of the environment coupled with the countless tales he told of the region provided a wellspring of inspiration.

Janice Holt Giles began writing a novel at night after an eight-hour workday. On the kitchen table after dinner, using a typewriter loaned by the seminary, she set for herself a stint of three hours every night, five nights a week. "Toothache, headache, flu, sinus trouble, no matter what," she wrote from 7:30 P.M. to 10:30 P.M. and, in three months' time, completed her first novel and submitted it to Westminster Press under the names of both Henry and Janice Giles.

The veterans' school was in existence only one year. During that time, Henry completed his course work, and the score of his GED examination was forwarded to Adair County. Nearing his thirty-first birthday, Henry Giles received his diploma from Adair County High School.

In the spring of 1947, Henry was ready to take up residence in the cabin. As the lease had terminated for their apartment, Janice and Henry stored their "city furniture" and left for Bullitt County. Henry wrote, "By the time we moved into our cottage, our old $150, 1930 model, toggle-switch Nash had run its race. So, each morning Janice would arise with the birds at daybreak, eat a little breakfast, then ride with someone into Shepherdsville—two miles from our cottage—to the bus station, take a bus to Louisville and the Seminary."

In late fall, the Gileses retrieved their furniture and moved back to Louisville into a third-floor apartment on Lexington Road. Henry was still unemployed. Janice's co-worker at the seminary, Maxine Strain, had a friend who was a foreman at the International Harvester plant. Jim Bench was successful in getting Henry a job at the plant, alternating on the second and third shifts.

At first, Henry "did a lot of sweeping and cleaning," but was told to observe the machine operators as much as his time allowed so that, when a position opened, he would be prepared to fill it. Henry followed the foreman's advice, and in a short time was reclassified as a machine operator and put on "piece work."

After nearly a year of waiting, Janice was informed by Westminster Press that her manuscript was one of five to reach the fiction contest finals. The 1947 prize recipient was Delia Gardner White, whose book, *No Trumpet Before Him,* was later serialized in *The Saturday Evening Post.* Westminster editor Olga Edmond wrote Janice and Henry that she considered their story publishable if certain sections could be rewritten adequately. Henry was "inherently pessimistic" and refused to have anything more to do with it. Furthermore, he instructed Janice "not to use his name on it again." Describing herself as "unquenchably optimistic," and with guidance from Olga Edmond, Janice diligently set about the rewriting.

Following "much blue pencilling" and assistance from the editor who patiently and understandingly worked with her all during the revision of the book, making Janice go back time and time again to rewrite a section until she was satisfied it was the best she could do, a revised manuscript was submitted in 1949. *The Enduring Hills* was accepted for publication, to appear in April 1950.

The book is the story of a man's search for himself. The plot, suggested and developed by Henry, closely paralleled his own life. There is great similarity between the fictional Hod and Mary Pierce and Henry and

Janice Giles. Wanting more than his father and grandfather had, Hod longed to go out into the world and make something of himself, but his family obligations kept him at home. Hod Pierce joined the Army for a chance to prove himself. Hod, who even has Henry's army serial number, met Mary on a bus during his furlough home before being shipped overseas. After marrying and working in Louisville, Hod and Mary Pierce returned to his homeland on the ridge when he realized "a man could search forever outside himself for the purpose of his life, but until he turned his eyes inward, he would never find the home he was seeking."

By the time her first novel was accepted, Janice was well into writing a second, titled *Miss Willie*. Henry was working at International Harvester, and there were weekend retreats to the cabin in the country. On the surface, all appeared to be well. But for a man born in the country who had grown up with the freedom of roaming the hills and hollows, "ennui eventually set in" with the confinement of a job on an assembly line in a factory. Henry wrote: "Gradually I realized that all I was doing was making money, eating and sleeping. Work so you can eat, eat and sleep so you can work, so you can . . . another proverbial vicious circle. Punch in, punch out, get your check on Friday, take a long weekend, have fun. Have fun if it kills you; but get back in time to punch in, punch out for five more days, eat and sleep, get your check, try to have more fun. Do it in spite of hell, or if you die doing it." Henry then shifted his musing to the relationship he and Janice shared, or failed to share: "Because Janice worked days at the Seminary, and I was either on the second or third shift at Harvester all the time, we merely waved at each other daily through the week. And after several months of waving in passing, the arrangement began to vex both of us. After all, if a man and woman are married to each other—they might as well *live* together.

"Children, I suppose, would force a conscientious father into a lifetime of enslavement such as that but we had no little ones to feed and water. (Thank goodness.) All I was was a short-tailed rat on a synthetic treadmill running a losing race into nothingness. So, as our future grandson was later to say to his mother when he got home from his first day of Vacation Bible School, 'I had to get out of that damn place.'

"By then there were many labor disputes and strikes at the plant, and I was losing a lot of work and time. Also by then Janice and I had a few hundred dollars saved for rainy days, so we decided to take to the woods."

With Henry's restlessness and unhappiness added to her own stress and work responsibilities, Janice developed ulcers. According to Maxine Strain, Janice called the seminary one morning to say she was hemorrhaging and would not be in to work. Janice later described the situation: "The next thing I knew Henry was packing. 'We're going to the farm,' he said grimly. 'The hell with this kind of life!'"

And they did. Shortly after Christmas, Janice received a five-hundred-dollar advance from Westminster following the signing of the contract for *The Enduring Hills.* With the advance, plus most of their savings, she and Henry paid eleven hundred dollars cash for "the little rocky, woodsy forty-acre farm" in Adair County they had heard about while visiting Henry's parents. After acquiring the land, Janice hoped they would not move to the ridge for several years—not until they had saved back the eleven hundred dollars and more to go with it to purchase farm equipment and remodel the house.

But six months of constant strikes at International Harvester, in addition to Janice's ulcers, altered those hopes. She summarized the transition: "I had written a novel. It had been accepted by a publisher. In sublime ignorance and supreme self-confidence, we quit our jobs in the city, spent all our savings on a forty-acre tract of timber hilariously miscalled a farm and moved to the ridge."

Janice laid her work on *Miss Willie* aside and moved to the ridge with her husband on May 30, 1949. The decision was made so hastily the house had not been cleaned or readied. Janice described the twenty-year-old structure as looking "ancient as time." It was a thin, spindling house, fifteen by thirty feet, with two rooms downstairs and one big room upstairs, which had neither floor nor ceiling; the house had neither electricity nor plumbing.

The Knifley post office was located four and one-half miles of dirt road from Janice and Henry's house, which sat right in the crest of a three-mile half-circle. To get to Knifley, one could go by Dunbar Hill in one direction or the Ray Williams Road in the other; both ways presented steep hills. In good weather, Dunbar was preferred; in bad, Ray Williams because it was rockier, thus making for a little less mud. There were times when neither passageway could be traveled. A week of spring rains left the road virtually impassable. Even if the wheels of the vehicle did not mire in the mud, there was still a flooded creek to ford. Other seasons could be worse. Janice explained, "The only things that can traverse the ridge in the middle of the winter are a mule, a jeep or tractor, and a helicopter." There were many occasions when even the mail could not get through.

Before Janice could return to writing *Miss Willie,* a garden had to be worked and a tobacco crop set. Gardens were usually planted on the ridge by early May and tobacco transplanted from plant bed to field between May 15 and June 1. Not moving until the end of May, Janice and Henry had some catching up to do. They purchased a hoe, rake, ax, spading fork, and scythe and went to work. Henry borrowed a team of mules and a plow from one of his cousins to break the ground for the vegetable garden and tobacco patch. To Janice, time had turned back to a lifestyle long past—that of her grandparents and parents in Kinta, Altus, and Charleston. To Henry, it was time to begin living—he was home at last, on the ridge.

In *40 Acres and No Mule*, Janice wrote about her adjustment to ridge life: "If it seems farfetched that I should be able to change practically every habit of my life without a great deal of trouble, I'm sorry, but it is true. Except for the lack of an electric iron and a refrigerator I didn't mind not having electricity at all.

"As for lamps, I loved the kerosene lamps. We had two good Aladdin lamps, the kind that use a mantle and give a very bright light. The light was soft and yellow, and it had a cozy, warm glow. Bringing in the wood, filling the lamps, drawing up the night water, those were a part of winding up the day. They became routine chores, and I remember thinking once as I brought in an armful of wood: How did I end the day in the city? With this feeling of content? With this simplicity of making ready for the night? With this knowledge of a day lived fully and richly? There is a significance to me in the evening chores. They settle my account for the day. They sum up, add, and total another turning of the earth, and generally I come to the end of the day replete with happiness. Even at first, when I was only beginning to sense these things, I knew a peace and contentment I had never known before.

"When we drove up, I could not help taking a little pride in our ownership of the place. I remember that as I stepped out of the car I thought, This is our own land! And there was a sense of miracle in the thought. It was the first time in my whole life that I had ever stepped foot on land to which I had clear title. My father and mother had been teachers, and we had moved constantly. They did not buy their first home until long after my first marriage, so that their home had never been my home. Libby and I had lived in apartments, moving as my work took us to different cities. And in the years of our marriage Henry and I had lived in an apartment, so that, even in the midst of being ill physically, the appalling heat of the day, the desolation of house and yard, I had a brief feeling of permanence, of coming home."

With the first summer of hard work on the ridge farm behind her, Janice returned to writing about the place where she now lived and the people that were her neighbors in an area she defined as "an island long isolated in the middle of America, a primitive society with its own mores and norms, its own peculiar ways and customs, its own social structure." By late fall 1949, the second manuscript, *Miss Willie,* was completed "sort of inbetweenst" the garden, housework, and tobacco crop and placed in the mail to Westminster Press.

9
Drawn from Real Life
1949-1950

"Meet Miss Willie!" Janice began the letter included with her manuscript to Olga Edmond, November 30, 1949. "I am very fond of her and I hope you like her too!" Janice had only to recall her parents for inspiration to begin her second novel about a schoolteacher who answered "the Macedonian call" from her niece, Mary Pierce, to "come over" into Piney Ridge and teach in the one-room ridge schoolhouse. Again, the fictional characters had their genesis in family and friends. The young boy, Rufe, grew from a story Henry told Janice about his boyhood. Until he was almost fourteen years old Henry believed he was the only person on the ridge who could hear the birds singing as he had never heard anyone else mention the songs of birds or even appear to hear them. Being too timid to talk about his feelings, Henry went through childhood, he thought, listening to the birds alone. "The rebellions in the Piney Ridge school, and Rufe's further rebellions" were also suggested by Henry, and Janice strongly suspected they had their basis in truth.

After reading the manuscript describing Miss Willie Payne's experiences of trying to enlighten ridge folks about a better way of doing things and learning a new way of life herself, including the romance with Wells Pierce, Olga congratulated Janice "on doing a fine job!" and informed her that there was no doubt concerning Westminster accepting the novel for publication.

After receiving the exciting news, Janice and Henry made plans to spend Christmas in Santa Fe with Libby and Nash and their growing family. Janice's first grandchild, Bartlett Neal Hancock, was born April 10, 1948; her second grandchild, John Graham Hancock, was born May 3, 1949, just weeks before the move to the ridge.

When Janice and Henry returned home from New Mexico, the contract for *Miss Willie* was awaiting Janice's signature. In a letter to Olga with the signed agreement, Janice included a most surprising announcement: "Henry has written his first book-length manuscript! I have been editing it and typing it for him and he's got a whale of a good book—in its field. It's a murder and suspense thing, set on the ridge, of course. He's sending it to Little, Brown & Company. We've just about worn out this typewriter, between us! I write days and poor Henry takes the night shift! Comes the book club check in August, and we get a brand new Royal!"

Soon after Olga received the news from Janice, she informed her she was resigning from Westminster Press in May as she was going to have a baby. Having great admiration and respect for Olga, Janice sent best wishes for her personal happiness but also expressed sadness in learning of the resignation. "Olga Edmond taught me how to write," Janice acknowledged, "and I mean that very literally. She took the time and had the patience to work with me for months, and what she gave me was actually a course in creative writing." Olga Victoria Edmond, a 1936 graduate of Wellesley College with majors in German and English Composition and an M.A. from Wellesley in English Composition, had been fiction editor for Westminster Press since 1945.

In late April, Janice received a letter from William Heyliger, who was filling in for Olga, that informed her the general opinion at Westminster was that her second book was "a better book than her first." Janice was delighted as she also was more fond of *Miss Willie* than of *The Enduring Hills* and was glad the editorial opinion sustained her feeling. "I was horribly afraid of being a one-book writer!" she admitted.

Before Olga left Westminster, Janice asked if she could recommend a literary agent. Olga shared the names of three agents in New York: Oliver Swan with the Paul R. Reynolds and Son agency, Bernice Baumgarten with Brandt and Brandt, and Martha Winston of Curtis Brown. Janice waited until the end of May before writing to Oliver Swan, as his name appeared first on the list. Following an introduction that he had been recommended by Olga Edmond, Janice informed him that Westminster had released *The Enduring Hills,* which was the May selection for Family Reading Club, and would be publishing her second book, *Miss Willie,* the following spring, which both Peoples Book Club and Family wanted. She presumed Westminster would decide which one to sell it to based on the best offer.

Janice explained to Swan that she was working on a third novel to complete the Piney Ridge trilogy, which she had planned with Olga's guidance. Following that book, she planned to write two personal stories, the first based on her life and relationship with her daughter and her work as a religious education director and the second an account of her first year living on a forty-acre ridge farm. Janice told Swan she did not have an agent but believed she had reached a place where she needed one for serialization, motion picture rights, and such things that were "completely over [her] head" that she might be missing. Janice had given some thought to changing publishers and solicited his opinion on that.

Janice also told Swan that Henry had begun "to write a little," and explained that his first short story had been sent to the *Ellery Queen Mystery Magazine* for their 1949 annual short mystery contest and won the first story award and $150 prize. Miss Jane Lawson of Little, Brown and Company had seen the manuscript and written him, asking him to try a full-length manuscript for their consideration. He did, and for the past three months they had been going over it, but Henry had received word that they were returning the manuscript because of disagreement among the staff concerning it. "Will you let us know whether you will undertake to handle our material?" Janice asked Oliver Swan, who responded immediately. On June 1 he wrote, "Replying to your letter of May 30, we'd be very happy to have a chance to consider your husband's manuscript and would be very much interested in you and your future work. We couldn't *promise* to act for either of you as we like to be genuinely enthusiastic about the work of the people we take up. However, I think the odds are very much in favor of this and I'll look forward to hearing from you further at your early convenience. In the meantime, we'll keep a lookout for Mr. Giles' manuscript which we'll do our best to read fairly promptly."

"Mr. Giles' manuscript" and the correspondence from Little, Brown and Company was mailed to Oliver Swan on June 5. Within two days of receipt of it, Swan wrote Janice that he had read it and remarked, "If your books interest us as much as this manuscript of your husband's, I can assure you we'd be very happy to handle your future work."

The expediency of Oliver Swan's response to Janice Holt Giles's work is indicative of his impression of her talent as a nascent author. He quickly discerned her ability to produce quality manuscripts and felt her capable of becoming a prolific writer. Without telephone service on the ridge, the dialogue exchanged in correspondence between the two became prolific as well. Everything they discussed in the next decade was through the written word. Even after telephone service was installed in north Adair County in 1961, most of their communication continued to be written.

Born in Waltham, Massachusetts, on July 27, 1904, Oliver Gould Swan was less than a year older than Janice Giles. In 1926 he joined the editorial staff of Macrae-Smith, a Philadelphia publishing firm. Seeking new material for the firm, he traveled to New York in 1946 to call on literary agents and contacted a former classmate, Paul Reynolds Jr., whose father founded the Paul R. Reynolds literary agency in 1893.

At that time, there were no literary agents in America serving as intermediaries between authors and editors. Paul Reynolds began to act on behalf of authors, presenting their manuscripts to editors and publishers, securing the best possible prices, and charging commissions for his services as agent. In doing so, Reynolds set himself up as the first literary agent in the United States. In the early years, Reynolds's dealings with book publishers took a secondary place to the selling of serial rights to magazine editors. One of his most noted sales was the serial rights of Paul Leicester Ford's *Janice Meredith* to *Collier's* for four thousand dollars. The book, published in 1899, had an impressive sale of 275,000 copies—one of which was read by Lucy McGraw Holt prior to the birth of her daughter, who then received the name of the heroine of the novel.

Reunited with his old friend, Paul Reynolds Jr. invited Oliver Swan to join him in the New York office at 599 Fifth Avenue. Recognized as being honorable and tremendously diligent, Swan submitted a book thirty, forty, or even fifty times if he believed in it. He soon became a partner in the firm that boasted an extraordinary clientele, including H.G. Wells, Edith Wharton, Winston Churchill, Willa Cather, and George Bernard Shaw.

Janice Holt Giles's first book, *The Enduring Hills,* received excellent reviews, one of which confirmed the widely held belief among editors that "the most fantastic material always seems to be based on actual truth" and was noticed by the editor of *Writer's Digest,* who wrote Janice asking that she submit an autobiographical article for their publication. Janice enthusiastically responded with "Hill Writer," in which she described meeting Henry Giles on a bus, their courtship and marriage, and how moving to the homeland of her husband's people became the theme and place for her first three novels. Summarizing the process of developing her first book, she concluded the article that appeared in the February 1951 issue: "Every writer must follow his own star. I know my limits. I'll never write the Great American Novel, but I'll write my heart out, just the same."

After the publication of *The Enduring Hills,* Janice received numerous pieces of correspondence from fans, including a letter from Francis Caldwell, president of the Louisville Presbyterian Seminary, who wrote, "Your vivid descriptions of things and people, your combination of chaste and choice language as the narrator, with your consistent use of the vocabulary, the idioms, and the characteristic grammatical structures of unschooled rural folk, and your characters all surpass the high expectations of your book that I had before reading it."

The consistent use of rural folk grammatical structure in her ridge books had not come easily. When the galley proofs of *Miss Willie* arrived from Westminster editor Paul Hoffman, Janice was appalled that someone had taken the liberty to change the ridge usage of the words "your" and "you're." She wrote Hoffman immediately to inform him that whoever authorized the changes had reversed the expressions. "The result is conversation that simply is not typical and I can't let it stand. I think if you will check my own manuscript with the galleys you will find, as I have done to my dismay, that great liberty has been taken with the dialect. Otherwise the editing has been excellent and entirely satisfactory." In reference to the use of dialect Janice commented: "It is impossible to reproduce the speech of the hill people exactly as it is spoken. There is no way to put it down in black and white. You have to hear it. I have therefore not attempted to use their forms with every word. I have, however, tried to do justice to the most common usages." With a gifted musical ear, Janice had heard the language of Henry's people for six years and combined a balanced blend of common language and the vernacular in her writing.

In August Henry and Janice drove to Santa Fe to await the birth of her third grandchild, James Scott Hancock, who was born September 1, 1950. Three weeks later, they returned to the ridge and Janice resumed work on the third book in the Piney Ridge trilogy. "I don't mind writing a book at all," she remarked, "but I hate like sin to do the final typing! And I have to do it because no one else can decipher a first draft of mine!"

On October 11, 1950, a letter to Oliver Swan with Henry's signature concerned a Harper and Row's reader's report of "his manuscript." At that time, Swan did not know that Janice had actually written the book, which would eventually be published as *Harbin's Ridge.* It might have been hard to imagine a story of the friendship of two men growing up in the Kentucky hill country with radically opposing natures could be so convincingly written by a woman, but Janice had heard the tales told by Henry over and over until they seemed inherent to her creative spirit. She skillfully wove the narrative of Jeff Harbin and Faleecy John Squires into a graphic portrayal of commonplace life in an isolated rural society.

As the work bore Henry's name as author, the correspondence from Harper and Row concerning it was directed to him. However, Janice wrote all the letters dealing with the criticism and frustrations about the book, but over Henry's signature. A Harper and Row reader had indicated that he did not know very much about the Kentucky hill people and therefore could not be trusted to judge accurately what was in character or out of character. He wanted Henry to set him straight on his remark concerning the southern male attitude in certain regions toward womanhood and sexual experiences. Growing up in the society, Henry knew from experience what the Appalachian male attitude was and expressed it in a response to Harper and Row, also revealing the origination of the novel: "Not at the turn of the century or at any other time have Kentucky hill men had such an attitude. Then, and now, it is far from chivalrous, as it is among all ignorant, uncouth people. It's purely animal—to put it bluntly, and in their terms, it's if she'll lay, then lay her! Whether she's another man's wife isn't important. And nine times out of ten, she'll lay! There's never been a time since my great-great-grandfather settled Giles Ridge down to the present time when you couldn't ride down the ridge and count on the fingers of one hand the women who didn't have their first 'youngun' anywhere from three to seven months too soon after marriage. That includes the Gileses, and the Gileses are the Harbins of this settlement.

"But, if this reader's attitude, and the editor's represent the typical response, then very likely we ought to try to do something about the plot—and we will. It probably was a mistake to take an old family story and make it into a book. But when I told Jan the story she went crazy about it and she's been digging around into the psychology of it ever since, all the tangled up emotions and hidden hates, etc. The people are all dead now, so we gave it a try, and we wrote it just about like it happened. Except for the end, and if we had used the real ending I wonder what the Harper reader would have said! Lucibel goes off with Faleecy John—not far away, just over into the neighboring hills, and Jeff tracked them down and caught Faleecy John out in the woods one day. He didn't shoot him. He broke both his legs and left him to die by inches. But I remember Jeff, and he was a gentle, kindly man to the end of his days! Out of character! Nuts!

"Another reason we used the plot was because all of our books are drawn from life. I've had a hand in the books published under Jan's name, and I know how real they are. Westminster did a pretty good job of taking a lot of the reality out of *The Enduring Hills,* around 25,000 words of it, for fear someone would be offended, and neither of us was satisfied with the puerile relationship they demanded between the boy Hod, and his ridge girl-friend. No ridge boy, including me, goes with a girl four years without taking her out in the bushes. But they wouldn't have it. When we wrote *Miss Willie* we made it pure as the driven snow—but there's reality in it just the same—Jan's horror at conditions here on the ridge, and the slow evolution of her own philosophy concerning it. And in the new book you are now reading, Ferdy Jones and Corinna are real, the belled ha'nt is real, Old Man Clark is real, and Hattie is very real. She's my own mother. Above all, the White Cap preacher is real. Maybe we're not writers at all. Maybe we're just pieces of blotting paper!"

Even though the reader for Harper's did not recommend publication of *Harbin's Ridge*, he found it "impressively beautiful writing that is sheer poetry in its evocation of the Kentucky hill country, its people, their life and character and even the flavor of their speech, which skillfully suggested by a selective choice of words and turns of phrase, conveys the essence without the tedious detail of hillbilly dialect."

Janice wrote Swan another letter in a further attempt to explain the attitudes and beliefs of ridge men that were used in describing the Harbins in "Henry's" manuscript: "Intellectually they *know* better, but emotionally they are still hill people. I don't think Henry would mind if I say that it is very evident in him. There isn't a kinder, gentler person in the world than Henry, and yet I saw him nearly kill a man one day because we caught him stealing walnuts from our woods. You can hunt all over any man's woods, or dig ginseng, or fish his streams. But you don't kill his fox when he's got one up, you don't snag down logs for wood without his permission, and you don't touch his walnuts—for generations of ridge folks have picked out walnut meats and sold them to add to their meager incomes. We didn't need the walnuts. There were more than I could use in the kitchen. But the mores of the settlement were so deeply ingrained in Henry that he reacted automatically, and it was fortunate he didn't have a gun with him! Henry's reaction to the criticism was typical, too. It just didn't make sense to him that murders by ordinarily gentle folk would be out of character! Being an outsider, though, I can see how it would appear unreal. Believe me, it has been *very* unreal to me more than once!"

Not only was Janice exposed to and learning a new culture, but it had become the context for her novels. "The first year Henry and I lived on the ridge," she wrote, "I was so eager to learn that I followed him everywhere he went. I dogged every footstep, up one hill and down every hollow." Defining writers as "sort of walking sponges, going around soaking up everything they see and hear to use in a story," Janice had been a keen observer with very impressive results.

10
His and Hers
1950-1951

John Scott Mabon, editor of the Peoples Choice Book Club, wrote Henry and Janice in the early fall of 1950 requesting "his and her" sketches about the author of *Miss Willie* to be included in their bulletin. The piece supposedly written by Henry contains descriptive information of "what it takes" to be the husband of an author. Having then lived with a writer for five years, "Henry" admitted, "you must have rare qualities of patience, understanding and tact," and elaborated: "Like a dope I supposed that the writing would be done in her leisure time and that meals would continue to be on time, she would keep on going fishing with me, and that she would be at my beck and call at any and all hours. How rudely I was awakened! She disappeared into her 'study' right after the breakfast dishes were done and frequently I didn't see her again until mid-afternoon. She was anguished when she realized she had worked past lunch, but that didn't put food in my stomach. Gradually I learned to feed myself, never to interrupt unless there was some sort of major catastrophe, and to adjust myself to bad days and good days according to how the writing was going.

"She writes very rapidly once she has her characters and her plot worked out, usually finishing the first draft in less than three months. Then she sweats over it polishing and re-writing. She hunches over her typewriter in an old pair of blue jeans, feet twisted around the chair legs, and drinks gallons of coffee from an old cracked cup which somehow has acquired personality for her. She says she writes better with it at her elbow!

"The people in her books are so real to her that she cries when something sad happens to one of them, giggles when something funny occurs, and gets tied up in knots when they are faced with trouble. I think that is why she has written three books with the same setting and many of the same characters. She loves them so much that she can't bear to tell them goodby!

"I know now that I shall spend the rest of my life with the people in Jan's books. They are part of the family, and I don't think I would like not having them around. In fact, I strongly suspect I would find life with the average housewife (which I thought I was getting) pretty dull and uninteresting. I've got used to dusty floors, books scattered everywhere, meals at odd hours and a cloud-walking helpmate. I'm even getting used to being pointed out as Janice Giles' husband. After all it isn't everyone who can live successfully with a writer. Besides, when she's writing I have an awful lot of time to go fishing!"

In "her" personal sketch, Janice described her first impression of Giles's Ridge as "a strange and alien land where time had stopped a hundred years ago." Regarding her marriage to Henry, she wrote, "This is not the life I had planned. Not by a long shot. But it is so much better that I have never ceased to marvel at the miracle of it and to give daily thanks for it. We never know what pattern the loom of life is going to weave for us. But in my case, long after I had expected it to have any new design or color, it slipped in a brilliant scarlet thread which has added excitement, adventure, love, and happiness."

In mid-October 1950 Janice learned that Family Reading Club had distributed over one hundred thousand copies of *The Enduring Hills,* which was applaudable for a first printing. To add to the excitement, in December Oliver Swan placed "Henry's" manuscript, which had a working title of *Faleecy John*, but was being referred to as *Harbin's Ridge,* with Houghton Mifflin. The novel had an expected publication date in 1951.

Houghton Mifflin editor Paul Brooks sent the following telegram to Oliver Swan, December 22, 1950: PLEASE SEND MY CONGRATULATIONS TO HENRY GILES FOR HARBIN'S RIDGE WHICH IS ONE OF THE BEST STORIES I'VE READ IN A LONG TIME. CONTRACTS WILL BE MAILED TO YOU TODAY. Swan immediately forwarded congratulatory news in both a telegram and a letter to the Gileses. A week later, Janice informed him that a telegram traveled by wire as far as Lebanon, Kentucky, fifty miles away, and was then mailed. The wire reached the ridge only one day before the letter.

On January 13, 1951, Janice wrote Swan that she had finished *40 Acres and No Mule,* her first autobiographical work relating their everyday lifestyle on the rugged ridge farm in the hills of Kentucky. She said that Henry was "turning to his next story" and that they hoped to get the worst of it behind them before the spring planting and fishing season opened, for there would be no chance of keeping him at a typewriter then. At the same time, Henry and Janice were eager for spring. Isolated by heavy snowfalls, they did not receive a letter written January 23 until February 4, when Henry finally managed to break open the road to the highway in his jeep with chains on all four tires.

In February Janice revealed a more honest description of "Henry's" writing to her agent by using plural pronouns: "The first chapter of our new book got written this week. That first one is always a desperate thing to get done. Tentatively we are calling the book 'Vengeance.' I have no idea how rapidly it will move, but we did *Harbin's Ridge* in three months. We do not work from a full or detailed outline. We let the action develop as the characters come alive." Janice also told Swan that Henry's short story would appear in the March 1951 issue of *Ellery Queen*.

In early March Janice traveled to her mother's home in Fort Smith, where she would be "under medical treatment." She admitted to Swan that she "kept company with a great many people who have stomach ulcers." Happily, she sent him news on March 28, her forty-sixth birthday, that she was "disgustingly healthy" after spending two weeks in the hospital to take care of "a few minor things" and that she hoped to return home within a week to ten days to get back to work.

By the first of May, Janice and Henry were happy to hear that *Harbin's Ridge* was selected by Doubleday Book Club. Concerning the novel, Janice wrote Swan, "Henry is stewing around because Houghton Mifflin have asked for a picture for the book jacket. He says he has a face like a horse and if they put it on the jacket it will scare everybody off buying a copy! The photographer and I finally got him settled long enough to get one, however he was still cussing blue blazes under his breath and I'm not sure there won't be a blur in front of his mouth!" Excited for Henry, Janice also shared, "Have you heard that Henry is to be one of several authors featured in a picture-text story in the September issue of *Glamour? Glamour!* He gets a kind of sick look on his face when it's mentioned! He says how the hell did he get left out of *Mademoiselle* and *Seventeen!*"

"A Message to Young Authors," with an introduction by Erskine Caldwell, featured twelve new authors that included such company as David Niven, J.D. Salinger, and William Styron. A photograph of Henry sauntering down a hallway with his fishing rod and tackle box appeared on the same page with Wirt Williams and Winston Brebner. Part of the text about Henry stated "Unless the long arm of Uncle Sam reaches out and grabs me once more I intend to keep on hunting, fishing and farming—with a little time out for another book once in a while."

Harbin's Ridge was the first Giles book to be reviewed in the *New York Herald Tribune*, which pronounced, "The structure of the novel is as tight and compact as a well built mountain cabin. The telling is simple and straightforward, but cadenced and richly poetic."

In early July 1951, Oliver Swan wrote Janice that he had just finished reading *Hill Man*, previously referred to as *Vengeance*, and had submitted it to Houghton Mifflin. After commenting on several passages, he expressed, "I'm sure I don't have to tell you that I'm very keen about this story and hope Houghton Mifflin will share my enthusiasm for it." Janice was delighted that Swan had submitted the manuscript to Houghton Mifflin as she had described her increasing discontent with Westminster Press in several letters to him. She felt she had fulfilled her obligation to Westminster for taking a chance on her in the beginning, but she had been somewhat restless under their restricted editorial policy since they whittled *The Enduring Hills* down "to pure sweetness and light" and she had deliberately tailored the next two books of the trilogy to meet their needs.

Janice told Swan it had been "a great joy to turn with freedom and a sense of integrity" to the joint effort of *Harbin's Ridge* and *Hill Man*. "I don't propose to write quite that kind of book myself in the future," she stated, "but I think I have finished with the kind that Westminster likes. I have in mind two things of my own. One, and probably the next in order, would have a historical setting, the location being only some thirty miles from us. The other is the story of a ridge woman, written with the same honesty we have brought to Henry's stories. Both books might be entirely acceptable to Westminster, but, as my next-door neighbor says, 'I misdoubt it!'"

While Oliver Swan was on vacation in August, Paul R. Reynolds corresponded with the Gileses concerning *Hill Man* and informed them that he and Houghton Mifflin editor Paul Brooks had considerable doubts about the manuscript unless extensive revision could be agreed upon. He assured them that he would try to do what they wanted in the matter and remarked, "I sometimes tell authors that the second hardest thing in the world to do is write a good first book and the first hardest thing to do in the world is write a good second book." Reynolds also stated that Houghton Mifflin was willing to pay Henry's round-trip expenses to Boston to discuss the book and desired to have him there September 24, the publication date for *Harbin's Ridge*. Reynolds added that Henry would probably want to bring his wife but that they could not pay Janice's expenses.

A response with Henry's signature was dated September 3 in which he told Reynolds it would be impossible for him to make the trip to Boston because Janice was not well enough to travel, and since they worked so closely together on all the writing, it would do no good to have a conference unless she could be present. "Aside from that," he remarked, "I'd just about as soon be shot at sunrise as to be in Boston the week *Harbin's Ridge* is published! It wouldn't scare me a bit worse."

When Oliver Swan returned from vacation, he wrote Henry immediately concerning the problems with *Hill Man.* Swan reported that Brooks "seems to feel that *Hill Man* isn't really a novel at all, that it is merely a series of four or five episodes around a not very attractive central character. They think the book lacks form; that is, an opening, a middle and an ending. They seem to feel that there really isn't any story but merely a pretty well done character portrayal. In view of this feeling, it is difficult for them to suggest either general or specific revision. I think what Brooks would really like to have you do would be to put this aside for the present at least and start work on something more nearly approaching a novel in form."

Swan did think there was a very good chance that he could place the manuscript elsewhere as it was or with relatively minor revision. Janice expressed her disagreement with the objections to *Hill Man* in a return letter but concluded that they were ready for him to withdraw the manuscript temporarily and hold on to it.

After six manuscripts in the regional setting of the ridge, Janice was ready to turn to writing historical fiction. In August she began doing the research for the novel with a working title "The Kentuckian." In two months, she had finished the greater part of her research for the new book with the exception of examining the Draper Manuscripts, an extensive collection of source materials about the early westward movement assembled by Lyman Copeland Draper. A western New Yorker born September 4, 1815, Draper was a devoted reader of frontier history and became fascinated with the American westward movement. In the 1840s and 1850s, he diligently gathered manuscripts and other source materials as well as numerous recorded oral history interviews with aging pioneers. The Draper Collection is housed at the Wisconsin Historical Society in Madison and was available to Janice on microfilm in the University of Kentucky library.

Janice had unbelievable good luck in discovering a man who had waded through three hundred volumes of the Draper collection while doing research for his dissertation, "The Life and Times of Benjamin Logan." Dr. Charles G. Talbert of Covington, Kentucky, conferred with Janice about her novel and generously shared his manuscript and bibliography, which saved her an immense amount of time. When the book was published, she gratefully acknowledged her indebtedness to Talbert.

Having informed Swan of her hospitalization in Fort Smith during the spring, Janice wrote in September that she was due back in Arkansas for a six-month checkup and that they were getting ready to "close the place for winter." Surprisingly, she wrote, "Doctors' orders are that I should not spend any more winters on the ridge."

Before leaving Kentucky for Arkansas, Janice revealed more information concerning her physical condition to Swan: "I didn't mean to give the impression that the decision not to spend the winter on the ridge was a recent one. We have known since I was ill in the spring that probably we should only be able to spend summers here for a time. When the possibility of malignancy was ruled out at that time, we had to realize that the difficulty was largely caused by nervous tension and the doctors agreed that the isolation of the ridge plus the actual physical hardships during winter were not good for me. I don't anticipate any radical change in the physical condition, and we are not at all uneasy about the check-up. It's just good sense with the type of lesions I have, and the spastic form of colitis to keep an eye on it."

Ironically, a review of *Forty Acres and No Mule* in the *Louisville Courier-Journal* by A.J. Beeler heralded "The Giles Story of Ridge Life" and stated, "Janice Giles is nothing if not honest, and in her discussion of her new life she extolls the beauty of the simple life and at the same time complains mildly of its disadvantages." Beeler concluded, "Most memorable, however, is the reflection of the personality of the author, a woman who despite a complete upheaval of her way of life managed to keep her good humor and equilibrium as well as a benevolent philosophy of life, succinctly expressed in these concluding sentences of her book: 'And in that great courage and heart, freshly revealed to us, we base a renewed faith in the indestructibility of the positive values of life. The ridge has given us a mood of optimism, in a pessimistic time. And for that we give thanks.'"

Janice felt it necessary to ask Oliver Swan to obtain an advance from Westminster Press and remarked, "We shall be glad to have the check. Frankly, this has been a rather expensive year, and just recently the Oldsmobile literally went to pieces and we had to buy a car. We probably had no business buying a Buick—it's much more than we should have paid for a car. But travel is difficult for me at best, and we rather felt justified in getting a comfortable car under those circumstances."

In an undated letter written during the first week of October from Fayetteville, Janice wrote that she and Henry had taken an apartment at 202 West Maple in Fayetteville, but a letter two weeks later gave her mother's address in Fort Smith. She explained the change in their address, thus in their plans: "We came down to Fort Smith early in the week for me to check in at the Clinic. It was pretty much a matter of form as far as I was concerned, for I knew I hadn't improved greatly, but I also knew I was no worse. These things that are caused by nervous tension are largely, I think, a matter of temperament and simply have to be lived with. Eventually you learn what you can do and what you can't do and regulate your life accordingly. I have been grateful that none of the doctors have suggested that the writing itself added to the problem. On the contrary they have seemed to agree that while undoubtedly it creates a type of tension, it also furnishes its own release. It will work itself out in time. Our plans for the winter have to be changed. I honestly don't know why we ever make any."

After Janice and Henry arrived in Fort Smith, they learned that Libby needed to have surgery and made arrangements to travel on to Santa Fe. Libby wanted to enjoy Christmas and then schedule the operation immediately afterward. She had been told to prepare for a convalescence of from six to eight weeks. Janice explained they were giving up the apartment in Fayetteville to stay at her mother's until they would go to Santa Fe around the first week of December.

Referring again to her problems of nervous tension and ulcers, Janice acknowledged Swan's attention to her liberal sprinkling of exclamation marks in her writing: "I can't thank you enough for catching them. I certainly did not realize I had fallen into such a bad habit. Not only have I eliminated them from this manuscript, but your suggestion came in time that I could catch most of them in the galleys of *40 Acres and No Mule*. They are a dead giveaway as to why I have ulcers. I react to everything too extravagantly. Life is one constant exclamation mark to me!"

That excitement for life is revealed in her novels. A letter written by Fleur Conkling Heyliger of Drexel Hill, Pennsylvania, on October 20, 1951, is indicative of readers' response to the writings of Janice Holt Giles: "For a long time I've been reading your books when my husband, William Heyliger, editor-in-chief of Westminster Press, brought them home to me, and for a long time I've been wanting to tell you how much I love them. The sheer poetry in them, the deep philosophies, the naturalness, and the fascination of those tales of the Ridge find my heart warm with understanding and happiness that you can so beautifully give all this of yourself.

"I do quite a bit of book reviewing for my husband, but never before have I been so stirred that I felt I must write to one of the Westminster authors. But this I must do for I feel that I am writing to an acquaintance which I wish I could really know better.

"We have both done a lot of enthusiastic talking about those books, for in our life together we find joy in sharing such things. I have an idea you and your husband have the same sort of life together too. We are among the fortunate ones, aren't we?

"I have also just finished *Harbin's Ridge* and feel its strange beauty and power still trembling through me. Last night we had dinner with a couple of *Saturday Evening Post* editors, and I did a heap of talking to them about it.

"Will you both please know that you have two friends here in the Heyligers who appreciate those Ridge stories and hope you will do more of them? I shall be waiting eagerly for books by Janice and Henry Giles."

11
Good Companions
1951-1952

At the time Janice received Fleur Heyliger's gracious letter, she did not feel she was among the "fortunate ones" in an idyllic marriage who found "joy in sharing." Whether she was "reacting too extravagantly" to what was transpiring in her mother's house in Fort Smith or whether Henry had simply been gone from home too long in the two months since they had left the ridge is not known, but on November 23, 1951, she wrote to Oliver Swan: "I'm sorry, but I have to share with you some unpleasant news. Reluctantly and regretfully, even agonizingly on my part, Henry and I have come to the conclusion that we must go our separate ways. With all the good will in the world toward each other we cannot reconcile the vast differences in our temperaments, backgrounds and interests, and we are compelled finally to face the fact that those differences are crippling both to the marriage and to us as individuals. Henry has already left to go back to the ridge."

Swan responded to Janice immediately on November 26, stating that he could not remember when a letter had shocked him as much as hers. On November 28 Janice offered her agent a lengthy insight to the intricacies of her life since her marriage to Henry Giles. She explained how two months after they were married Henry disappeared, just walked out. "There had been nothing to warn me, no ill temper, no appearance of unhappiness. A note came about a week later saying he'd decided he didn't like being married and that was that. I was working, of course, and I went on without telling anyone, not even my family, what had happened. I talked with only one person about it, Dr. Sherrill, who advised me just to wait and not to judge him too critically, saying that after all he had had a big adjustment to make, everything being so new to him, civilian life after five years in the Army, the United States again after two years overseas, and especially marriage, after thirty-odd years of being single. I thought very much the same thing, so when, in a month or so he returned, stony broke and repentant, I was glad and happy to have him home.

"He had never worked of course, so finding a job was very difficult for him. My own work was of a kind so professional in nature that I had no experience with ordinary job-hunting and I couldn't be of much help to him there. Several months went by and finally I suggested that he return to school. I thought it would at least occupy his mind and time, and that the subsistence paid by the government under the GI bill would make him feel he was helping financially."

Janice revealed to Swan that Henry hated the veterans' school from the first, and at least twice quit and talked of reenlisting, but each time she persuaded him to go back. "Probably that was wrong," she admitted, "but I was trying to do the best I could. The school closed after a year and he was again thrown on his own with no idea what to do. In all of this time our own relations were pleasant. In our entire six years of marriage there has never been any bickering or quarreling. For the next six months Henry was idle, restless naturally and not very happy. In an effort to build up his self-respect, from the start I had insisted that all the funds were family funds and I had opened a joint bank account to save him from the humiliation of even discussing his own financial needs with me. He did not draw on this too heavily during this time."

Six months later, Janice wrote, Henry got a job at International Harvester and seemed happy. He worked well, although with not much interest for a year and a half and talked occasionally of wanting to buy some acreage outside of Louisville. Janice understood his need for some land of his own. Then his talk turned to buying a farm down on the ridge. "We had about $1500 saved by then," Janice told Swan, "and he said we could buy a farm for less than that, while it would only be a drop in the bucket towards buying something near Louisville. I was reluctant. I knew that my job was our only real security, and frankly I thought it was not very wise economically to make the move. But I had developed this colitis and was getting very run down. I had written *The Enduring Hills* and it was in process of being printed. I felt the royalties would add enough income to help us get started, and I truly thought Henry was enough of a farmer that he could provide us a basic security. So I agreed to the move and we paid the small sum we had saved for the '40 acres' and started out with practically nothing. You know from the book how that first year went. Even so the difficulties would have been nothing had there been real happiness between us. You can take that kind of external differences when there is a good, solid ground under a marriage.

"I should have foreseen what would happen, but I didn't. It was perhaps very stupid of me not to, but the fact remains that I had a great deal of faith in Henry now that he was in his own environment. I just didn't know the environment very well. For Henry became a typical 'ridge' man, for which certainly he cannot be blamed. At its best it isn't too nice. At its worst it is extremely difficult. I think I could have taken his lack of niceness, his not shaving or bathing often, his reversion to a kind of uncouthness, but when it became evident that he was also sinking into that inertia that is so typical of the hill people, I was almost desperate. *40 Acres* does not tell the whole truth, after all, it couldn't. It wouldn't do to read. I helped make that tobacco crop because it was the only way it got made. I canned all the food I could that summer literally to keep us from going hungry. And I borrowed and borrowed until by the time the first royalty check came from Westminster I owed $1200. In all the time we were on the ridge (two and one half years) Henry earned by his own efforts, including the tobacco crop that first year, $230, and he earned that in the first six or eight months.

"When we first moved to the ridge he talked a great deal of clearing more land, making good crops, of cutting the timber, etc. None of it ever got done, and when the royalties started coming nothing more was ever said of it. He spent all his time hunting and fishing, and I didn't inquire about his other activities. Since he was a ridge man I thought I knew what they were, and they were best left alone. He has always had access to the bank account, and although I have now made something like $10,000 on *The Enduring Hills* all of it has gone. I never knew what his checks were for, never asked, but they were constantly drawn and spent, usually labeled 'For cash.'

"You will understand how a person with as much pride as I have would be compelled to build and to keep built a very big front. No one, absolutely no one, not his family or mine, ever knew one thing about this. I said 'we' all the time, and I tried very hard to think 'we' and to feel 'we.' But it was the most hollow 'we' that was ever invented. Henry never had anything at all to do with the writing, was never interested in it except for the money, rarely read what I wrote or if he did laughed at it as tripe, and frequently made me feel I was a failure when a royalty check was small.

"I don't know how unethical I was in writing *Harbin's Ridge* and submitting it under his name. I didn't think of it as being unethical at all. It came about so queerly. Of course it was I who wrote the short story *Ellery Queen* accepted, and thinking it would have a better chance under a man's name I asked Henry if I could use his name. It was all right with him, but that story started a chain of events I could not foresee. When Little, Brown & Co. asked for a book I was happy to have an opportunity to do something different from the Piney Ridge books and Henry was again willing to have his name used, so I just sat down and wrote the book. It may seem very odd to you, but I felt as if I were Henry writing it. It came out of a man, rather than out of myself. Perhaps out of the Henry I would have liked him to be. Do you understand how that could be? I should certainly, however, have been frank with you about it, and I regret so much now that I wasn't. But I hoped so much that Henry might be sufficiently interested that a real collaboration might evolve, and I guess I was merely trying once again to make the 'we' come true.

"As you know I had to borrow, or rather ask for an advance from Westminster this fall. I think when I had to do that, with all the money earned this past year and a half, I saw the whole situation realistically for the first time. I'm such a darn fool idealist. But it's hopeless—just dry bones. I've given it up, and when I told Henry the other day, most unflatteringly he was just as glad to get out of the marriage as I. Truly he went his way rejoicing. I will have to bear much censure for this when it becomes known, for no one could possibly understand the circumstances, and it goes without saying that only the family will ever know what lies underneath. I have told you, not to excuse myself because I've certainly made many mistakes, and not in any spirit of criticism of Henry. I know that he cannot help being as he is. But I have a kind of wistful desire that you shall know how things really are. I suppose, actually, I am trying to save myself from your censure to a certain extent, though."

The letter to Oliver Swan verbalized tensions and exasperations that had been repressed during six years of marriage and were now surfacing into major confrontations. Henry's actual departure occurred while Janice was talking to her mother in another part of her home in Fort Smith. Henry left a note on the kitchen table that stated simply: "I'm gone. Back to Kentucky." He slipped out the back door, went straight to the station, and boarded the first bus headed in the direction of his native land.

In addition to the numerous adjustments the transition of personal lifestyle had entailed for Janice since their move from Louisville to the ridge in May 1949, she had completed *Miss Willie* and in two years written *Tara's Healing, Harbin's Ridge, 40 Acres and No Mule,* and *Hill Man.* Interspersed with countless chores of house and garden work on the ridge, she revised the manuscript about Libby's childhood, wrote several articles for magazine submission, and completed most of the research for and began writing her first historical novel. At the time Henry left Fort Smith, Janice Holt Giles was exhausted—mentally, physically, and emotionally.

Before they traveled to Arkansas, much tension had been mounting over the correspondence concerning the authorship of the *Ellery Queen* story and *Harbin's Ridge,* particularly following the request from Houghton Mifflin that the "author" appear in New York at the publication of the book. The fear of a critical reaction from her literary agent at this deception, in addition to the opinion of her readers at a time of increasing success and appreciation of her work weighed heavily on Janice's conscience. Henry offered no consolation because he apparently "did not worry about things." Janice, therefore, bore all the financial burdens of the Giles household as well as the weight of "their" literary career.

Oliver Swan's response to her concerns was most meaningful to Janice in her precarious emotional state. "It was good of you to have written me at such length," he told her, "and I now well understand why a reconciliation is out of the question although I'm still terribly sorry that you've had to be involved in such an unpleasant situation.

"After reading *The Enduring Hills* and *Miss Willie* it was pretty apparent to me that your contribution to *Harbin's Ridge* was more than that of a mere collaborator and this became even more obvious when Henry balked at coming to Boston. However, that's now water over the dam and I hope your conscience won't bother you further in the matter."

Swan felt *Hill Man* could be placed with another publisher in the event that Houghton Mifflin decided they did not want it, and added, "Eventually I suppose they'll have to know the real story behind it, and of course they are going to be disappointed when they realize that there aren't going to be any more Henry Giles books." In pen, he scrawled across the bottom of the page, "This was dictated before speaking to you on the phone this morning."

From her mother's home, Janice responded to Swan's kindness on December 1: "I can't tell you how nice it was to talk with you yesterday. Your warm, friendly voice and your assurance of concern was a morale lifter of the highest sort. My last worry has gone now.

"There is no way I can express my gratitude to you, but you must know something of what it means to have you as kind and interested as ever. I do hope to come to New York as soon as the trip would be fun for me and not a burden. I am very anxious to come, as a matter of fact, it may soon be possible."

Enclosed with her letter was the itemized statement of her income for 1951 Janice had promised to submit. From January 5 to November 26, royalties and advances from Westminster Press, Houghton Mifflin, Family Book Club, and Peoples Book Club totaled $7,527.86. It was an impressive accomplishment for a beginning author who spent much time worrying about the "insecurity of a writer's life." Janice had not revealed to Swan the extreme degree to which anxieties taxed her nervous system. Going in debt for the new car at a time of profound worry concerning the consequences when the truth surfaced about "Henry's writing" caused an alarming incident during their travel.

On the way to Arkansas, Janice and Henry stopped to eat at a restaurant. In the middle of her meal, Janice felt she could not swallow. She "literally could not force another bite of food down" and developed "a nervous chill." For the remainder of the trip, she could not eat, nor could she relax. When they arrived in Fort Smith, Janice's mother phoned the family physician, who suggested that she consult another doctor. Ten days later, having eaten very little solid food, Janice was hospitalized and heavily sedated. Gradually, during two weeks of medical care, she began to eat again.

The symptoms that had their beginnings before her divorce from Otto Moore would continue to plague the author during stressful times throughout her lifetime. The sensation of a lump in her throat was always there, "sometimes tolerable, sometimes intense," depending on the circumstances that aggravated her nervous system. Traveling in a car could cause major or minor flare-ups, and eating anywhere away from home or family would always be difficult.

When Janice was dismissed from the hospital and returned to her mother's home, Henry fled from the intensity of the experiences and departed for Kentucky. His wife remained in Fort Smith until December 13, then traveled to Santa Fe as they had originally planned to do. Janice needed to be near her daughter and was eager to see her grandsons. She also hoped to continue writing. However, because of the emotional stress of the past few weeks, she could not relax or concentrate in Libby's home amid the noise and confusion created by three energetic little boys.

Janice rented a small apartment in downtown Santa Fe at La Posada, which allowed her to be near Libby and still have the privacy of her own space so she could come to grips with what was happening in her life. The maturity, kindness, understanding, and concern of her son-in-law, Nash Hancock, was a tremendous source of consolation to her. Janice had great appreciation and respect for her daughter's husband, who had become a very successful businessman, establishing the Hancock-Old Chrysler Plymouth dealership in Santa Fe.

The years leading to the realization that she could write books had not been easy years for Janice Holt Giles. Her youthful first marriage and motherhood within a year had given rise to feelings of uncertainty and depression because of Otto Moore's lack of emotional support and financial security. Janice's later infatuation during the brief encounter and almost daily correspondence with a Kentucky soldier promised love and hope for a brighter future. The initial happiness she found in her hasty marriage to Henry Giles helped sustain her through his difficult adjustment to becoming a civilian and finding a job in Louisville. The discovery that she could write and the publishing of *The Enduring Hills* renewed

her strength and buoyed her self-esteem. With her intrinsic talent and sensitivity, Janice was obsessively compelled to produce the succeeding books that flowed rapidly from the ceaseless stories shared by her husband concerning the people and places of his Adair County homeland.

But with the good came the bad, and with the bad, the frustrations. Janice was confronting the startling reality that, in both her marriages, the financial responsibility fell to her. While the writing was pleasurable, exciting, and rewarding, being burdened with the entire load of monetary demands produced much tension and extreme anxiety. If Henry did not work, how many books could she write? How long would the prosperity last? Would it be enough to sustain them over an extended period of time?

In the postwar years following their marriage, the economy of the country reached new heights, and most of the world was recovering from the conflict in material comfort. Janice and Henry continued to live in second- and third-floor apartments in Louisville. In the old pioneering spirit of her mother and grandmother, she followed her husband on an adventure into a culture foreign to her own. She had left the comfort and security of a professional job with educated colleagues at the Presbyterian seminary, where love and hope and peace and morality were taught and practiced, in exchange for two and a half years of living on a dirt road in a ramshackle house with no electricity or indoor plumbing in a region of Kentucky where the stark realities of isolation and poverty were constantly in evidence. Once again, the choice she had made provoked a test of her endurance.

A description of Janice's personal reaction to ridge life might best be seen in the narrative of her second book, *Miss Willie.* The protagonist, Miss Willie Payne, complains about the harshness of the ridge to her friend, Wells Pierce, from whom she has received a proposal of marriage. Defending herself as to why she would rather return to her home in Texas than remain in Kentucky, Miss Willie lashes out at Wells with strong words that address the local culture: "Nothing will ever be different on this ridge. Folks will always go right on doing things the same old way. They don't want to do any different. They're your folks, Wells, but they're not mine, and I've got to say it. They live so poorly and they're content that way. Most of them are dirty, uncouth, don't-care people. They live and die without even the common decencies of life. Patched-up old houses, patched-up old barns, patched-up old fields! Flies, dirt, disease! Water from springs and old wells! Never a balanced meal in the whole of their lives! And you can't get them to do any different! You could bear all of it, if they'd just try! But you can't even get them to eat wholesome food if they had it! They wouldn't like! And here on this horrible ridge, if folks don't like, that's all the excuse they need not to do a thing!"

Wells Pierce's son, Rufus, overhears the banter and confronts Miss Willie about her feelings toward ridge folks. He then chastises her for her snobbishness in what he perceives are her reasons to return to Texas: "Back where they's some easy livin', ain't that what you mean, Miss Willie? . . . Back where you won't have nothin' hard, like we do on the ridge. Back where you flip a thing on the wall an' yer lights come on. Back where you turn a faucet an' the water runs out. Where yer bed is soft an' springy an' they's rugs under yer feet. Where you turn a little gadget an' yer fire's lit. No coal oil lamps, no drawin' water, no bare floors, an' no choppin' kindlin' ever' night. Back where things is easy an' soft, an' they's nothin' to turn yer stummick, like Lutie Jasper alayin' in her own blood!"

"I reckon ever'thing's clean an' sweet an' pure-like back in Texas! I reckon they ain't no dirt nor craziness nor moonshinin', like they is here on the ridge! Nor no flies nor no dishwater throwed out the back door nor no windowpanes out! . . . You know they is. You know good an' well they is! They's meanness an' dirtiness an' poreness an' craziness ever'-wheres! You've jist shet yer eyes to it all yer life! You've lived nice an' easy an' never looked at the nastiness! Hit was there, though, all the time."

The self-examination Janice experienced in her frustrations and previously unvented anger toward Henry Giles must have been very similar to the thoughts she revealed in Miss Willie: "Humbly now [Miss Willie] sought the truth. With relentless honesty she compelled her mind to look upon herself and to face reality. She must search herself, discover her motives, find her utmost integrity and courage. She must learn, now, what manner of person was Miss Willie Payne.

"You want an easy way of living, the young voice had accused. You want things soft and nice. You don't want it hard. That's not fair, Rufe. And it's not entirely true. I haven't had it too easy this year. And I haven't missed the easy ways of life outside too much. I've built my own fires and done my own washing, and carried water from the spring. And I haven't minded too much. It's only human to want life to be as gentle as possible. . . . Out of a dim, long memory Miss Willie remembered a text of her father's. 'Take my yoke . . . and I will make it easy.' . . . Take my yoke! But it was going to drag mighty heavy sometimes, just the same. Go back to Texas and dry up like a piece of withered moss! Go back to Texas! Not in a hundred years!"

For Janice, the choice was whether to remain in Santa Fe near Libby or return to the ridge and its hardships with Henry. Although she needed occasionally to be near her only child, Janice realized Libby's life revolved around her husband and their three sons. Elizabeth Moore Hancock had her own active and fulfilling life. Libby was proud that her mother could love with "open hands," totally unpossessively, which was particularly difficult to do with an only child and a distance of fourteen hundred miles. She and her mother would always maintain a close, loving relationship, but Janice recognized and respected that Libby's first devotion was to her husband.

Janice also realized that her devotion was now to Henry, in spite of all their distresses and the demands on her emotions. Alone in Santa Fe, like Miss Willie, she would "dry up like a piece of withered moss!" She also knew her yoke "was going to drag mighty heavy sometimes," but she missed the companionship of Henry Giles, and Henry missed his wife. He began sending dozens of roses to Janice and making numerous telephone calls seeking her forgiveness. He asked her to overlook their differences and return to Kentucky. Recognizing the sacrifices his wife had made since their move to the ridge, Henry was ready to compromise. He promised Janice that, if she would come home, he would be willing to sell the forty-acre place, return to Louisville, and get his old job back at International Harvester.

In her aloneness after Henry's return to the ridge without her, Janice examined her feelings concerning their marriage and came to the startling realization that there was more "real happiness between them" than she had admitted to Oliver Swan during the peak of her frustrations. Janice packed her suitcase at La Posada, went to the Hancocks' house, and told her daughter, "Libby, I can't write without him. I'm going home." Within three weeks of informing Swan that she had an apartment in Santa Fe and would probably be there until spring, Janice wrote him that she was returning "home."

Janice was happy to be home again in Kentucky with Henry, even if she did have to pay for the roses. "People do not change," Janice wrote Libby almost two years later. "What they are inherently, they remain. When people of unalterably opposed temperaments find themselves linked together there are only two things to do. One is to judge as objectively as possible whether the good outweighs the bad, and then to accept things as they are. That is, of course, what I have done with Henry. The marriage is basically good. There is sparkle and fun and a common meeting of minds. I have accepted the fact that I must make the money and he will always piddle along. It isn't any longer important for he brings too much that I love and enjoy to let it be important. The other course is what I did with Otto. It simply wasn't worth it.

"In the last analysis marriage boils down to one thing—good companionship. Nothing else in it is very important compared to that. Romantic love passes. Children grow up and leave. Financial security comes and maybe goes. But if, more than anything else in the world two people like each other, like to be together, can talk or be quiet in perfect understanding, differ and agree sometimes passionately, sometimes dispassionately, but down deep are rooted in one another—that is good. There are some people who simply cannot live together without drying up and wasting away. Their personalities, their hopes, their very minds are wasted. Otto and I were like that. Henry and I are not."

With introspection, at forty-six years of age, Janice now knew that Henry had become an indispensable part of her life. In needing to be loved, she needed to love, to nurture, to care for someone. She needed companionship, and being with Henry fulfilled that need. In the novel *Hill Man*, Janice wrote: "The place for a man and woman that's married is together. They might sleep better apart, but they'd lose more than they'd gain. For there isn't anything better in being married than the plain and simple act of sharing a bed. Outside the loving, it's the knowing the other one is there. To lie in the dark and talk to, maybe. To snuggle to and get warm. To roll against in the night and feel good because they're there to touch."

The forty-acre farm Henry and Janice purchased from Welby Allen and his wife, Creola Allen, May 7, 1949, was deeded to A.W. Cheek of Knifley on December 22, 1951. From that point in time, whatever Henry and Janice Giles determined to do, they determined to do it together.

12
Back to the Ridge and Beyond
1952-1954

When Janice resigned from her position at the seminary, Dr. Sherrill had insisted that she take the large mahogany desk that had been hers during the ten years she worked as his assistant. For Janice the desk became symbolic. From it, she had typed hundreds of letters to Henry while he was overseas. Following her marriage, she worked at the desk by day and began writing her first novel in the apartment at night. Many a thought of Hod and Mary Pierce and *The Enduring Hills* carried over to the next morning when she uncovered her office typewriter to begin a new day. "It is more than my writing desk," Janice said, "it is my study; for where that desk is set down, there I can write. The work habits of years have been formed at it, and I need only to open the typewriter to be completely and easily at home."

Henry and Janice were in a rented apartment on Cherokee Road for a month before the desk and their other furnishings were moved from the forty-acre ridge house. Their belongings barely in place, there was already talk of yet another move. They found a small farm seventeen miles south of Louisville that Janice described as, "the sort of thing I wanted for us from the beginning," but added, "although I don't by any means regret the years spent on the ridge. They were fruitful, although I am inclined to think their greatest value lay in the publicity, for I have so quick an ear and absorb characterization so readily that the writing material would have come through our regular visits there anyhow."

They made plans to purchase the fifty-two acres with a very sturdy house, a good barn, and other outbuildings, located just a thirty-minute drive from downtown Louisville. "The farm is productive," Janice wrote Swan, "and there is a tenant who will work it on the shares. Henry is within ten miles of his work, and I may continue writing with great peace of mind."

However, Janice was once again in the embarrassing situation of having to appeal for a monetary advance. Explaining she needed "exactly

$2,500 to close the deal," she concluded her request to Swan by stating, "I do hope this is the last time I shall have to bother you with my personal affairs, but I think you will feel happier about me yourself when I am settled again."

Within days, Janice was in receipt of twenty-five hundred dollars from Houghton Mifflin, the book club advance for *Harbin's Ridge,* and, in addition, Swan had arranged for an advance from Westminster Press for *Tara's Healing* in the amount of five hundred dollars. Incredibly, *Tara's Healing* was the third Giles title to be published in 1951. The novel completed Janice's Piney Ridge trilogy with connecting themes described by Westminster Press: *The Enduring Hills* concerns man's search for his own identity, *Miss Willie* explores man's responsibility to his neighbor, and *Tara's Healing* develops the idea of the power of love as a way of life.

In the story of Tara Cochrane, M.D., an army friend of Hod Pierce's, Janice takes the men through many experiences on the ridge, all of which contribute to the physician's emotional healing. Tara, who had never known the warmth of a sustained and loving relationship, meets Hod Pierce when he is recovering in a field hospital and is invited by Hod to recuperate in Piney Ridge. The story concerns Tara's salvation as he involves himself in the affairs of the ridge families, which gives him less time to think about himself. In his review of the novel in the *Louisville Courier-Journal*, A.J. Beeler wrote, "Janice Holt Giles is in love with life and writes her stories from the head and heart."

On February 26, 1952, Richard Lee and Katherine Kitterman deeded fifty-two acres on Bells Mill Road in Bullitt County to Henry and Janice Giles for four thousand dollars. A man of the hills who loved to fish and hunt, Henry was happy to be in the country again. Ecstatic with the abundance of wildlife on the new property, he later described the tract as having "rabbits in the fields, squirrels in the woods, some fish in the creek, and a few families of groundhogs scattered all over the place."

Having returned to full-time work at International Harvester as a machine operator in Department 46 and without farming equipment of his own, Henry rented the land to a tenant who planted the acreage in soybeans. Trusting the local folks, he had not even bothered to ask the farmer his name. A couple of months later, Henry began to inquire at the barbershop as to why the man had not shown up to harvest the crop. He was greatly surprised to learn the tenant was no longer in Kentucky. He had overextended himself, declared bankruptcy, and left the state.

As the tenant had paid for the planting, the Gileses did not suffer a loss. Actually, in Henry's way of thinking, they had gained. In early summer, his mother had given them half a dozen old hens and a dozen or more biddies. “The matured soybeans fattened the chickens,” Henry wrote, “as well as predator rabbits, squirrels, and groundhogs. The chickens ate the beans and outdid themselves laying eggs, and the soybean-fed broilers we had that fall were truly something to write home about. Those broilers had fatty spots all over their fat places; the most delectable fried chicken I had, or have, ever tasted.”

Janice continued a steady exchange of correspondence with her agent throughout the spring and summer months. Most of the letters concerned the fate of *Hill Man*. Janice admitted she did not believe the book should be published in her name. “It would probably be a ruinous thing to do,” she wrote. She decided the book should be published in Henry’s name and indicated that he was working on an army story. She assured Swan that in the future, they would “always give the exact source of all materials.”

However, in July, Henry “laid aside the material he had accumulated for the war story” as he was extremely busy with his job in Louisville and on the farm. Janice added that she thought it “very unlikely” that he would “ever pick it up again.” She asked Swan if he would please inform Houghton Mifflin editor Paul Brooks that Henry Giles was not working on anything at the present nor was he interested in working on anything in the immediate future. “That, literally, is true,” she said, “and I think can serve as the death and burial of the use of his name.”

Swan submitted *Hill Man* to Houghton Mifflin, Harcourt Brace, and Harper and Brothers, all without success, before inquiring of Janice, “Shall we try one more publisher?” She responded, “Do exactly what you think best to do about that dratted book! If you want to, and you mentioned the possibility in conversation with me, dream up some pseudonym and let it go to one of the paper-bound companies. It’s kind of a dead duck with me.” So *Hill Man* was the first and only book to appear under the pseudonym John Garth. It was published in paperback by Pyramid Books of New York with an advance of one thousand dollars against royalties to be earned at the rate of one cent per copy for the first 150,000 copies sold, and one and a half cents per copy for all in excess of that number.

Paul Reynolds confessed that what bothered him about the novel was that it “would not fit too well to the *Harbin’s Ridge* market.” He felt that *Hill Man* would be “ruinous” to the reputation of the author whose first four books were published by a religious press and the fifth by Houghton Mifflin.

Hill Man was the most sexually provocative book written by Janice Holt Giles and it may be that the experience in getting “the dratted book” published prevented her from writing more in that genre. Having accepted the manuscript, Ray Compton of Pyramid Books made three editorial suggestions to the author: "The time taken to build up to the seduction is unnecessarily long. The seduction scene itself could be more graphically described. It seems to me that two people who generate as much static electricity as do Miz Rowe and Rady Cromwell should certainly discharge a much bigger spark than the authors grant on page 186. The scene itself should be a high point in the narrative, granting the reader both the reactions and sensations of both Rady and Miz Rowe. We would also like to see more of the terror, fear and horror written into the death of Annie coupled with Rady's fruitless attempt to save her."

Janice responded that she thought the requests of Mr. Compton were very reasonable and she would be glad to make the suggested changes. "Golly, do you remember the very first manuscript, with the detailed seduction scene? If I can find it, it's already written. But we've moved several times since then and it may have got lost in the shuffle." Two days later, she found a carbon of the original manuscript and forwarded the pages to Swan.

The aforesaid scene began with Rady Cromwell telling the wife of his neighbor, Jim Rowe, that he would be waiting for her down by the branch if she wanted to meet him there. Rady assured "Miz Rowe" that he would be there "the same time of evenin' ever' day." Rady waited each day, confident she would come. On the fourth day, Cordelia Rowe appeared: "She came from the house, in a white dress like a bride's, and she was crying when she came. Rady saw her stop at the gate and look back at the house, and then duck her head and hurry into the woods. He went to meet her, his hair still wet from the bath he'd taken in the brook.

"He went to meet her and she came straight to him, not making a sound with her crying, just letting the tears roll unhindered down her face. But even with her face wet with tears there was still a look of pride on it. She didn't come gladly, nor she didn't even come willingly, but she did come pridefully.

"And she went straight into Rady's arms like a homing pigeon, fierce and eager and hungry. Hill men don't talk at such times. They don't make love by talkin'; they just take, and even if Rady had wanted to talk, he knew she wouldn't. She'd come . . . she was ready. He held her, and like they were one body they touched and pressed and flattened, melting together in the hardness of their touching. Like a water-dry deer, they slaked the long thirst of their mouths, drinking deep and greedy, until neither of them had any breath left. Like starved pieces of living flesh seeking food, their hands and their mouths looked for and found the places of love, neither of them saying a word, neither of them even knowing when they sank to the bed of moss on the bank of the brook. All they knew was, it was now . . . the joining and the finishing of what they had started. They were shaking with the need, impatient of the end. They didn't even take off their clothes that first time. It wasn't Rady that took her . . . they took each other, she matching his heat with her own, following him in the mounting rhythm, in the hurried sweeping away of all things real and solid, completely joined, one flesh. Followed him, or led him, into the quick breathing, the quivering, shivering suns and shaking earth, until the dam was broken, the flood spilled."

When Janice Holt Giles returned the galleys of *Hill Man,* she wrote, "This was the first time I had read the book entirely through since it was completed, and I was struck by its strength. It is the most realistic ridge book we have written, completely honest and presenting the truest picture of most of the ridge men. The narrator is especially typical. Well, at least it will get read."

Janice thanked Swan for prechecking the cover design of the book and added, "I didn't expect too much of it. Just so it isn't actually indecent." When the book appeared in print, the words "The earthy story of a Kentucky mountaineer and a city woman" were above the title. The cover illustrated a buxom woman sitting at the edge of a field casting a seductive glance toward a barefoot, muscular young man. Standing above her, Rady Cromwell is returning the gaze of Cordelia Rowe while wiping perspiration from his neck with one hand and holding fast to a horse-drawn plow with the other.

To Janice, Rady was a "thoroughly likeable" character whose positive virtues were his "indomitableness and his unwillingness to be beaten." He cut a rather wide, immoral swath through life, never regretting a thing he did or learning from his actions. Referring to Rady as a "moral blank," Janice revealed, "The inbreeding and introversion of the hills produces many such men. Men who know no law but their own wills and desires, and have no evidence of conscience. Rady is not fiction. He is fact."

On the back of the book, a description of the protagonist gives a pretty good indication as to why the manuscript was not presented to Westminster Press:

"He hungered for land . . . and the love of three women. He married the widow Annie for her farm. He became the lover of a rich city woman to increase his property. And to bear his children, he took a young mountain girl called Flary. But Rady Cromwell surrendered his soul to none of them. His fierce ambitions and fertile dreams made his life a lusty struggle, dedicated to the fulfillment of his manhood. Rooted in the Kentucky hills, this forceful novel portrays an earthy people whose elemental passions give rise to violence and desperate desire."

Swan wrote Janice that he could see no reason why she should hide the identity of John Garth or deny writing *Hill Man.* He sent her a list of the Kentucky papers that were forwarded review copies and suggested that she use her influence with reviewers if she wished to do so.

On April 4, 1954, Lois Decker O'Neill published in her *Courier-Journal* column, "Looks at Books," the pseudonyms of well-known writers who had turned to pocketbook publishing to reach a new audience for their work. "The intention was not necessarily to smoke any of them out," O'Neill wrote, "but in the case of one John Garth, by golly, that is what happened." O'Neill later devoted a paragraph from Janice's somewhat-stretched-from-the-truth letter that she felt was of great interest to her readers as well as local and would-be writers. In defense of *Hill Man,* Janice wrote: "You do understand, I'm sure, that the pseudonym is not something to hide behind. We are not committed to secrecy—but one's own name is under contract to a hard-cover publisher. This is my first experience and I shall be greatly interested in the outcome. The prospects are that the soft-cover people can do very well indeed for a writer, and as far as a contract and advance royalty are concerned, they were quite as satisfactory as any other. I found, too, a very real respect for the author (perhaps even more than one is accustomed to), excellent, clean galleys—and because I objected to a lurid cover, an honest effort to compromise at that point."

O'Neill injected an editor's note: "The black-haired beauty on the jacket of *Hill Man* still isn't what you'd call all buttoned up," and continued with information from Janice's letter about the novel: "The first printing is 300,000 which guarantees a writer as much money as a hard-cover book which doesn't happen to make a book club. The whole writing 'front' is so very fluid right now what with paper-back magazines, such as *New World Writing* and *Discovery* and paper-back originals, that it is very hard to tell what the next move may be. I have been eager to experiment with this soft-cover thing for a long time and was glad to take advantage of the opportunity when it was proposed to me. This is a fascinating time to be a writer."

By the end of July 1952, Janice had completed 320 pages of *The Kentuckians,* her manuscript in progress. Turning from writing about the region of her husband's homeland to historical fiction, she had a very ambitious project in mind. Janice wanted to create a series of novels about the opening of the American West that would combine drama with scrupulous adherence to historical fact. Beginning in Kentucky, the series would bridge two centuries and move westward to include the Arkansas Territory where the author herself grew up, and continue on to the Santa Fe trail.

While working on *The Kentuckians,* Janice explained to Swan that she worked very hard in her research and intended her writing to be factual. "All the historical events are true, the dates are correct, even the weather and the movements of the people accurate." In June one more trip was taken to the location of Logan's Fort and the headwaters of the Green River so Janice could be certain how it looked during that time of the year. Her diligence to factual information is reinforced by her statement, "I suppose I could assume that the growth of vegetation in one part of Kentucky is very similar to that in another, but I want to be sure." As Janice did not drive, Henry was always the chauffeur for such trips and travel.

The Kentuckians, completed December 6, 1952, was the fifth book published by Janice Holt Giles and exemplified her steady development as a literary craftsman. "It is a proud book, proudly written, about a proud people," she wrote Swan, "and it is going to have a proud look and a proud presentation or, so help me, it will go into my desk drawer and gather dust. Either you or I must have proofs on the dust jacket, for I don't want a glamorous young woodsman leaning on a long rifle with a coonskin cap perched on his head. We must approve the binding. If that is the only way I can get a decent binding, then that's the way it has to be. And I want to see page proof so I may be certain the chapters are not run together. I don't like the style of printing Plimpton Press does for Westminster, and should much prefer a cleaner, more open type, but I realize that may not be possible. The other things, however, can be safe-guarded. And darn it, they can spend a little money on some advertising."

By mid-January Janice learned that the kidney surgery Libby had originally planned to have soon after Christmas had been rescheduled for the end of February. Nash Hancock and Janice left Kentucky on February 22, 1953. While Janice was in Santa Fe, Henry learned that a farm they both had long admired and hoped would someday be available was for sale. Through numerous telephone calls to Janice and the assistance of a notary public, he purchased the property in Knifley. Before the end of her six-week stay, Henry moved their belongings from Bells Mill Road back to the ridge.

During the preceding winter, strikes and layoffs at International Harvester had forced Henry to stay at home more days than he worked. In his unpublished autobiography, he explained their return to the ridge: "This still un-rehabilitated and un-adjusted Appalachian—and former

GI—got restless again. Bullitt County wasn't Adair County. And the Bullitt County people weren't Adair County people. I wanted to go home.

"When we talked the matter over, Janice was as ready to return to Adair as I. By then we could afford a better place and more acres. When the word got around that we were looking for a place, we soon found one. Cousin Fred Giles was ready to sell out and move to Illinois. He set a price on his 106 acres of land, the house, outbuildings, and farming machinery and we took him up."

A deed was made and entered on March 17, 1953, between Fred Giles and Alcy Giles, and Henry Giles and Jenice [sic] Giles, for 106 acres in Adair County at a cost of six thousand dollars. This farm, known to ridge folks as "the Felix Price place," was across the road and within sight of their earlier forty-acre farm and about a mile and a half from Henry's boyhood home. The Bells Mill Road farm in Bullitt County was sold to Ray V. and Madeline B. Conkling on May 1, 1953. In further explanation of their decision to move again so soon, Henry elaborated: "We could leave the hills and hollows, but always we had to come back. And the we used here means Janice and me. It wasn't easy at first—for a long time at first—for Janice to leave the city and try to make a go of it down here in Adair County with an Appalachian husband. And I know now that she went through a lot more in adjusting to me and the country life than she ever told me. Once when she was ailing—physically—a doctor told her that what she needed to do was get the hell out of the country. Go back to the city life where people are decent and civilized, the doctor recommended. We tried it, and Janice was the first to decide that was exactly what she *shouldn't* have done."

Janice described herself as a "darn fool idealist, always a romantic, always filled with hope and trust and faith and love." In a letter to Swan, she mused, "I don't know why in the last analysis I have so much trouble making a central character unhappy, but I do. I shrink from it so much that if there is any way at all around it, I'll try to find it." The "happy ever after" ending of Hod and Mary Pierce's story in *The Enduring Hills* might have reflected Janice's idealism as she and Henry returned to the ridge. Mary's thoughts as she stood by Hod's side when he showed her their home were perhaps reflective of Janice's feelings as she stood by Henry's side: Hod said,

"It's our house."

"Mary was still. There was no mistaking Hod's meaning. This was his answer. She must have known it all the time. Known that this was where they would make out their lives together. Known it even that day long ago when he had boarded a bus and racked his bag above her and sat down beside her. Known that this man would take her by the hand and lead her here. Known it, and wanted it. Something in her was fulfilled now.

"Oh, it wouldn't all be as simple as that! She would have to change every habit of her life . . . remake herself . . . strip herself of many small vanities and prides. She would hate it sometimes. She would cry from weariness and ache from the hardness of it. She would feel sorry for herself sometimes. She would be frightened and ill sometimes, borne down by the strangeness. But even as she knew all this, she knew another thing. She had it in her to be that much of a woman. By this man's side, she had it. He would call it out of her . . . expect it of her, and make her that big. She could take on that stature to walk beside him."

Janice had proven she "had it in her" to be flexible in sharing her life with Henry. In adjusting to the culture and traditions in the region of his birth, her husband did "call it out of her, expect it of her." When she returned from Santa Fe, Janice wrote Swan that not only was she happy to be home, she was happy to be home again on the ridge.

In early May she described the farming activities on the new place: "We are both working very hard right now. Henry is putting ninety acres into cultivation this year, and even with a tractor it keeps him busy from early morning till night. I am struggling with carpenters, painters, paperers etc., helping with the garden and trying to get some baby chickens off to a good start. We certainly have 'something to tend' finally! We are fast becoming respectable citizens of the ridge.

"We have a beautiful location, the loveliest, perhaps, on the entire ridge. The house is a six-room white frame structure which sits in a grove of trees—silver poplars, locusts and some fruit and walnut trees, with a view across the valley directly before it. We have 106 acres. On one boundary they directly adjoin our old forty acres, and of course we rather wish now that we had never sold the old place—purely for sentimental reasons because there are only about ten acres of the entire forty that would add anything to the present farm. Well, maybe some day we'll buy it back."

On May 17, 1953, she wrote to Swan, "Yes, I think we can come to New York in July. Henry surprised me, and of course made me happy, by agreeing to come with me. I look forward to seeing you and Mr. Reynolds and the Houghton Mifflin people—but just what kind of personal appearances would they expect us to make?" Swan replied, "As to personal appearances, these will depend pretty largely on how extensively you will want to get involved in this sort of thing, and I'm sure I don't have to tell you there's no reason for you to do anything you don't want to do along these lines."

Henry had good intentions but he did not get to fulfill them. A month before their proposed date of departure, he learned that he must have his teeth extracted, so it was impossible for him to make the trip with Janice. On July 12, 1953, Janice wrote her agent, "Libby and the three boys will arrive this week. Henry thinks he can manage them all with the help of a girl to cook, so I am hoping to persuade Libby to come with me. In that case we may stay over a day to do a little running around. Henry, incidentally, has finished his extractions and is doing nicely."

Janice and Libby departed the Louisville airport Sunday afternoon, July 19, 1953, for one of the most exciting times in the author's life. The soldier Janice met on a bus in Bowling Green, Kentucky, stood at the airport and waved goodbye. A decade after their happenstance meeting, he stood beside her daughter's three small boys—Bart, Mike, and Scott, ages five, four, and almost three.

It was a thrilling experience for Libby Hancock to walk with her mother into the Paul R. Reynolds Literary Agency office and down the hall containing photographs of their impressive clients: Emile Zola, Willa Cather, George Bernard Shaw, H.G. Wells, Stephen Crane, Conrad Richter, Edith Wharton, Jack London, Dorothy Canfield. Included in the long gallery was a photograph of her mother, Janice Holt Giles.

The Reynolds agency, located in the modern Scribner's building, retained the flavor of its 1893 founding with rolltop desks of rich woods and oriental rugs of deep hues. Most memorable were the meetings with Oliver Swan and Houghton Mifflin editor Paul Brooks, with whom Janice had been corresponding since May 1950.

Meanwhile, in Kentucky, Henry wrestled with the three grandsons for the ninety-six hours their mother and grandmother were away. Libby laughingly recalled the sight of them upon their return. "When Henry and the boys picked us up, they were the funniest little troop at the Louisville airport. Their shirts were on backwards or wrong side out and their socks didn't precisely match, but they were happy and safe—even Henry."

13
The Plum Thicket
1954-1955

In September Janice was "spinning away at the new book," writing five to seven hours a day. By mid-December she had composed 250 pages of what Oliver Swan expected to be the second novel in the projected historical series. In a letter to him January 14, 1954, Janice happily announced, "The book is finished! Of course I mean the first draft is finished." All that remained was revision, but she expected to have the manuscript in his hands within a month and explained it was not the historical novel they discussed during her New York visit. "It is a thing, however, which that trip to some extent set in motion, and which has sort of boiled over."

When Janice sat down to tell the story about a sturdy pioneer woman in Kentucky in 1780, she kept seeing a little girl in western Arkansas in 1912; rather than Indian wars and settlers' forts, she saw an old man in a battered gray uniform hoisting the Confederate flag to lead a reunion parade. During one of their recent trips to Fort Smith to visit Janice's mother, she and Henry decided to detour and pass through the small town of Charleston, Arkansas, where her father's people lived. They drove out to the old home place, only to find a new school built exactly where her grandparents' house once stood. "The only thing I found that was familiar," Janice wrote, "was a gnarled old mulberry tree which was in the front yard and which I used to climb as a child and sit, hidden in the upper branches to read. I was sent to my grandparents for part of each summer and their great old square farmhouse, with its four massive fieldstone chimneys has always been, emotionally, home to me."

That visit began a chain of reactions that Janice "did not realize were going so deep" until she was in New York in July for the conference with Swan and Paul Brooks. While in New York, memories of childhood stories about a "beloved aunt" who studied music there stirred her creativity. On the flight back, the whole book began to shape up. Janice kept seeing where the old farmhouse stood, the cotton fields, the barns, the huge mulberry tree, the old well, the plum thicket that contained a little child's grave, and Choctaw Bill. "The plot is entirely fictitious," she wrote, "but the props are very real."

The Plum Thicket is one of the most compelling novels written by Janice Holt Giles and presents a psychologically penetrating self-portrait of her childhood. She constructed a fictive world from the actuality of people, places, and events of her youthful years. Reading *The Kinta Years*, the autobiography of her childhood from age four to ten, one can readily discern that the context of the novel includes a bounty of factual elements. A fascinating interplay between reality and fiction merges in the narrative to tell a compelling story. The countless memories stirred by her return visit as an adult stimulated her creative mind and now "had to come out." Katie Rogers was forty-eight years old when she told the story; Janice Holt Giles was forty-eight when she wrote it and commented, "Out of my forty-odd years of living, much of whatever wisdom I have acquired has been distilled into this book."

"Much of the book is so real that writing it was at once a joy and a grief," Janice explained. "The grandfather is my own beloved Grandfather Holt and the little girl Katie is all too much myself. I was just as nosy, full of curiosity, just as eager, earnest, timid, fearful as she. The father and mother are much like my own parents. But there reality ends and fiction begins."

Continuing her explanation of *The Plum Thicket* to Swan, Janice commented, "There was certainly no warped and bitter grandmother and I hope my own fat, jolly Grandmother Holt, no longer living even when the book was written, would have forgiven me the invention of this hateful woman. The plot, woven as it is into the reality of the setting, is pure fiction, but always the dank, dense darkness of the plum thicket and its small mysterious grave hangs over it. The plum thicket hung over me as a child. I wondered about it, why it was allowed to be so dense, who the small child was, buried there in that darkness."

By early February 1954 Janice had completed the revision of *The Plum Thicket* and mailed a copy to Paul Brooks. In the enclosed letter, she confessed, "I am so bone weary I am limp. I can't recall feeling so tired at the conclusion of any other book but no other book of mine has been dredged up out of such depths, either. Perhaps that is the answer." Revealing her attachment for the book, she concluded with a plea, "Be as kind to my child as you can."

After reading the manuscript, Brooks sent Janice a telegram stating: THE PLUM THICKET MAKES ME PROUDER THAN EVER TO BE YOUR PUBLISHER. In a follow-up letter, he expressed that he felt this book was the

author's best work thus far and that it "has all the qualities of depth, wisdom, perception, and literary style that go to make a first-class piece of writing." Brooks concluded, "I can see why you felt compelled to turn to this book before you went ahead with anything else. I'm very glad that you did."

Janice was now ready to return to her former commitment of writing a second historical novel. Paul Brooks suggested that, since *The Kentuckians* was about a man, the next book in the series should be about a woman. From the beginning, Janice planned to create several families to carry the series forward. Ready to move the Kentucky settlers out of the forts and onto the farms, she liked the idea of writing the second novel from a woman's perspective but quickly recognized it was not going to be an easy task. The challenge was to create what she envisioned as "the new woman—a physically strong, enduring woman, who must furnish the seed for the future generations of strong men and women to carry the balance of the series forward."

Janice admitted her fear of beginning the book. "I do not like this book and I do not really want to write it," she stated. The writing of the ridge trilogy and the autobiographical *40 Acres and No Mule* had "rolled out happily and easily." Her struggle was how to write an entire book about the daily activities of a pioneer woman. "What does such a woman do every day of her life?" she pondered. "What does she think? How does she meet this kind of life?" There is little doubt that the strong feminine members in Janice's family provided idealistic imagery for such characters in her novels. It is not surprising that she gave the heroine the maiden name Moore to reflect her own personal identity in the adventurous spirit and enduring strength of the character.

Janice created Hannah as "tall, and big in every way. Her shoulders were square, her hips were broad, the reach of her legs was long. She was strongly built, not gaunt, but angular and spare fleshed." Her strength earned the respect of her father who said she "c'n do as good as e'er man." In contrast to the heroine's vitality, the author designed Hannah with a spirit of quietude very unlike her own expressive nature. The death of Hannah's mother occurred when she was five, and the child was reared entirely by her father, reared almost as if she were a son, taught all he knew of living off the land, hunting, dressing skins, and hewing logs, while she also learned to cook, raise a garden, spin, and weave. Missing the social interaction of brothers and sisters, Hannah knew only the placid companionship of her father and the men who were his friends.

Janice felt it imperative to "get inside" her characters. "My real problem with Hannah," she admitted, "is that this silent strong woman is not me," for she described herself as "high-strung and chattery." She explained, "I have yet to write a book which does not live vividly for me during its writing." Wanting to do "full justice" to the second historical novel, she continued to ponder a solution.

Recognized as an established and successful author, Janice received numerous requests for lectures and other engagements. In February 1954 she mailed Swan a copy of a bulletin from the University of Kentucky Extension Department that announced that she would be a featured speaker for their Literary, Speech, and Dramatic Series, and in a letter, confided, "This, as you know, is the first thing of this sort I have ever attempted to do, and I think it is a little presumptuous of me, but a good bit of pressure was brought to bear. Writing this last book [*The Plum Thicket*] has given me more insight into several traits of mine and I decided my reluctance to speak and to appear publicly was not so much shyness as a carry-over of that little-girl superstition—you know, don't make too big a wish on a star—if I don't admit I'm a writer, and don't allow much to be made of it, perhaps I'll go on being one. That won't do, so I have accepted several engagements for this spring." Some years later, Janice elaborated. "One of the most difficult things to explain is that a writer's commitment is total and unending and that his books must be his 'good works.' There is simply not time for more. With a writer an interruption causes a hiatus in the rhythm of work, in broken concentration, which cannot easily be picked up or quickly abridged. A meeting which lasts only one hour, can cause a distraction of concentration with a writer that may take two days to mend. A talk or speech of even the most informal kind, when a book is in progress, may disrupt for as long as two weeks. I despair of having this understood however and have resigned myself to being thought coldly selfish and uninterested. It is one of the prices that must be paid for that yearly book."

In late March 1954, Janice traveled to Lexington to lecture at the University of Kentucky. Boyd Keenan's report of the presentation in his column "Blades of Bluegrass" for the Lexington newspaper revealed a few inconsistencies in "Mrs. Giles's review of her literary career," which Keenan stated was "marked by unusual success from the beginning. Almost unbelievable was her account of how she sold her first novel to the first publisher contacted." Keenan quoted Janice as saying, "I submitted my novel to the publisher, and it was accepted without a single rewriting or revision. It was just that easy." Keenan described Janice as "an Adair County woman whose novels have been among the bestsellers for several years who wants most of all to be a good farmer's wife. Mrs. Giles assured her listeners that she and her husband really farmed." Again, quoting

Janice, who liked to project a rosy glow to reality, he recorded, "My writing time is sandwiched between my farm chores, and those duties always come first." Janice explained that she did "most of her writing in the morning, very little in the afternoon and none during the evening." The best time for creative work, she declared, "is in the morning after breakfast and before she has to stop and 'prepare a hot meal for Henry when he comes in from the fields.'"

Janice had not addressed her literary agent on a first-name basis until three years of correspondence and the visit in New York had transpired between them. A letter written August 1, 1954, was the first to begin simply, "Dear Ollie," in which she shared with him that the grandsons had been visiting for six weeks. As both her parents were teachers, Janice had long established an internal school-year calendar. She liked to begin a book in September and complete it by the first of June. When a book was finished, she eagerly looked forward to a change of pace and sent word to her daughter, "Libby, send me the boys!" Janice wrote affectionately about the grandsons' summer visits and their attachment to Henry, whom Mike declared to be his "favoritest" grandfather in the whole world. The boys would follow Henry's every footstep to the barn and through the fields or be "forever underfoot" in their grandmother's presence in the kitchen.

During the summer of 1954, Libby stayed the last two weeks before returning with the boys to Santa Fe. "In Libby," Janice wrote, "I have my best friend. Not only do I love her deeply but I also find her a stimulating individual, a good, clear thinker, a witty, bubbling personality, a gay and lovely woman with an educated mind and heart." The vacations passed all too swiftly, and parting was painful. "To say goodbye is to die a little," she confessed, and it took her several days to "feel resurrected." After Libby and the boys left, Janice wrote to Swan, "We have just begun to settle down," and added, "I expect to start work very soon."

But much would occur before Janice really settled down to write *Hannah Fowler.* As they neared the end of their second summer on the farm, in the midst of intense heat and prolonged drought, Henry became bored with farming. Janice described her husband as "a countryman, something of a naturalist, that wanted a few chickens for the good country eggs and a cow for milk and butter." But the "gentleman farmer" was beginning to realize he had a full-time operation with acres of cultivatable land, farm equipment, and sundry livestock that neither he nor his wife were finding very enjoyable. "We were working ourselves to death and losing money on it too," Janice lamented.

For diversion, Henry began volunteering three days a week in the Taylor County newspaper office, nineteen miles away. "Simply to learn the trade," he worked as "a printer, linotype operator, pressman, and general factotum" for the *Campbellsville News-Journal.* Late one summer afternoon, Janice stopped by to talk to Henry "about something to do with needing money" and "stuck her head in the editor's office to say hello." When she returned home, she wrote Ollie, "You'll never guess—I am going to try my hand at a weekly column in the county newspaper!" While she was in his office, George Trotter, the *News-Journal* editor, invited Janice to do a column in which she could "say what she pleased, on any subject under the sun, at whatever length she wanted to say it" and suggested that she call it, "The Book Shelf."

Janice accepted Trotter's invitation with great enthusiasm for what she viewed as the opportunity of a lifetime for "an already garrulous woman." Her first "Book Shelf" appeared August 26, 1954, and began a two-year association with the *News-Journal.* Initially, she used the space for "a rather folksy book review" but within six months learned from reader response that the most popular columns were her more personal ones in which she shared what she had been reading, thinking, and doing. In January 1956 Janice changed the title to "Around Our House" and continued to write the column until November 1956.

In addition to working on a book and writing the newspaper column, Janice submitted more short stories to Ollie. There were several reasons she wanted to do them, she explained: "One, and the most obvious, is that it would be a way of earning extra money in 'short' book years. But actually more important is that I do not feel I have much mastery of the craft of writing until I can successfully do several forms."

Janice sent "Miz Poopey Lives Here" to Ollie, suggesting that he try *Good Housekeeping, Woman's Day,* or *Farm Journal.* He replied, "Personally, I once again have to express doubts as to whether it can be sold to a major magazine—though it is charming!" In spite of Ollie's reluctance, Janice did successfully master the short story. Examples include "The Gift" in January 1957 *Good Housekeeping,* reprinted July 1958 in *Women's Weekly,* Sydney, Australia; "Adios, Miss Em" in February 1958 *McCalls,* reprinted in September 1958 in *Wife and Home,* Great Britain.

In mid-August 1954 Janice received complimentary copies of *The Plum Thicket.* John Beecroft, editor-in-chief of the Doubleday Book Club system, informed Houghton Mifflin that he could not accept *The Plum Thicket* for various channels of distribution because he used only "good, wholesome, family-type" books. Janice remarked, "This book definitely was neither wholesome nor family-type," but added, "I have never regretted writing it."

Throughout the early fall, Janice wrestled with the second historical novel. The characters were firmly fixed in her mind—the woman's name being Hannah; her husband's, Matthias Fowler, which was inspired when Janice glanced up and rested her eyes on a copy of Fowler's *Modern English Usage.* With sixty pages written, she often walked the ridge farm in the early mornings, continually vexed with how to write three hundred more pages about Hannah and Tice Fowler's daily lifestyle, what they thought, what they did, and how they did it. "It's a very strange thing—writing," Janice declared. "The more I learn of it, the less certain I am that it's a healthy thing to do. Not only must I cope with all the fears, anxieties, emotions, angers, loves and problems of my own, I must daily live with and cope with these same feelings in the characters I have created. It is a truly wearing thing and I predict that one day either my problems or *theirs* are going to get the best of me!" In short, Janice felt "twice-torn, twice-anguished, twice-worn."

Lucy McGraw Holt reared her children on pungent jabs calculated to make them self-reliant: "Stand on your own two feet. Figure it out for yourself. *Can't* never got to the top of the hill. Finish what you start." And above all, "Where there's a will, there's a way." No doubt those words echoed in Janice's subconscious when she noted, "I will work out the problem of this book somehow. It is simply a challenge. I think I shall not be very happy writing it, but I can do it." In that positive, determined spirit, Janice put the work aside temporarily while she and Henry made arrangements to spend Christmas in Santa Fe.

Janice felt a change of scenery and a break from the manuscript would provide time and opportunity to collect her thoughts and renew her writing energies. She knew that Libby was a chatterbox. "She will talk and I will talk, and the grandsons will chatter," Janice said. "When we return I will be talked out. Perhaps Hannah Fowler and her quietness will seem very restful to me."

14
Hannah Fowler
1955-1956

The three grandsons roaring through the house in wild anticipation of Santa Claus were most successful in removing Hannah Fowler far from their grandmother's mind, but the holiday visit ended all too soon. With gifts from the boys packed in their car and promises made for a summer visit, Janice and Henry waved goodbye and drove home to Kentucky with Janice eager to plunge back into writing the story of a pioneer woman.

Soon after their arrival, she began plugging away with the manuscript but lamented "the woman story" still did not come right. "While Hannah would not mind that dark cabin to which I am now taking her," Janice wrote, "would not mind, does indeed wish for the wilderness and the lack of people, the isolation, I *would* mind it. Indeed I have minded the isolation of north Adair County. Very much."

When Janice and Henry moved to the ridge in 1949, their house was located on a cut-bank dirt road that was not graveled until 1951. The first winter, they were marooned for six weeks during January and February, and Janice suffered from the extreme seclusion. "Maybe Gileses were used to such isolation," she said, "but Janice Holt wasn't and wasn't about to get used to it." The isolation of the ridge plus the fourteen-hundred-mile distance from Libby and her family was compounded by the solitude Janice experienced in writing. "I have never discussed the problems of my writing with any member of my family," she disclosed. "To them, writing is simply one more thing 'Mother' or 'Janice' is doing. Is apparently successfully doing, and the success is also assumed by my family. In the work I had done before Henry and I were married, I had never failed. It has been taken for granted, I think, by my family that naturally if I decided to write books I would be successful at that, too." She admitted that since she completed the ridge trilogy, Henry had not been "much interested" in her writing. "He always knows what I am working on," she said, "but to the best of my knowledge he has not read either *The Kentuckians* or *The Plum Thicket*." "At first this hurt me," she confessed, "until I realized he never read fiction of any kind. He read my first four books and eagerly discussed them with me, their characters and story line, only because they dealt with the life he knew, and he was pleased that I seemed to have understood it so well and had written about that life so successfully." While Henry did not take the time to read her newer fictional works, Janice claimed to understand. "This is not to say he is not proud of me. He is. But I have my work and it is not his problem. I am lucky that he reads George Santayana, Bertrand Russell and Will Durant."

Bearing the stress of their financial worries and the nagging pressure of the next book, Janice was admitted to the Taylor County Hospital in mid-January with viral pneumonia. Henry had quickly recovered from the flu they both had contracted soon after their arrival home from Santa Fe. While brooding in a hospital bed, Janice was able to think through her problem with Hannah Fowler and "had a brilliant idea" for the solution. Rather than write the novel in first-person "because Hannah was too inarticulate to tell it herself," she decided to use author-narrative to relate the pioneer woman's story. This presentation would also allow selective dialect usage, "the use of many of the old words and sayings as if the author had lived and been present at that time and knew Hannah's story and was telling it." After rewriting the first hundred pages in the vernacular, Janice happily expressed, "I *know* I have found the answer. It reads beautifully and there is not too much to irritate readers who don't like dialect." Relieved and excited to be on the right track, she added, "I have finally found my way of doing a good job on this book."

While Janice was busy writing, Henry attempted to keep up with the daily care of the livestock and continued to drive three days a week to Campbellsville to work at the newspaper office. By March 28, Janice's fiftieth birthday, she was near completion of *The Wilderness*, the working title for *Hannah Fowler*.

When the manuscript of Hannah's story was complete, Janice unashamedly declared, "I have done a very beautiful book and I know it, but at what a cost! My God, at what a cost! I have written my heart out in Hannah. It cost me all kinds of trouble and grief and anguish to find a way to write it at all. Then, the way being found, it has cost me loss of appetite, nervous tensions, and a weight loss of fifteen pounds. I am glad to have the book finished, yet I shall miss Hannah greatly."

When Ollie and Paul Reynolds completed reading the manuscript, they both expressed disbelief that a story such as Hannah's abduction by the Indians could have evolved from the truth. In defense, Janice explained that the captivity scene was very much the story of Jenny Wiley, a Kentucky pioneer woman. "Wherever I go and whatever I do, I am soaking up material, reading, studying and making notes. . . . When did I get the idea for *Hannah Fowler?* Ten years before when I first read the story of Jenny Wiley."

"This is a documented story," she told Ollie, "it is not from history books. It is from Jenny Wiley's own narrative, as told to Dr. Draper. And there are so many others. Mary Ingles, for instance, who gave birth to her child (remember that pioneer women were pregnant most of the time) on the march, got up and carried it on the next day. You know my passion for truth in these things—I don't write melodrama in these historical novels. You don't have to—what really happened is too melodramatic itself, as your reaction and Mr. Reynolds' bears out."

After many suggestions and much revision, Paul Brooks wrote Janice, "Hannah is a wonderful character and I feel more than ever that this will be your strongest book and I believe that the rewards to you will be worth the effort."

Janice signed and returned a contract for *Hannah Fowler* with a letter to Ollie dated July 16. Within a week, she received a telegram from Paul Reynolds with more exciting news: SOLD "THE GIFT" GOOD HOUSEKEEPING ONE THOUSAND DOLLARS CONGRATULATIONS. Submitted in April, the sale of "The Gift" was a wonderful surprise in July.

August, to Janice, was a "nothing month." By August the grandsons and their mother had come and gone. It was "the gray time" of thinking through another book, hoping to begin writing again in September. August was in the middle of the period of depression she experienced following the completion of a book. She explained, "It is only that one says goodbye to some old friends with whom one has lived for so long and so intensely."

In August 1955 Janice was also plagued by feelings of loneliness with Henry's being at the newspaper office in Campbellsville all day. "For years now," she confessed, "I have had the comfortable knowledge of Henry's presence near me, if not in the actual room, then somewhere within calling distance on the farm. As that kind of life becomes acceptable and pleasant one grows to lean upon it, and suddenly thrown, as I was, into a long, lonely day, all my habits were disrupted, even my habits of work. I kept listening for a whistled note, for the sound of a footstep, for the slam of a door, and the silence was more disconcerting than the sounds had ever been."

With Henry's cousin renting and farming the land, there was less work for him to do on the farm. Becoming more and more interested in the newspaper work, Henry decided to sell all the livestock in hopes that George Trotter would hire him full-time to assist in printing the weekly newspaper.

In the later autobiographical *Around Our House,* Janice presented a different perspective on their decision to give up farming so Henry could work at the newspaper office. "The pay would be small," she admitted, "but that doesn't matter. If Henry is doing what he most wants to do that is the most important thing and it is quite plain he is *not* a farmer. It was the only way of life he knew and he believed that if we had a pretty good farm, with all the equipment needed to operate it, he would like it and do fairly well at it." In hindsight, Janice related, "From the day he was old enough to be put to work, Henry had detested everything about the whole process of farming. But he did love the country and by now I had become an enthusiastic convert to country living myself. There is a lot of ham in me and for a while, as usual, I was able to slip into the role, the role for the time being acting like a farmer's wife." Janice's later remarks had a different tone, "Nothing I ever did in my entire life filled me with such dreadful, dreary, deadly, monotonous, killing boredom." Three years on the farm, she claimed, "stunted what creative ability I have and because I was too bone-tired most of the time to think, much less write, they made what had been such a joy to me just one more dreary chore through which I had to drag myself. . . . I consider those three years of our lives a vast wasteland, the stupidest thing we ever did."[21]

By the end of August 1955 Janice and Henry had rented an apartment at 106 North Central in Campbellsville. As Janice did not drive a car, she wanted an apartment in town so she would have access to Henry at the newspaper office, the post office, and stores. "There's no point in living in town unless we practically pitch a tent on Main Street," she said, and described the apartment they rented from Ira Vaughn as being an entire floor above a business building immediately behind the Taylor County Bank with a living room "twenty by thirty feet and ten-foot ceilings!"

Before the move to Campbellsville, Janice had written and mailed a short story to Ollie that had surfaced in her mind from a childhood memory. About age four, she believed that the earth was round and flat like a saucer and was convinced that the horizon was the edge of the world. If she walked to the edge of it, she would fall off. In "Patteran" she told the story from a small boy's perspective and included descriptions of the colorful gypsies from recollections of their springtime encampments on the Oklahoma prairie.

On October 11 Paul Reynolds wrote that he had sold "Patteran" to *Woman's Day* for six hundred dollars and was afraid Janice would be disappointed with the amount. He remarked, "I'm not wiring you because I suppose you may be displeased about the price although I really think you've done pretty well. Despite your luck with this story and *Good House-*

keeping I hope you are planning to do another novel. An author's reputation and prestige is built by the long story rather than the short." Janice's view of the sale was quite contrary to Reynolds's skepticism. She responded, "Why in the world should you think I wouldn't be happy over the sale of 'Patteran' to *Woman's Day*? That price doesn't bother me. Of course I am practical enough to want as good a price as you can get for me—but I don't write only for money, and actually I am deeply pleased that *Woman's Day* took the story—at any price!

"I'll try not to do any more children's stories for awhile. I realize these two sales are a little miraculous and I won't push it too hard. But the things just sort of boil up and I don't know what to do about them but write them. But pretty soon I'll be into the research for the new novel and these things will have little chance to get born." "Patteran" was published as "The Edge of the World" in November 1958.

Plans to spend the weekends at the farm after the move to Campbellsville lasted about a month. A young couple asked to rent the furnished ridge house and were granted their wishes. "But," Janice noted, "every Sunday morning of the world, before daylight sometimes, Henry is out in the country. Not at our home, not even at his parents' home, but just out in the country. He will fish until the river freezes over, or just roam the woods. He is so good and I feel so sorry for this angst of his. He likes his work, but he must have the country."

15
Dedicated Writer
1956-1957

In January 1956 Paul Brooks wired Janice that *Hannah Fowler* had been selected by Family Book Club for July and Dollar Book Club for September, with guarantees of two thousand dollars and seventy-five hundred dollars, respectively. Brooks informed her that publication was set for March 7 and added his warmest congratulations. As the distinction of double selection had never before been bestowed upon any other book they represented, Ollie telephoned Janice his praise of the accomplishment.

In *Hannah Fowler,* Janice Holt Giles had written a novel of considerable substance and was about to realize what her agent had predicted, that the rewards would be worth the effort. She felt "the most beautiful tribute" to the book was a letter lovingly written by Libby, dated February 1956: "Dear Mom, . . . This is a thank you note. To thank you for writing *Hannah Fowler.* It is a warm, lovely, strong book. Hannah is a dear person—once again a reader finds himself transported right into the center of that time, living right with the people. They are so alive—you are an artist at smooth dialogue. I believe the reason for the 'aliveness' of this book, even though it seemed another story to you—is that the description, history and action came alive through dialogue."

After completing the second historical novel, Janice pondered a theme for her third. She had intended to write only three books with a Kentucky setting with the last one to be about the ten statehood conventions, but she had been reading a great deal about "the peculiar religious sect which came into Kentucky about 1807, during the period of the Great Awakening." She decided to focus the third novel on this group, known as Shakers. The Shakers, founded in England by Mother Ann Lee, came to America in 1774 to escape religious persecution. Their missionary work in Kentucky began as the result of a vision Mother Ann had in which she was told the movement would come to fruition in the West, which in the late 1700s included Kentucky.

"The interesting thing to me," Janice wrote Ollie, "is that they successfully practiced communal living, and most unsuccessfully practiced celibacy. A married couple going to live in a Shaker community were separated forever from each other, and children were separated not only into sexes, but from their natural parents. An idea, a very dim one, is shaping up in my mind. What would a woman, happily married, not converted to this queer theology at all, but loyal to her man, feel and think if he insisted on joining the Shakers? Well, we'll see. Four books with a Kentucky setting won't be too many."

While walking on the ridge farm in contemplation of the new novel, Janice began to reflect on how seriously she had become involved as a writer: "I faced squarely the fact that I am scared . . . scared to death by the fact that there is no longer any doubt that I have become a dedicated writer. That the writing is the most important fact of my life. I did not want that.

"I wanted my writing to stay in proportion to the balance of my life, not to tip the scales so heavily as it does. It never occurred to me it would become so important. I wanted to write, lightly and easily, simply to make certain there was enough income that I could live on my own scale of comfortable living, and mostly to fill the void in my life I knew would be there when I left the city and my professional work.

"I knew it was very unlikely that at my age Henry and I would have any children to take up the slack for me. I knew that housework could not do it, nor could farming or civic and community work. Having done work of the sort that required mental activity, which was purposeful and meaningful for me, rather than physical work, I knew country living could not fill that dreadful loss of purpose and meaning.

"I thought I was so lucky to discover I could write publishable books at all. But I was too ignorant to know that there would inevitably come this day when I finally and truly and probably forever am, by nature a writer."

Within two months of beginning the Shaker novel, Janice had completed almost half of the manuscript. At Ollie's suggestion, she mailed the completed work to him for his opinion before continuing. Her first working title was *The Great Adventure;* the second, *Wind of the Spirit.*

After reading the manuscript, Paul Reynolds wrote that he and Ollie had both read what she had sent. Her background was "as good as always," he said and followed with a lengthy critique of the characters' strengths and weaknesses. Reynolds concluded that Janice would have a good book, but he did not feel the Shaker book would have the readership possibilities of *Hannah Fowler.* Janice responded, "Thank you very much for a full and frank opinion about the new book. It is going to be a little difficult to go ahead with any confidence or enthusiasm, in the face of it, but I see no alternative."

Receiving those words from Janice, Reynolds wrote, "I feel badly that I've discouraged you about the new book. An author writes with a two-fold purpose in mind for prestige and for money, and I'm not sure that the prestige doesn't loom larger with you than the money. I think the new book may receive as good or even better critical praise than *Hannah Fowler.* What I fear is that this book won't be a possibility for a book club and the money and wide circulation is very much connected with the book clubs."

"I don't think I care *more* for prestige than for money, Mr. Reynolds," she retorted. "They are about equal in my thinking. I have a very healthy respect for money, and I'd like to make a lot of it. Essentially I am quite practical about it, or I would never have conformed so readily to a popular pattern. I never did have and do not now have any intention of starving for art's sake. For that matter I am a lot like Chekhov—the words 'art' and 'artistry' have little meaning for me—I only know what I like and what I don't like in literature. But I think it is true that you cannot be a well-read person without hoping that some day you will have both the idea and the skill to do a book you yourself would want to read.

"Actually I have done two—*Harbin's Ridge* and *The Plum Thicket,* which would have interested me as a reader. *Hannah* is a good enough book, in many ways, but I don't care much for historical fiction. But this doesn't mean that from here on I am only going to try to do the books I most enjoy. I'll go right ahead, doing the best I can—with a very sensible eye on the balance sheet."

In the spring of 1956, Janice and Henry had a buyer for the ridge farm. Janice viewed the sale as part of a very eventful year, with Henry "finally finding himself," and such interesting possibilities opening up for him. "I know people have wondered why we have stayed on a farm so long," she wrote Ollie, "but in any marriage there are two to be considered, and he was happier there than as a misfit in any other kind of work he ever tried. Newspaper work is where he seems to belong though—for in addition to the writing he does, he loves the shop and machinery and is rapidly learning every phase of it. As you said, things work out—if you have the patience and the love. My patience has run thin at times, but I guess, not ever the love."

At the time of writing this news, Henry and Janice had celebrated their tenth wedding anniversary. Aware that her husband no longer read her work, in the Shaker book Janice perhaps utilized a subtle irony concerning their finances in describing a character whose name is Henry Akin, the last name closely resembling the vernacular, "achin'," or "a kin." Janice's heroine, Rebecca Fowler Cooper, enters her room in the South Union dwelling house to discover one of the sisters crying. When Rebecca asks her what has happened, Sister Lacey Akins replies, "Henry is takin' us away." Sister Lacey did not want to leave the Shaker community because she and her children "had never had it so good" as they had while living there. Lacey Akins knew when they returned to their farm her husband would resort to his old ways. "Hit'll be the same old things," she mourned. "Not enough to eat, nothin' handy, jist gittin' by, same as allus." But Rebecca was optimistic about Sister Lacey's husband and said, "Maybe not. Maybe Henry will work harder now." As the Akins family left the security of communal living, another sister wept as she watched the big family of children follow their parents. "They'll go hungry," Sister Susan said. "Henry can't provide for them."

After the publication and success of her books, strangers were finding their way to Janice's door—just to see the author, to see her home, to meet her and talk with her. "I can't stretch myself that far," she responded to the increasing demands. "I must begin right now to decide precisely how far I can stretch myself. Beyond my own duties and responsibilities to my family, and the research and the writing, not very far. All of these things are so new and strange to me and I did not foresee them. All I want to do is write. And I do most honestly believe that what I write is all of me the public is entitled to."

What had become most important to Janice was writing a book a year, and she was growing more and more reclusive to accomplish it. By the first of April she was within two chapters of completing the rough draft of *Wind of the Spirit*. She hoped to have it revised, retyped, and ready to mail to New York by May 1.

In mid-April 1956, Paul Reynolds inquired if Saturday, June 16, would be a convenient time for him to visit Kentucky. He may have been surprised with Janice's reply, "In light of my disappointment and unhappiness over the Houghton Mifflin treatment of *Hannah Fowler*, plus the fact that I have another book practically ready to go to the publisher, it seems to me we ought to have our conference earlier than June 16th." She explained that she did not intend to go to Santa Fe until she finished the Shaker manuscript and needed to have "a good bit" of dental work done. Planning to be at home through May, she asked if Reynolds could arrange a trip within the next six weeks.

Elaborating her frustrations with Houghton Mifflin, she told Reynolds she had been so disappointed with the handling of *Hannah Fowler*, in light of the hard, hard work she had done on it, that she was most reluctant to continue an association with them. The decision distressed her a great deal, because she had taken pride in being one of their authors and enjoyed the relationship with Paul Brooks. "But," she concluded, "there simply is no point in throwing away books."

It is interesting to note that Willa Cather was also a client of the Paul R. Reynolds literary agency for a decade and grew continually more disenchanted with Houghton Mifflin's policies. Cather's biographer, James Woodress, claims that other publishers were more aware of Cather's future as a "literary property" than Houghton Mifflin and that they, as an old, long-established book publisher, saw her as "just another of their many authors and far from their most profitable one." Cather felt that her reputation among reviewers and the public had surpassed the recognition she received from Houghton Mifflin. Following the success of her first two novels, Cather received propositions from three New York publishers for her next book, *The Song of the Lark,* each promising advances and higher royalties than she was receiving from Houghton Mifflin. They also offered to spend more in advertising her works. As Cather explained, "The firm didn't believe it could make much money on me; so they were careful not to lose very much either."

One of the publishers pursuing Cather was Alfred Knopf, who founded his publishing house in 1915. Cather began comparing Knopf's advertisements with Houghton Mifflin's and came to the conclusion that the young firm pushed its books with much more spirit and effect than her Boston publisher. She made the decision to change in 1921 and began a publishing relationship with Knopf that lasted until her death twenty-six years later.

According to James Woodward, Alfred Knopf gave Willa Cather great encouragement and absolute liberty to write exactly as she chose; protected her in every manner he could from outside pressures and interruptions; and made evident, not only to her but to the world in general, his great admiration and belief in her. Knopf treated her like a very important person, gave her as much say in the physical format of her books as she wished, allowed her to write jacket copy or advertising blurbs, and "made her a wealthy woman."

One has to wonder what would have happened if Paul Reynolds Jr. had encouraged Janice Holt Giles to change publishing houses. Although Janice proved to be a very successful, highly respected author, she never achieved the acclaim of Willa Cather. In his letter of reply to Janice's concerns, Reynolds nonchalantly wrote, "You of course can leave Houghton Mifflin and we'll do our best to do what you want. However, I think you're perhaps a little hasty and a little unduly worried." In their defense Reynolds informed her he was getting a copy of their advertising schedule to date and added, "I don't say that Houghton Mifflin has done enough but they have done much more than I think you realize." Reynolds's advice at that time was that if Janice wanted to leave her present publisher, he didn't think that the next book was the one to do it with. He assured Janice that he was going to make the trip to see her but would rather wait until he had read the manuscript of the Shaker novel; however, if she insisted that he come to Campbellsville in the next couple of weeks, he would try to do so.

Janice, who claimed she could "stand on her own two feet and roar," wrote Reynolds a lengthy rebuttal. After examining Houghton Mifflin's advertising schedule for *Hannah Fowler,* she stated: "The sales, I think, indicate the kind of advertising that has been done. I have seen the two *Courier-Journal* ads, and if those scattered over the rest of the country have been the same, they are a little larger than postage stamps." She clearly stated her belief in her work and her devotion to *Hannah Fowler.* "*Hannah is* a good book. It is the book which, to quote Paul Brooks, had 'possibilities of being a best seller.' How? With two-inch, one-column ads?"

Paul Reynolds scheduled a flight and a hotel reservation in Louisville for Sunday night, May 13, and made arrangements to pick up a rented car to drive to the apartment so Janice and Henry would not have to meet him at the airport.

The jaunt to Campbellsville turned out to be the easiest part of Reynolds's journey. Learning that his flight had been canceled at La Guardia because of mechanical problems, he left New York by train, missed his connection in Indianapolis, and did not arrive in Louisville until late afternoon. Reynolds appeared at the Gileses' in time for dinner and had time for only a brief early evening visit before he had to return to Louisville for a scheduled flight to Georgia. "Mr. Reynolds has been and gone," Janice wrote. "He is so nice. Shabby nice in that way Bostonians and nice Easterners have who have always had so much money, so much culture, so much education that they never have to give it a thought. His suit needed pressing. His shoes were old and needed shining. His hat looked as if he had sat on it every mile of the way. His old briefcase was bulging and looked as if it would burst any minute. He is of medium height and wears a mustache, a sort of stiff, wiry, bristly one and iron-gray."

In spite of his seemingly Eastern stiffness, Janice was immediately drawn to Reynolds's personality. She had prepared their meal and, as he had arrived a little late, dinner had to be served very promptly so he and Henry had time for only "one short drink." During dinner, they discussed

Hannah Fowler and her earlier books, and he predicted "a good future" for her. Janice acknowledged, "He gave me confidence in myself," and he convinced her that her idea for the historical novel was an excellent one. She later expressed her opinion of that genre: "Historical novels are not held in very high esteem by the critics and intellectuals, because in general they are not very creative. The history itself is the creative part and the author simply grafts some fictional characters onto the history and moves them through the historical plot of figures and events.

"But I am not myself an intellectual. I realize I shall become known, with some contempt perhaps, as a writer of historical novels and dismissed. But I choose this anyway, for I love history and I know I can do this kind of novel well and to try to do something foreign to my own nature, above my ability, would be false."

The decade Janice was born was marked by births of an impressive list of contemporaries: F. Scott Fitzgerald and Marjorie Kinnan Rawlings (1896), William Faulkner (1897), Ernest Hemingway (1898), Thomas Wolfe (1900), John Steinbeck (1902), Robert Penn Warren (1905), Jesse Stuart and Jessamyn West (1907), Harriette Arnow (1908), Eudora Welty, Wallace Stegner, and James Agee (1909). "As a writer, just as with any human being," Janice wrote, "I am responsible only for doing what *I* can do. I must dream high, keep working to improve. But because I am no Willa Cather, or William Faulkner, or Ernest Hemingway, I refuse to admit that there is no place for Janice Holt Giles. The place may be humble, but the place is there and I shall fill it to the best of my abilities."

Catherine Ophelia Babb McGraw, 1884. *Back row:* Fred, Florence, and Mamie. *In front:* Grover, Ophelia, and Lucy, age two

The Holt family, circa 1899. *Back row*: John, Jim, Harrison, Elizabeth, Belle, and George. *In front*: Billie, James Knox Polk Holt, Grace, Mary Tolleson Holt, and Emma

Wedding photograph of John Albert and Lucy McGraw Holt, August 31, 1901.

Janice Meredith Holt, 1905

Lucy Elizabeth and John Albert Holt, 1929, with John Albert Jr., Janice Meredith, and Mary Catherine

Henrietta Crabtree Moore, circa 1907. *Back row:* Oren, Erie, and Otto. *In front:* Lenore, Annie, and Mae

Janice Meredith Holt, engagement photograph, 1923

Otto Jackson Moore, 1923

Janice Meredith and Otto Jackson Moore soon after their wedding in November 1923

Janice Holt Moore and Elizabeth Ann Moore, 1924 and 1925

1437 Hepburn Avenue

Dr. Lewis J. Sherrill

The Presbyterian Theological Seminary, Louisville, Ky.

Janice Moore at Presbyterian Seminary, 1943

Janice and Libby Moore, spring 1944

Thomas Franklin and Bessie Hazel Bottoms Giles, Knifley, Ky., 1945

Henry and Janice Holt Giles at log cabin in Shepherdsville, Ky., 1947

Henry and Janice Giles gardening in front of the "forty acres" farm house, 1949. House built around 1929

Frank and Bessie Giles, circa 1954. *Back row:* Irene, Frank, Bessie, and Cora Mae. *In front:* Henry, Robert, and Kenneth, circa 1954

Janice and Henry Giles at work in the "forty acres" house, Knifley, Ky., 1951, and in front of W.K. Stewart's, Louisville, Ky., following release of her first book, *The Enduring Hills,* April 1950

Janice Holt Giles holding first grandson, Bart Hancock, with Henry, great-grandmother Lucy, and mother Libby, Louisville, Ky., 1948; *below,* Henry and Janice with grandsons Mike and Bart, Christmas, 1949

Olga Victoria Edmond, 1936.
Wellesley College Archives

Paul Brooks. Courtesy Susan Brooks Morris

Oliver Gould "Ollie" Swan.
Courtesy Dana Swan

The first literary agent in the United States!

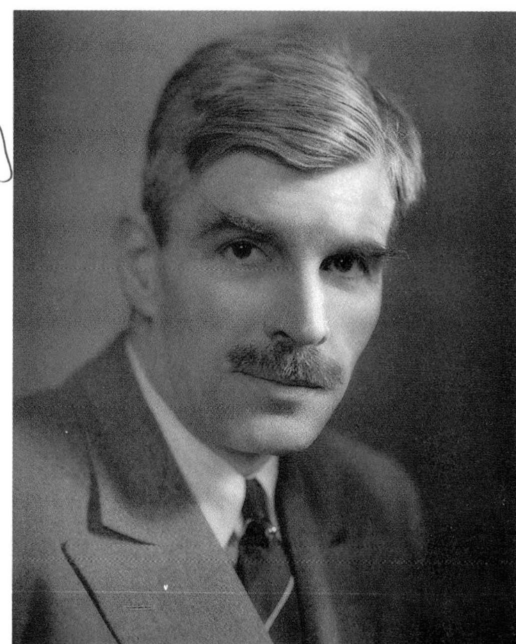

Paul R. Reynolds Jr. Courtesy Robin Reynolds

Janice with Anne Barrett at the autographing party for *A Little Better than Plumb*, 1963

Janice Holt Giles, circa 1956

Henry with Mike, Scott, and Bart Hancock, circa 1956

Henry and Janice Holt Giles beside log house, Spout Springs Road, Knifley, Ky., 1958

The log house, Spout Springs Road, Knifley, Ky., 1991

Janice Holt Giles, 1965

16
Dead Ducks
1957

The isolation of the ridge and the self-contained work of writing and farming did not allow much time or opportunity for Janice and Henry to develop many friendships. "Long ago we began to budget our social life," Janice said. "Almost too self-contained we found much of it unrewarding. It was also expensive and there were other things we liked better to do with our money. Partly we were simply lazy, but mostly we found too much of it deadly boring." Describing the closeness in their relationship, she added, "Except for the first few years of our marriage when we lived in the city, it has been our good fortune to be together daily in a way which certainly gave validity to the marriage vows themselves. No two people could have ever forsaken all others and cleaved only unto each other more literally."

A native of the region where they lived, Henry knew almost everyone and they knew him; many were his kin. "There are literally dozens and dozens of Gileses on the ridge and down in the hollows and valleys. I am never called Mrs. Giles," Janice wrote. "What would be the use? No one would know which Mrs. Giles was meant for there's Luther, William, Walter, Russell, Wesley, Owen, Lee, Milt, Fred, Welby, Charlie, Dewey, Sammie, Johnnie, Elby, Edgar, Frank, and Van. No doubt I've left out as many as I've named, but those are the ones I know. I am either Henry's woman, or Janice, Janet, Jenny, and even, heaven help me, Jennet!"

Janice was often misunderstood by her neighbors. When ridge women got their house and garden work done, they liked to go visiting, or "just stop by and sit a spell." Elvin Giles explained, "Even if your neighbor was busy, you should be welcomed to drop in whenever you wanted to, to say hello," but when Janice was writing, she did not want to be disturbed. Folks just did not understand that attitude. "They would have understood it if she went out to work in Columbia or Campbellsville but if she was 'working' at home she should welcome company. A lot of the women got upset and quit going to see her on that account. Most didn't dare go near the house when Henry told them she was writing." Neighbor Joe Spires related, "She just didn't jive with other people around here with that type of living. Her way was altogether different. She didn't bother their business and she didn't want them to bother with hers." Only in the late afternoon, when her "workday" was over, did she like to visit or be visited.

Ridge folks treated Janice all right but they often felt she was too nosy, trying to find out too much about the way they lived. The few families that read the Piney Ridge books were offended by the "stories" she told. According to Spires, "A lot of things she wrote may have happened, but those things had settled down and folks did not want them brought back up." They were friendly to "Henry's woman," but not many were her real friends. Janice was fascinated with the folklife traditions of the ridge families and used their stories freely in her books, but she had very little in common with her neighbors socially or intellectually.

The move to Campbellsville in the fall of 1955 and Henry's association with the newspaper provided an opportunity to make new acquaintances. A young bachelor, William Marshall "Buddy" Lowe, stopped by the *News-Journal* office almost every day to talk to society editor Ann Newton. During one of his many visits Buddy met Henry, who enjoyed his witty conversation. Henry wanted Janice to meet Buddy and took him by their apartment. Buddy, in turn, introduced his friends Steve Pendergast and Ann Newton.

The three young people began meeting at the Giles's apartment on Saturday evenings to enjoy Janice's home cooking. Chicken tetrazzini became a favorite meal, and Janice prepared it often. They usually stayed until well past midnight talking, laughing, singing, and having a wonderful time together. Buddy Lowe described Janice as an extremely bright person who liked to talk and often dominated the conversation, but he, Ann, and Steve looked forward to their times together and remarked that the only topics most folks they knew talked about were "tobacco prices, whether it was going to rain or snow, and who was stepping out with whose wife or husband." It was invigorating to know there were people who had accomplished something outside of their region and had New York agents and were aware of a different culture. The many Saturday night gatherings were spiced with refreshing and intelligent conversation about numerous issues.

During the winter in Campbellsville when Janice was writing about the Kentucky Shakers, she wanted to visit a village where they had once lived. The fivesome traveled one weekend to Shakertown at Pleasant Hill. As Janice did not drive and Henry did not like to, Buddy became the designated chauffeur.

When they arrived at the abandoned Shaker settlement in Mercer County, they wandered around the village and took photographs of the architecture and landscape. At that time, Pleasant Hill was not open to the public as a historic site and many of the buildings, constructed in the nineteenth century, were in terrible disrepair. Even though the setting of her new novel was South Union in Logan County, the Kentucky villages were similar in nature; Janice knew that seeing Pleasant Hill would help her evoke a sense of place for the community as it might have been when the Shakers lived there a century before.

While standing under a bare tree on that winter day, an indiscreet bird perched on a branch above left a dropping on Buddy's head. Janice would eventually dedicate the book "To Buddy, who in the line of duty ran afoul of a 'Shaker' bird, and to Ann and Steve because of all our fun."

With the arrival of spring 1956, Janice was nearing completion of the Shaker story. In spite of their newfound friends and Saturday night fun, she and Henry were growing restless in town. "Nothing of this sort lasts forever," Janice wrote of the Campbellsville gatherings. Throughout her lifetime, Janice remained close to few friends, in part because of her transient lifestyle. "There is no one living, except the members of my own family, who have known me since my childhood," she said. "People can say of me, 'I knew her when she was ten years old, or fifteen years old, or twenty years old, or thirty or forty years old.' But they are not the same people, and they have not known me continuously throughout my life. My own memories are full of hundreds of people and places, different towns, different cities, different schools, for I have moved around over the country most of my days. I have been as peripatetic a human being as ever lived. I have moved probably forty or fifty times in my restless shifting about."

Because of that feeling of rootlessness, Janice began to yearn for the two things she had wanted most of her adult life—a log house and a body of water. "I was born with one foot in the past and a log house is to me the most beautiful structure man ever built," she explained in *A Little Better than Plumb*. "I had also lived most of my life with some mystic love of water and a great longing to live beside it. Having all his life lived on land his forefathers owned, having all his life lived under a roof they established for him, Henry cannot know the effect upon my soul the transient life circumstances have forced on me. It *is* my necessity to build a house. There comes a time, when one can no longer go about carrying his possessions on his back. There must be a place to put them, without change or alteration, for the rest of his life. That time has come for me."

The time had come for Henry to make a change too, as he was "becoming tired of the back shop at the newspaper." Always concerned for Henry, Janice wrote in his defense, "Since World War II, he has had arthritic knees. His back has a pinched nerve. The long hours of standing on that concrete floor at the newspaper office are beginning to hurt him. On press days, when that old flatbed press inevitably breaks down and everybody has to pitch in and often work eighteen or twenty hours, he is so tired he can't sleep. This can't go on much longer. We must find the country place soon so he can have some peace and rest." Henry did not wait for ownership of a country place for "rest and peace." On the back of a letter Janice received from Paul Reynolds, dated May 28, 1956, he scrawled in penciled, inch-high letters, "Out at lake—be back around dark. H."

In early summer Buddy Lowe invited Janice to attend an art show with him in his hometown, Greensburg, Kentucky. Pansy Phillips, a friend of Buddy's and a resident of the small town, was exhibiting her paintings. Janice was immediately impressed with the artist, whom she later described as "a tall, five feet nine inches, rawboned woman" much like herself at five feet seven. Pansy and Janice were within three months of the same age, and both had married younger men. Russell Phillips, whom Janice described as "tall, thin, beautifully groomed and a bundle of nerves," managed the local movie theater. Janice contrasted Henry as "pudgy, always rumpled, but wholly nice and relaxed."

In July Janice returned the signed contract with Houghton Mifflin for *Fruit of Innocence*, declaring that she had "loved writing the Shaker book" and "had a healthy nine months working on it." She did not have the feeling of being beyond her depth with the Shaker novel. "While no book is easy to write none will ever again be as anguishing as *Hannah,*" Janice declared. To her delight, Doubleday Book Club offered the same terms for *Fruit of Innocence* as were offered for *Hannah Fowler*.

After Janice completed proofing the galleys for *Fruit of Innocence*, she asked Ollie what he thought about *The Believers* for a title instead. He responded that he rather liked it, although he suspected it might be too late to change it. Janice wrote Anne Barrett, the editor who had handled her manuscript, and asked if it was too late to change and was delighted to learn it was not. "Funny about titles," Janice wrote. "Sometimes they just won't come. I was never in love with *Fruit of Innocence* but none of us could think of anything better. Then when I was reading proofs the other day the title hit me right square in the face—and it was there all the time. If I spoke of the Believers once I must have used the term a hundred times!"

With the tremendous success of *Hannah Fowler* and the acceptance of *The Believers*, Janice felt more relaxed in the fall of 1956. Sheldon and Mabel Willock invited Janice and Henry to spend a weekend at their fishing camp on Green River. Janice had not realized how much she had missed the country until the enjoyment of the weekend. "It has been a year since we moved to town," she wrote, "and in that year I have not once watched a sunset, seen the dark drop down over the trees, listened to the hum of the locusts and the sawing of the katy-did, looked at the stars, or sat on the hearth by a blazing fire. Saturday night, almost achingly I realized how much I missed such homely things.

"It was cool enough for a fire Saturday night. Everyone but me pulled up a chair. I like the floor, with Henry's knees for a back-rest. We turned out the lights and watched the flames, and talked and talked and talked. Then someone handed Henry his guitar. Do you know how lovely a guitar sounds, in the late hours which end a happy day—when the fire has almost burned out and you are sleepy and content?

"It was lovely, every minute of it—but I'm looking for my own half-acre on the river, and a set of logs for my own fishing camp."

By October 15, Janice and Henry became the proud owners "lock, stock and barrel, of a log house, a little plot of land, and a skiff already christened 'The Chokeberry Belle,' for less than the cost of a new car." Their fishing camp was dubbed Chokeberry because "in the language of slightly mad friends it stands for all the things that are a little beyond the horizon, expeditions to circumnavigate the west, the million-dollar income, the Fountain of Youth, the Nobel Prize for Literature."

Even though Janice and Henry expected to spend the 1956 Thanksgiving holiday alone in their apartment, Janice prepared a hearty traditional meal. Around noon, Buddy Lowe telephoned and said some friends of his that he would like for them to meet were on their way from nearby Bowling Green. At 1:00 P.M., Buddy knocked on the door and introduced two bachelors, Mitchell Leichhardt, owner of a landscape business, and Joe Covington, an attorney. Janice served dinner around 3:00 P.M., after which the celebration lasted until nearly 3:00 A.M. and began a tradition for many years to come. Future years would also include Pansy and Russell Phillips.

Janice had ceased writing her column for the *News-Journal the* first of November, and the Thanksgiving issue of the paper was the last to be produced with Henry's assistance. After Christmas in Santa Fe, Henry would begin working for the *Adair County News* in Columbia and, even though the two small towns were only twenty miles apart, the shift in work meant a change in residence. Soon after their return, on January 10, 1957, Janice and Henry moved into the five-room lower floor of 305 Guardian Street, within walking distance of town. The second floor of the private residence was vacant at the time they moved in.

During the latter part of January, Janice's sister, Mary Catherine

Sullivan, who had not been well for several months, became seriously ill. Lucy Holt phoned Janice and asked her to come home and help care for her sister as she was "too distraught to bear the strain of it alone." With Henry "unhappy in his work" in the fall, the travel to Santa Fe for Christmas, and the move from Campbellsville to Columbia the first of the year, Janice had not been able to make much progress on the next book in the historical series in which she planned to tell the story of Kentucky's ten-year struggle to achieve statehood. Now faced with her sister's illness, she was even further delayed.

Thankfully, with equity from the sale of the ridge farm, income from the successful *Hannah Fowler* book club royalties, and assurance of the same for *The Believers,* Janice did not experience the usual financial pressure, so the delay in the book's beginning did not cause the "dreadful feeling of insecurity." In *Around Our House* she explained, "This insecurity has always been mostly in my mind, caused by my training during childhood and the hard depression years of my young womanhood when, literally, not to have the rent money meant to be put out on the street. There never was a time Henry Giles could have supported us, at least livably.

"It did bother me not to be earning, but the biggest problem was that a writer—and I was now committed and dedicated beyond any turning back as a writer—is lost unless he is working. There is a deep inner misery which rides with him through every hour of every lost day."

When her sister was back in her home with a combination nurse and housekeeper, Janice returned to Kentucky only to learn that Dr. Lewis J. Sherrill, with whom she worked for ten years at the Presbyterian Seminary, had died of a heart attack. Weighted down by all the recent happenings, Janice wrote Ollie, "It's good to be home—but I don't know how the writing is going to fare for a while. We'll see."

To add to Janice's mental and emotional distractions, a young couple moved into the upstairs apartment. The irritation of the tap, tap, tapping of the woman's high-heeled shoes on the uncarpeted floor was compounded by her requests to both make and receive telephone calls from the Gileses' apartment. "In these circumstances," Janice explained, "I postponed beginning the historical novel." Instead, she began writing a novel dealing with a rule the Catholic church imposed on its members: that once baptized people are married in the church, they are forever married and there can be no sanctioned divorce. Janice had known two young Catholic women who had fallen in love with devout Catholic men who were divorced but who could not face a lifetime of being excommunicated from the church by remarrying.

Janice had also recently completed and submitted to Ollie *The Fig-*

uring Man which was developed "with great humor" from the short story "Tetch 'N Take" she had written for *Kentucky Writing*. Janice defined the manuscript as potential for a novelette, based on true incidents within the enormous Giles clan. Ollie's response to her was that he was "sorry to have been so slow in writing about the book" and even sorrier that he was "not wholly enthusiastic about it." As always, Janice assured Ollie that she had a strong feeling about the book but admitted, "It's entirely possible that I'm wrong—but I also believed in *The Believers* and neither you nor Mr. Reynolds much cared for it. I also believed in *The Plum Thicket* and while you were right about its lack of financial success, it was worth publishing."

By April 8, Janice had completed thirty thousand words of *Walk on the Water*, the book dealing with Catholicism. "It isn't the next historical novel," she wrote Ollie, "and for some reason I find myself not wanting to talk about it yet. I think I'd rather finish it, without your comments, for criticism does make a block when I'm working. It should be finished by late June." Janice had begun the novel around the first of March, writing all day every day except Sunday, at which time she and Henry drove into the country looking for the perfect place to build their home. By April 30 they had found it.

Janice described the events to Ollie: "We are going to be moving back to the country some time in May. We have slowly been bitten by the building fever, but thought of it as some time in the future. Once you're bitten, however, it colors everything and of course we couldn't help thinking of sites. Sunday we were merely out driving around and went up a small cove near the ridge where we used to live to see an uncle of Henry's. Henry remembered a beautiful little valley farther on up, which his uncle owned, and thought he might sell it. He did—on the spot. The odd thing about it is that it is the Spout Springs Hollow, and four generations of Gileses went to school in the old schoolhouse there. Our water supply will come from that tremendous 'spouting spring' which is about sixty feet up the hillside. The house will sit on the bank of a lovely little stream, called Boyer's Branch, and the valley opens up for several miles behind it. It is very secluded and quiet, very beautiful—about half a mile off the highway. The post office address will again be Knifley, for it serves all that end of the county. We shall make do with the house on the place until the new one is finished. We're taking on quite a job, for we plan to build it ourselves—that is, Henry and a friend of his, with me overseeing. Henry hasn't decided yet how much of the newspaper work to continue—probably only three days a week."

Janice also reported that "the new book is almost finished. It doesn't seem possible, but I have frequently done an entire chapter at one sitting. There are some 97,000 words completed and about another 30,000 to go. This book has haunted me so that I have had no peace from it and instead of working half a day as I usually do, I often spend seven or eight hours at it. I haven't been able to get away from it even at night, and ideas come almost too fast to get down. I hope it's as good as I think."

On May 8, 1957, Janice wrote, "*Walk on the Water* is finished—at three o'clock this afternoon. I am as limp as a rag. The last two chapters were very hard work, and so very important. There is very little revision to be done. It has poured out with remarkably little need for change, even as I went along. It should be ready to send along to you fairly soon."

On May 27, 1957, Janice and Henry moved a few pieces of furniture into the small house in Spout Springs that would be their temporary quarters while the log house was being built. The remainder of their furniture was stored in a neighbor's unused tenant house. Also on that date, Henry wrote his first column for the *Adair County News,* which he called "Spout Springs Splashes." Designed to relate everyday happenings in and about the ridge, he began with their move to Spout Springs Hollow and would continue writing the column for thirteen years.

During the first week of the grandsons' summer visit, Janice wrote a short story about three mischievous little boys titled "Adios, Miss Em" and sent it to Ollie. In his letter acknowledging receipt of it, Ollie approached a matter that he had been "at least in part deliberately avoiding and evading"—Janice's manuscript, *Walk on the Water*. "Lord knows I've had plenty of time to think about this," he wrote, "although I confess that I don't know what to tell you about it except that both Paul and I have been disappointed and I suppose as much because of the subject matter as for any other reason. Consciously or unconsciously, I am sure we have been hoping for and expecting another *Hannah Fowler* or another *Kentuckians,* so that a modern novel has taken us both somewhat by surprise.

"I suppose that what bothers me most is that in a sense you have the Catholic Church as the villain of the piece (whether intentional or not I don't know, but the effect is the same). This bothers me principally because of your, until now, very cordial relationship with the Doubleday Book Clubs and John Beecroft. What you probably don't know and had no way of knowing is that Beecroft is a recent convert and in addition a rather spiteful little man. I hate to think what might happen if he were to have a look at *Walk on the Water,* and for various reasons, I don't see how Houghton Mifflin could avoid showing it to him. I hope you don't think we are being too squeamish or too commercial!"

Ollie felt that the book would be publishable but informed Janice, "whether it will enhance or detract from your reputation is another matter." He intended to send the manuscript to Paul Brooks without comment and see what he and his colleagues at Houghton Mifflin had to say. Assuring Janice again that his letter was not an easy one to write, Ollie admitted that he had at least made an attempt to be frank, which is what he thought she wanted him to be.

What Ollie found most "appalling" about the manuscript was that, having committed to an engagement, Regina Browning, a young widow, and Dr. Michael Panelli, a devout Catholic and the small-town physician, have a premarital sexual relationship before he is legally divorced. Michael's wife, Eva, who is "incapable of faithfulness," has left him for another man but will not seek a divorce; therefore, he would be forced to do so. Michael cannot go to confession and truthfully say, "I have committed a mortal sin and I repent." If he does not repent, he cannot take Communion. Having married Eva in the church, Michael cannot remarry or he will be excommunicated and never again allowed to take Communion. "With a Catholic, there is no divorce," Regina is told by Father Vincent. "Catholicism does not recognize divorce." Regina responds, "I cannot believe that God is without mercy Himself. Surely He must love His creatures more than that. He couldn't want them condemned to unhappiness."

Ollie believed "the frank but not pornographic descriptions of the lovers" would harm Janice's reputation as a writer of clean, wholesome books and would "literally ruin" her rapidly growing national and international readership. Paul Brooks found the entire book in bad taste and even found it difficult to believe that Janice had written it. Brooks likewise felt publication of *Walk on the* Water would do her "irreparable harm" and hoped she would not insist on publication but, instead, withdraw the manuscript.

Janice thanked Ollie for his frankness but, rather than seeing the book as an insurmountable problem, tried to persuade him that it was a sympathetic portrayal of the rules of the Catholic church. She so strongly believed the story offered "a special understanding to the agony this particular rule costs so many young people" that after suggestions for making the story more palatable, John Beecroft would be happy with it. "What you don't know," Janice confided, "is that I studied for a year to become a convert myself, and that not even the priest knew what my status could be until he had consulted the bishop in Louisville. It was too legalistic for me, in the end, but I certainly learned a lot."

Ollie Swan's flinching accusation that Janice portrayed "the Catholic Church as the villain" in the 404-page manuscript might be seen in her depiction of Father Vincent as "an implacable enemy." In arguing with him concerning the "Holy Word," Regina lashes out, "I know what the Holy Word says. I also know it says many other things, which may be variously interpreted. Not your church nor any other puts into practice everything it says. All of you pick and choose, according to your own needs and understanding. This one thing your church has picked and I think it did it very shrewdly. It was a very certain way of holding Catholic families together and in the Church."

Michael's sister, Rosa, now Sister Mary Marguerite, accuses Regina of condemning her brother's immortal soul. Regina's patience breaks under the sting of her words. "I am not condemning anyone's immortal soul, Sister. You are . . . and your Church. It is you who should examine your conscience." When the nun "swished by her, without pity or mercy," irreverently Regina thinks that "she would forever hate that black garb, now." As she and Michael leave his mother's home and Regina glimpses Sister Mary Marguerite standing at the window, her hands busy with her rosary, she angrily thinks, "Tell your beads, tell them to the very end and see if they can forgive you for what you've done!" Recognizing that Michael does not have the strength to end their relationship, Regina knows that the decision is hers. "It must be her cross to give Mike back his Cross."

Janice wrote Ollie, "I meant to end the book with the renunciation, built the entire book up to it, then my failing crept in and I tacked on a more or less happy ending. The cracks rather show, too, I guess. I don't know why in the last analysis I have so much trouble making a central character unhappy, but I do. I shrink from it so much that if there is any way at all around it, I'll try to find it. Probably I am still infected with fairy tales!"

As in *The Plum Thicket,* Janice patterned the image of the child Regina with her self-described youthful appearance and nature, "fat—freckled—stubborn," whose own will and her mother's "too frequently clashed," as do the characters in the novel. Janice's experience of working in a library while she was in high school is utilized in Regina, a librarian at a small midwestern college. Regina also shared Janice's love of classical music and accomplishment at the piano as well as an acute interest in remodeling and redecorating her home. In the strangeness of new surroundings, Regina realized "how much she had missed her own familiar countryside. It surprised her a little, for she had always prided herself on her adaptability." As did Janice, Regina "would have to make these new hills and streams her own."

By the end of July 1957, Janice was distressed by Houghton Mifflin's lack of interest in her last two manuscripts, the strongest rejection she had experienced since the publication of her first book. Janice wanted Ollie to try placing *The Pigeons* (first called *The Figuring Man*) with another publisher but confessed she was "still on the fence" concerning *Walk on the Water.* She suggested Random House, Doubleday, and William A. Morrow as prospective publishers but admitted she did not know their "virtues or faults" and asked Ollie to "please be frank" about them. Ollie wrote back that he would send *The Pigeons* to the publishers she mentioned, beginning with Random House, but acknowledged he was "a little pessimistic" about its acceptance and that he was "for the moment ignoring, but not forgetting *Walk on the Water.*" Enclosed in the letter was a check in the amount of $1,125 for the placement of "Adios, Miss Em," to be published in the February 1959 issue of *McCall's.*

William Morrow's reaction to *The Pigeons* was very similar to that of Random House. Returned with the manuscript to Oliver Swan were the comments: "As fetching as this author is, I'm afraid that this particular off-beat manuscript just didn't appeal to us. Even with Mrs. Giles' potent name on it, I just don't see how we could distribute it successfully."

After forwarding their responses to Janice, Ollie heard in turn from her: "Thank you for letting me see the reactions to *The Pigeons.* That convinces me, and unless you have already sent it elsewhere, let's just consider it a dead duck. I have also decided, after much weighing and balancing, to do nothing about *Walk on the Water,* unless you think it might sell, under a pseudonym, to one of the paperback original companies. Outside of that, as far as I am concerned, it's just another dead duck. I expect that is very good news to you and will make you feel greatly relieved. But I think you know, after all these years, that I can be counted on in the final analysis to be pretty practical. This winter's book will be historical—that apparently is my field and I'd better stick to it and be very grateful to have a field."

Ollie's letter to Janice of August 30, 1957, did indeed agree with her expectancy: "I confess I am quite relieved that you are willing to put aside both *The Pigeons* and *Walk on the Water.*" Janice considered *Walk on the Water* one of the best books she had ever written, but because she valued her "happy association with Ollie Swan and Paul Brooks far too much to quarrel with them," she withdrew the book without "further ado." Surprisingly, she chose to ignore the rejections Ollie received on the two manuscripts and offered a more flattering explanation in *Around Our House.* "This does not mean the book was rejected for publication. That has never happened to me. It does mean that I accepted the opinion of two men, both genuinely concerned with my welfare as a writer, and I voluntarily withdrew the book."

However, neither decision concerning the "two dead ducks" affected Janice's excitement and happiness at that particular time. The log house of her dreams was finally going to be built beside her longed-for stream of water. She could now turn to writing the next historical novel surrounded by her "own" place.

17
A Place of Her Own
1957-1958

After twelve years of marriage, Janice felt she and Henry had finally come to a time of understanding their needs and wants. She defined their needs as simply "uninterrupted time and rather solitary living" and realized that "the country did, after all, offer it best." No more cows and chickens to complicate living—just land, water, and solitude. Desiring to be "fenced by the hills of home and the Green River," they were delighted to have found the fourteen valley acres hugging the banks of the Spout Springs Branch with fifty-six acres of woodland stretching up the hollow. The seventy acres would later be increased by six additional acres that included the Spout Springs schoolhouse. Henry Giles was home again and his wife had found the perfect place, "a very secluded and quiet, very beautiful place," to build their house.

Janice was fifty-two years of age in 1957 when she wrote: "Though, as the saying goes, 'Home is where the heart is,' in the middle years the heart itself may grow homesick. One faces the fact that a corner has been turned. There are not as many tomorrows as yesterdays and a quiet preparation had better be made for the years that remain. Neither the flesh nor the spirit are as resilient as they once were and both now crave a certainty in life. Where once adventure called a high, bugling note and the next day, the next month, the next year unpredictable were not only acceptable but preferable to me, I now am willing, desirous even, of adventuring more quietly and predictably and I want at least one thing unchanging to my death—my home. I want my own hearth and fire, my own land, my own dwelling, built to my design, to which, wherever I wander in the future, I may always come back and find solid and changeless, unalterably mine, my books, my desk, my papers, my trees, my soil, my possessions so materially comforting because they are old and familiar and mine.

"My husband, sensing, as he always does, the cold winds that shrivel me and make me afraid and small, was willing. He could, he said, drive back and forth to the town, for of course when it came to building this home there was only one possible place to build it—near the hills, the river, the valleys of his ancestors. It is one of the strange turns of fate that

I should have come to love this country more than he. Perhaps it is because I have written about it so much that I have absorbed it until it is part of my bone and flesh."

When Libby and the boys, ages nine, eight, and six, returned to Santa Fe at the end of July following their summer visit, Janice and Henry rented and moved into a small house about half a mile down the road. The little white house they had used for temporary quarters to accommodate the grandsons could now be torn down, as it occupied the building site for the new house. Janice explicitly described in *A Little Better than Plumb* how she and Henry, in August 1957, intensified their search for old log structures to purchase, dismantle, and move to Spout Springs for use in constructing their home.

The spacious cabin at the fishing camp, eighteen by twenty-two feet, a story and a half in height, became the first set of logs for the new house. By September, three other abandoned log structures had been located and purchased. Edgar Giles began taking them apart and hauling the logs to the Spout Springs site. Janice busily sketched house plans on pieces of cardboard Henry brought home from the stockroom of the *Adair County News.* "The plan" included five rooms, entrance hall, and bath downstairs and three dormer bedrooms upstairs, which were later relinquished to attic space when the downstairs' ceiling height was raised.

In mid-September, Janice mailed Ollie the first four chapters of the new book, first titled *Bright Star,* then changed to *The Glory Road.* Janice was inspired to write the novel while reading a biography of General James Wilkinson and planned in her book about Kentucky's struggle for statehood to recount the Spanish conspiracy in which Wilkinson secured from the Spanish authorities a trade monopoly on the Mississippi River. Wilkinson sought to detach Kentucky from Virginia as well as the United States in order to create a vast western empire with himself as the "Washington of the West." Using the intriguing Wilkinson as the main historical character, Janice introduced the fictional protagonist, Major Cassius Cartwright, to infuse new blood into the Fowler and Cooper genealogy of the preceding novels. Cartwright would carry the generations forward as the families continued their settlement of the American West.

Cartwright, narrator of the story, is portrayed as a wealthy, educated Virginian who crossed the mountains into Kentucky to establish a settlement of his own on the Green River. Janice explained to Ollie that following chapters would bring a group of settlers who had lost their land through overlapping titles to Cartwright's station. "I hope in this book to give a good picture of a settlement, not a lone settler," she stated. Further explaining a conflicting love interest for Cass Cartwright, Janice concluded by telling Ollie that he did not have to be in a hurry to read the partial manuscript as she and Henry were leaving October 16 with Pansy and Russell Phillips for a vacation in Florida and would not be home until October 27. Upon their return, Janice had a letter from Ollie with news that he and Paul Reynolds had read and liked the first chapters of the new book and felt the plot was headed in the right direction.

Assuring Ollie that she had come home "rested and refreshed and eager to be at work again," she wrote that she hoped the book would be finished about the usual time—May or June. "It depends on how much interruption there is during the balance of winter. The most difficult part of the writing is behind me now and as you know I work pretty fast after I get into the stretch, so it may wind up as early as April."

Janice received word from Ollie in mid-November that a check was forthcoming for the book club royalties on *The Believers,* which Anne Barrett of Houghton Mifflin informed her had reached the eight thousand mark in sales. Having received a "huge book club check" for *Hannah Fowler* earlier in the year, Janice was stunned by the news that she must accept another significant sum in the same calendar year. In addition she was "horrified to learn" that Henry's "tiny salary" at the *Adair County News,* which she described as "just a stipend because he worked more for the love of the work than the salary," had been "just enough to put them in a higher tax bracket."

In *Around Our House,* Janice stated that Henry was "working six days a week, and happily," at the *Adair County News* office and writing his weekly column, "Spout Springs Splashes." Even though they realized the meager stipend he received was exactly the amount that put them into the next tax bracket, neither was willing for Henry to give up the newspaper job, for it was truly a labor of love. So they "just paid up and he continued as before." She related it differently in A *Little Better than Plumb,* stating flatly that when they realized the situation, "in complete disgust he quit." Either way, the resulting check to the director of Internal Revenue amounted to almost the entire sum Janice received from the book club for *The Believers*. "I just practically wrote one book for the government!" she moaned to Ollie.

Though extremely frustrated that foresight could have prevented the sizable tax payment, the success of the previous historical novels was all the more incentive for Janice to forge ahead undaunted in the writing of the next one in the series. When she mailed four additional chapters of *The Glory Road* to Ollie in mid-November, she pleasantly informed him,

"I'm very fond of these characters and am thoroughly enjoying working with a masculine protagonist again for a change. I had grown a little weary of petticoats."

Progress on the log house was moving slowly, largely because of bad weather. Janice was elated they were to have hand-riven shingles; Henry's father was busy splitting out the ten thousand shingle boards necessary for the roof. In her own rural section of Appalachia, Janice was surrounded by the same everyday tasks of the diverse tenants of Cass Cartwright's settlement that provided flesh for *The Glory Road.* She was at her best when describing early Kentucky folklife, which she had only to glean from personal experience and observation in her tradition-saturated environment. Janice and Henry were building a house of century-old, handhewn logs for which his father was riving shingles in an age-old manner befitting the Cartwright settlement.

Having herself practiced many of the traditional ways, Janice knew firsthand the phrases she used in writing. She knew the scents of "wood smoke as thin tendrils from fresh-laid fires spiraled out of the chimneys," of meat roasting on an open hearth, of bread baking, of stews simmering, and the "acrid smell of stock, heavy and sweaty and animal from stables and stalls back of the houses."

"Henry's people" continued to make use of "a man and a mule and a plow." During her first years of living on the ridge, Janice experienced the "routine chores of bringing in the wood, filling the lamps with kerosene, drawing up the night water." She confessed a contentment for having shared some years as a member of the ridge society before it began to change. "I am glad I saw it lit by kerosene lamps and warmed by woodburning stoves. I am even glad I made use of an outdoor privy and walked a dirt road. I am glad I helped spring-pole a well and raise a tobacco crop."

Janice located the mythical Cartwright's Mill in the Green River Valley and patterned the setting after the "lovely banks of Boyer's Branch" in Spout Springs Hollow. Once again she skillfully employed the soft-spoken language she heard daily for authenticity in the settlers' speech. The behavior of the Green River and its tributaries was easily described as she witnessed it. "We have had a flood this week," Janice wrote Ollie in November. "A month of rains kept the streams swollen, and a cloudburst Monday sent all of them all over the valley. Our own little creek, which normally is about three feet wide, became a booming torrent, shifted its channel and washed away a few pieces of lumber that were stacked in the yard. But it did not reach the house and no great damage was done."

Unexpected sources of research were revealed to Janice in preparation for her historical novels. Aware that she was writing about the period when Kentucky achieved statehood, Allan M. Trout, columnist and news reporter for the *Louisville Courier-Journal*, directed her attention to a small pamphlet on the history of Frankfort that traced Wilkinson's activities in the founding of that city. In mid-December Janice spent several days in Frankfort at the library of the Kentucky Historical Society examining the pamphlet and other source materials to fill in research gaps for the novel in progress.

If, while in Frankfort, Janice recalled the year she spent there as secretary and director of religious education in the First Christian Church and the ladies of the church who encouraged her resignation, she had to have done so with satisfaction. In the eighteen intervening years, she had served as assistant to the dean of the Louisville Presbyterian Seminary and become an established author with ten books in print and a secure reputation in the field of historical fiction.

In January 1958 Elizabeth Coombs, librarian of the Kentucky Library at Western Kentucky State College (now University) in Bowling Green, informed Janice about a Ph.D. dissertation by Percy Willis Christian on "Wilkinson and Separatism." Feeling it might "turn up something new on Wilkinson," Janice traveled to Bowling Green. To her delight she found "a scholarly, well-proven work," and the material was extremely useful. It meant rewriting three chapters, but she was happy to do so as she could confirm some suspicions about Wilkinson she had previously been unable to prove.

Janice never wearied in her efforts of intensive research as she plumbed archives and endless resources to document the factual background in her historical fiction. She tirelessly familiarized herself with the countryside involved in the setting of her novels and was invigorated by the experience. "If I only enjoyed writing as much as I do the research all would be well," she noted, "but alas the writing is a heavy piece of work."

Four months after sending Ollie the first four chapters of *The Glory Road*, Janice mailed him the completed manuscript. In her enclosed letter of February 10, 1958, she stated: "Here it is—all of it; finished, done, the end! As usual I'm worn to a nub—so very tired I feel as if I could barely lift my hand."

Except for suggesting minor changes and shortening of the manuscript, Ollie Swan and Paul Reynolds both liked *The Glory Road*. Janice immediately went to work on their suggestions for revisions and, by March 26, informed them that 104 pages had been cut in addition to tightening and sharpening the story wherever possible.

Janice was hoping the Literary Guild would select *The Glory Road,* "largely for the prestige." She felt the novel had more possibilities for attracting a movie contract than anything else she had written except *The Kentuckians.* "But it would have very little opportunity to be considered without the prestige of a major book club selection." She realized the fate of her book depended on Houghton Mifflin and John Beecroft. "That man terrifies me," she wrote Ollie. "My fate, and it is especially important right now, depends to such an extent upon his decisions. I have to write historical novels to please Houghton Mifflin and it looks as if I have to write them about women to please Mr. Beecroft."

John William Richard Beecroft, a 1924 graduate of Columbia University with additional study at the Sorbonne, became associated with Literary Guild of America in 1928. The mid-1920s was a distinctive time for "entrepreneurs of the word." DeWitt and Lila Wallace founded the *Reader's Digest* in 1922; Henry Luce and Britin Hadden began *Time* in 1923; Henry Canby became founding editor of *The Saturday Review of Literature* in 1924; *The New Yorker* was created by Harold Ross in 1925; and in 1926, Harry Scherman designed the Book-of-the-Month Club. Beecroft became the Literary Guild editor-in-chief in 1937, and the next year concurrently served as editor of Doubleday Dollar Book Club and Book League of America. He was also editor of two other Doubleday clubs, the Family Reading Club from 1946 to 1960; and Dollar Mystery Guild from 1948 to 1960.

For her next book, Janice told Ollie that for some years she had written a series of weekly letters to Libby's boys that dealt with the many animal frolics on the farm. She described the stories as imaginary, with the animals often talking to Henry, and claimed that Libby read them to the grandsons as well as their neighborhood friends "who were very fond of them." She queried Ollie to see if he would be interested in a small children's book titled *Dear Boys,* describing the stories as "a labor of love."

Janice compiled the stories and sent them to Ollie. After he read the manuscript, he passed it on to Mary Silva Cosgrave, editor of children's books for Houghton Mifflin, who responded that she was sorry that the decision was not a favorable one. She explained that the letters were certainly enjoyable but did not "lend themselves particularly to a book for a wide general reading audience."

Janice, in defiance of Cosgrave's report, informed Ollie in no uncertain terms that enjoyment by all the children on Santa Rosa in Santa Fe as well as Libby's use of the letters in a children's story hour at the library had already given them "a general reading appeal." Feeling Cosgrave's judgment was inappropriate, Janice wrote, "But of course there is no point arguing. If half the children in the United States had had these stories read to them and liked them, it still wouldn't matter since they don't fit into a certain groove and pattern. Which is largely the reason, it seems to me, why there are so few good children's stories these days. We have to go back to *Winnie the Pooh,* to *Alice in Wonderland,* to *The Wind in the Willows,* to Rudyard Kipling, or else we have to write our own. Of course there is now Dr. Seuss—and how he ever managed to get in print I can't imagine."

Janice asked Ollie to try *Dear Boys* another place or two before giving up. At the same time, she informed Ollie that she had been "doing a sort of personal and autobiographical document" during the building of the log house and was calling it *The Home Place.* She had completed ten chapters, some 160 pages, that included recollections of her childhood homes and would like for him to examine the work if he was interested. "Incidentally," she informed him, "unfinished though it will be, we hope to move into the new house around July 1st."

Janice mailed Ollie the first ten chapters of *The Home Place,* which he read with "enormous personal interest" and deemed her device of "opening each chapter with the progress of the house and then flashing back to autobiographical materials" an interesting one. He wondered, though, if she was not "skimming the cream off" what would someday be her "straight autobiography." He forwarded the manuscript to Paul Brooks, who replied to him, "Janice Giles' *The Home Place* is such an interesting book in its quiet way that I really regret having to return it without a publishing offer. The way she has gone about this shows the professional writer. I like the tone of it and I think that she has succeeded very well in what she set out to do. At the same time I haven't the remotest idea how we would go about selling such a book."

Janice was content to momentarily lay aside *The Home Place.* By the end of May, just at a time when "the world was lovely," she learned that she was facing major surgery with the possibility of malignancy. As a person who "didn't much hold to running to the Lord in crisis" but believed "one's whole life should be a prayer," Janice did admit to being frightened to the point that she wanted Libby to be by her side during the ordeal. "I needed her gaiety and I knew it would not falter," she said. "Even though I was asking her to come and be frightened with me, and I was frightened, I knew that no amount of fear would keep her from providing me with the high jinks of the old days when we two stood alone but together against the world."

A week before she was to enter Norton's Infirmary Female Surgical Ward in Louisville, Janice's "jangled hypertensive nervous system promptly erupted into a bad case of shingles." Three weeks later, on June 23, Henry's forty-second birthday, she had a hysterectomy and "extensive internal repairs," which required a month's recovery in the hospital. Henry drove back and forth from the ridge to Louisville three or four times each week to visit his wife and give her a progress report on the log house.

When Janice was dismissed from the hospital, Lucy Holt arrived from Fort Smith to take over the management of the household and her daughter's continuing convalescence. Janice was home only a few days when a "violent recurrence" of shingles sent her back to the hospital for another week.

With Lucy's help and Janice's directions, the move became a reality August 19, 1958. When she had finally settled into the house that was built with the royalties she earned from putting to pen the many stories Henry had shared as well as those from her own creative imagination, Janice wrote: "A great peace settled over me and as the flames licked up the dry wood of the fire Henry had built and it began to crackle and spark, I knew that nothing ever again would really threaten that inner peace. Whatever storms came, and I knew they would come, Henry and I had a home, of the spirit as well as of the body."

18
West with the Fiction
1958-1959

Persuaded that her daughter had regained strength from her surgery in June and that the duties of the new house were less demanding, Lucy Holt returned to Fort Smith in mid-September. Nestled in her Kentucky log home, Janice shifted her thoughts to the fifth historical novel, which would be the first to place characters in her native Arkansas.

Janice had long looked forward to writing about the West. In the conclusion of *The Believers*, she had set the stage for the beginning of the westward movement by sending her protagonist, Rebecca Fowler, to the old Missouri Territory with her husband, Stephen Burke. Janice Holt Giles could now literally "go home" with her writing.

On a rainy afternoon with ideas brewing, Janice retrieved her research notes from the summer of 1956 when she had spent three weeks in Fayetteville with her sister. Together, she and Mary had traversed the region of eastern Oklahoma and western Arkansas while Janice searched out sites and locations for the novel that would take the second-generation Fowlers out of Kentucky and on their adventurous trek westward.

Janice was elated to place the book to be called *Johnny Osage* in country she knew so well. She had studied numerous chronicles of Oklahoma, including personal narratives and journals, and was extremely pleased a month after her trip with Mary when the librarian of the Oklahoma Historical Society offered to send her a copy of the typescript of the *Union Mission Journal,* which provided great detail of the daily activities and tribulations of the first missionary effort among the Osage Indians.

Janice had been intensely interested in locating the actual site of the mission station. She and Mary had stopped for lunch one day in Muskogee, and Janice asked their waitress if anyone knew where the early mission had been. To her absolute amazement, she discovered that the young woman's grandmother knew the exact spot. It was an overwhelming experience for the author, who wanted to transpose a lasting narrative of the mission days to the printed page, when she stood on the shelf of land where the buildings once stood "well above the flood waters of the Neosho River." A powerful sensitivity to place embraced Janice as she knelt beside the tombstone of Epaphras Chapman, the man who had led the little band of ministers and teachers to the territory, and traced the chiseled letters on his headstone: "In Memory Of Epaphras Chapman Who died 7 June, 1825 Aged 32, First Missionary to the Osages, Say among the heathen the Lord Reigneth."

This man of cloth would take his place among the military and political historical characters in the projected novel. Several young unmarried women were a part of the teaching staff assembled by Chapman, which inspired Janice to create a fictional character named Judith Lowell. The male protagonist, Johnny Fowler, was Hannah Fowler's youngest child. Johnny would follow his sister Rebecca to the Missouri Territory and work in the trading post that her husband had organized. Janice's sentimentality to heritage is evident in Hannah Fowler's children. When Johnny left Kentucky he took with him a small particle of the old home place on Hanging Fork. In remembrance of his mother, he transported a coal from Hannah's hearth fire to the Three Forks trading post.

As previously instructed, Janice mailed the first few chapters of *Johnny Osage* to Ollie and Paul Reynolds for their review. Reynolds responded that he and Ollie had read what she had submitted and at that point "had to be discouraging." They did not feel Janice was "off to a good start" and yet could not tell her why. "I think," Reynolds wrote, "part of the trouble is that your heroine doesn't seem to have too much appeal to the reader. A group of religious people with an unmarried girl going up the river to start a mission and convert the Indians certainly has all the elements of an engrossing novel and yet I wondered as I read this whether you really sympathized with your characters. Somehow I didn't get any genuine religious feeling in the book even though that is what actuates your characters." Janice replied: "What I did not count on was my inherent dislike for missionaries. I wrote well about the Shakers because they were so different as to be queer and unknown, and because I made them the villains of the book. Also I had real respect for them. They were competent and genuinely spiritual, and with their schools and orphanages, their excellence as farmers, they made a real contribution anywhere they settled. These Union Mission people are not attractive any way you look at them. They blindly followed a bigot and zealot who, because of a fiery and self-centered conviction, was able to convince a board of missions to do what he wanted them to do.

"I don't like missionaries anywhere, anytime. The kind of person who can go into any land and say to its people, your religion is all wrong, your way of life is bad, I have the truth and the only truth, is not a person I can admire and respect. My personal feeling about Epaphras Chapman (and wouldn't you know his name would be Epaphras?) is how dare he go to the Osages with his narrow, limited conception of religion, with his smug conviction they were pagans and heathens, and try to teach them anything. They could have taught him much. The Osage religion was a beautiful, profound thing—Wa-kon-dah was a comforting, lovely conception—that which the children of the earth do not understand as they walk the face of the earth, and which is not explained to them until they pass on into the Great Mystery. It was no more superstitious for an Indian to dip his pipe in the four directions, toward the earth and the sky, than for a man to kneel in prayer, to take communion, to be baptized, to belong to a church. It is all directed toward the Great Mystery. But the Osages had enough humility not to limit the Mystery with any qualifications. Well—I needn't preach you a sermon."

The problems Janice encountered during the winter, once she had chosen the right technique for writing *Johnny Osage,* were unrelated to the book. They were physical and financial. The enormous state and federal income tax payments, hospital and medical bills, continued medications, and building supplies and labor for the log house had drained her financial resources. She had borrowed funds using copyrights as collateral to pay the tax and building debts, but little remained for daily living expenditures.

Since her surgery, Janice had lost weight, was nervous, and felt bad, physically, most of the time. In trying to trim costs while building the log house, proper insulation had not been installed, particularly in the attic. They burned wood in the fireplace and heating stoves but by the middle of winter finally resigned themselves to living in three rooms as "all the heat promptly went right out the beautiful hand-riven shingleboard roof."

"I remember writing *Johnny Osage* in great physical discomfort," Janice wrote in *Around Our House*, "my legs wrapped in a blanket, a small electric heater at my feet, and my hands so cold I could barely type. I noticed the cold more then because I was not well. Occasionally self-pity got the best of me and I wrote with tears running down my cheeks—but I wrote."

Houghton Mifflin suggested that The *Land Beyond the Mountains* would be an excellent title for her last book about Kentucky's statehood, previously called *The Glory Road.* Ollie agreed and felt that it would be "pretty much in keeping with *The Kentuckians, Hannah Fowler,* etc." The publishing date for *The Land Beyond the Mountains* was set for March 4, 1959. Paul Brooks sent Janice a telegram: OFF TO A GOOD START WITH

ADVANCE SALE OF OVER SIX THOUSAND COPIES. John Beecroft accepted it for the Family Book Club, continuing Janice's admirable record of book club editions for her novels.

In a lecture in Owensboro at Kentucky Wesleyan College to the FreeLancers, Janice told the group as reported in the *Messenger and Inquirer,* May 16, 1959: "I have read that the average book nets $1,500 for the author. We have found that unless you get a book club you do well to realize $4,500 to $5,000. With acceptance by a good book club the author will get from $15,000 to $20,000." Janice shared the fact that eight of her eleven published volumes had been accepted by book clubs with the "most lucrative step being chosen by a company such as Doubleday, in which case a book might be selected for the Family, Dollar and Youth Clubs, then used as a dividend with one or two other clubs." She expressed joy in having "had that pleasant experience."

Johnny Osage was completed in May 1959 and immediately accepted by John Beecroft for the Doubleday Book Club. "It won me my first true national and international fame," Janice wrote. To Janice, *Johnny Osage* had been "unalloyed joy to write, from the writing standpoint." Reclaiming her heritage and revealing less devotion to her adopted state, she explained: "I was on home ground and I knew the country from firsthand experience in my childhood. I knew and felt the entire country in my bones and blood and nerves. Because of this, I not only had no writing problems with *Johnny Osage,* I have never had any with any of the historical books after I got my people out of Kentucky into my own southwest country. It was Kentucky that was my alien land, although I had come to love it and it was my home. But spiritually probably Kentucky has never really become my home.

"I am the only member of my family who lives east of the Mississippi River and to most of my people my removal to Kentucky was turning backward, both in history and in the breezy, free-blowing western spirit. I never meant to live in Kentucky forever when I came here in 1939. It was only a job that brought me. But I married a Kentuckian and here I have been ever since."

To ease their mountainous gas bills during the second winter in the uninsulated log house, Henry built flues in the kitchen and the dining/sitting room and installed two woodburning stoves. On a "black, black January day" when the plumbing pipes had been frozen for three days and the only water in the house was a bucket of creek water at the kitchen sink, Janice smelled something burning. She jumped up from her desk chair and discovered black, billowing smoke boiling all around the red-hot flue hole in the sitting room. She was sure that at any instant the room would burst into flames.

Henry was not at home. "In the winter," Janice explained, "as with all the other men of the community, he makes a daily sashay to the country store to catch up on news, prognosticate about the weather, play a game or two of checkers, loaf and whittle an hour or two. It's a countryman's coffee break. But at that moment I bitterly resented it. It seemed to me that in every crisis of my life since the day we were married [Henry] had not been where I needed him. He was always away, up the hollow, on the ridge, at the river, or at the store, when his man's strength was needed."

Horrified, but with no time to panic, Janice grabbed the bucket of creek water near the kitchen sink and tossed the water up through the smoke. She fled to the creek for bucket after bucket of water until no more was escaping around the stovepipe. In a last magnanimous effort to save her house, Janice yanked the pipe down and carried it outside. She furiously began to clean up the wet, sooty mess. When Henry returned he had only a charred log to chip out and a flue hole to mend. His wife had handled the crisis.

Gradually the task emerged that became Henry Giles's full-time job when he was home—that of providing the critically needed privacy for Janice's writing. The soldier who had written, "I could never see a wife of mine working. I believe it's a man's responsibility to do the earning and providing" was, by 1959, "keeper of the gate." Henry's major role was to "head 'em off at the pass" when people tried to invade Janice's privacy—the "long silence" that was so necessary to her writing. Perhaps the fact that Janice stayed home to do the work that earned their living, which also allowed her to be available to cook their meals, assuaged some of Henry's purported "shame to be seen" he had claimed he would suffer "if his wife had to earn or even help earn" their income.

Though he might not be there in a crisis, "My Henry," Janice acknowledged, "is the dearest man in the world. There is no doubt I love him with all my heart." She elaborated on "some very special things" about Henry that gave her life "added richness": she felt grateful for "the twinkle in my husband's eye. I take for granted his love, for in a good marriage love is something so basic and inseparable that it is hardly necessary to speak of it. It speaks for itself and like food and sleep and breath, it is always there. But it is a happy boon that my husband should have so grand a sense of humor. That his everyday speech should be so pungent with it and his wit that it is a constant delight to me, that we should often laugh together. It makes him a very special companion. It also smooths over some rough places and takes even unkindnesses to him or to me in good stride."

By the end of September 1959, Janice still had not settled into the beginning of the next book. When she did, it was not the historical novel to follow *Johnny Osage* but a contemporary story with the present-day setting in fictional Cartwright's Mill, which was patterned after her own environment. On October 8, Janice wrote Ollie, "We have had an oil boom all around us in the last two years, which has slowly been creeping toward our neck of the woods." Janice had been observing with interest how the thought of sudden riches changed relationships and the lives of people touched by it.

Her creativity astir, Janice began to plot a story seen through the eyes of an older woman wisely observing, with the maturity of her years, weighing events shrewdly. The woman would run an old-fashioned, hand-set weekly newspaper—*The Mill Wheel,* which would also be the title of the book. The novel would include romance, threatened violence, and "much seething and tossing before the whole thing is smoothed over." It would also link the Fowler and Cooper descendants with the Cartwrights and Pierces of earlier books. "This Green River country is a world unto itself," Janice remarked, "with a rich history and an intriguing present. It is so typical of Kentucky that unto the seventh generation families are connected and inter-related that the way I want to work with them seems peculiarly appropriate."

By October 12, Janice wrote Ollie that she was plugging away at the new book, though there had been so many interruptions that she had not made much headway. "I think the crew of an oil rig just down the road from us are fearful I'm going to put *them* in a book," she wrote, "but it's only by haunting such an outfit I can get the feel of it and hear the language. Much excitement in this valley right now, which I personally can't believe will come to anything."

The day before Thanksgiving, Janice mailed Ollie chapters of *The Mill Wheel* and was pleased when he wrote that he thought favorably of what she had sent, even though he felt it was "a little loose" and would need considerable revision.

Janice and Henry made plans to spend Christmas in Santa Fe and remain in the West after the holiday so Janice could to do some "refresher work" on the Santa Fe Trail book she had planned "in her mind" for years to write.

19
Religion and Politics
1959-1962

In the autobiographical *Around Our House*, Janice presents information concerning the writing of most of her books; however, she does not mention *The Mill Wheel*, the novel begun in October 1959. Instead she wrote that in September 1959 she began *Savanna*, the sixth historical novel, and had written about 150 pages before the Christmas holidays. Plans for that season included a stop in Fort Smith to spend time with Janice's mother before she and Henry traveled to Santa Fe for the celebration with the Hancocks.

When they reached Fort Smith, Janice was appalled to find her seventy-seven-year-old mother "in bad physical condition." Like her daughter, Lucy Holt always "presented a bold front," so Janice had no idea she had been suffering digestive problems and mild attacks of angina. Janice described her mother as "very thin, nervous and shaky and almost everything she ate hurt her." She felt that her nervousness was partly associated with worry, because Lucy was experiencing financial problems for the first time since her retirement. She had mortgaged her home to pay for badly needed roof and paint repairs and had allowed her income-producing rental property to become so run down she could not attract desirable people, so her earnings were "badly curtailed."

Written ten years after the event, Janice's account in *Around Our House* implied that during the holidays she and Henry worked out a scheme to help her mother. They planned to tell Lucy that Janice needed to be in the western region for further research on the next historical novel. They would move in with her and, while there, pay all the household expenses as they customarily did, which would give Lucy a chance to recoup her finances. Janice felt that she could be comfortable in Fort Smith and work on *Savanna* while she took care of her mother's house. "My thought was that if we paid all the household bills, if I planned and cooked the meals, her poor appetite would be helped, she would not worry about money, and her digestion would be improved."

"Unfortunately," Janice wrote, "we could not put this plan into action until March of 1960. We got caught in the season of snow blizzards in

Santa Fe and could not leave until the middle of January. Ollie Swan and his wife had planned to visit us in February on their way to the Mardi Gras in Mobile, Alabama. We had to come home to receive them. But once our obligation to them was over, we wrote my mother in such a way that she could feel she was doing us a favor in allowing us to come to Fort Smith and stay with her."

In mid-March Janice wrote Ollie from Fort Smith that "comfortable arrangements were made to rent an apartment from my mother, and I, at least have begun work. Henry is still a little up in the air trying to get the garden house furnished and heated properly for his use as a study." No doubt, Henry would have preferred to call it a "getaway house." Janice's sister, Mary, remarked that Henry was "lovable, so sweet and so good, but when he got mad you knew it. He'd storm out of the house. He always had little diggings of his own to go to."

From her mother's home, Janice admitted to Ollie she could use another thousand dollars if Houghton Mifflin was willing to advance it against the book club contract and asked him to send it directly to her bank in Columbia. She also informed him that they would be at her mother's address indefinitely. "I'm going to try to write the new book here. With air-conditioning I think I can write in the summer and I would like very much to have a fall publication next time. But whether or not we shall stay here all summer depends on many things—and to some extent at least on how hot the summer is this far south."

Ollie managed an advance for Janice and, as instructed, sent it to her bank in Kentucky. Soon after, she wrote him extensively "about money" and concluded, "What would actually be most helpful to me would be to have book club money prorated over the balance of the year, which would be $500 per month." She ended the lengthy missive by stating, "The past two years have been such a fearful struggle, financially, and I am so weary of it and the whole precarious business of writing that I am strongly tempted to chuck it and go back on a regular salary. I can't even fool myself that the books I write are even worth writing. They're just a way of earning a living and a darned uncertain one at that."

Janice sent Ollie the first section of *Savanna* on June 7, along with "a rather comprehensive outline of the continuing story." Feeling that he was going to "yell" at her "immediately" about the length, she remarked that, while the sixth historical novel was certainly going to be longer than any other, it would not reach "mammoth proportions." Janice explained that the additional length was necessary to completely develop the background of the fictional character, Savanna, "because she turns into such a complex person with such fascinating facets of personality." Confessing that she was not willing to "turn her loose" until she explored as much of Savanna's character as she could perceive, Janice added, "Of course I am in love with her, but not, I think, sentimental about her. She is, I think, the best woman character I have ever done, including Hannah."

Savanna Fowler, daughter of Matthew, second son of Hannah and Matthias Fowler of Hanging Fork, was contrived in the image of Libby Hancock. Her name was chosen "simply for its euphony with Fowler." Savanna had the enduring strength of her grandmother Hannah and the "gamin qualities, some vulgarity and greed" of her grandmother Tattie Cartwright. Like Elizabeth Moore Hancock, Savanna was beautiful. "To me a beautiful woman always looks like my daughter," Janice wrote. "Savanna had Libby's dark hair and eyes and tawny skin. When I dressed Savanna for the colonel's ball at old Fort Gibson I remembered Libby's gold bangles and Libby's gold hoops. Indeed, I could not have helped it, for Libby is all through the character of Savanna! The same independence, the same 'by myself' attitude, the same come-a-cropper and pick-myself-up again fortitude, the same color and flair and life and gypsy vividness. Libby was sweeter and gentler and less self-centered, but she provided a form on which I could drape a pioneer character."

Janice was immensely pleased when Ollie wrote that he, too, liked Savanna. In return, she divulged, "I don't think I've ever had a character before who so charmed me. I have the oddest feeling that she really lived, that she was perhaps my own great-great-grandmother, and I have the most tremendous admiration for her! I think it may be that the device I used of having her keep a journal, without making the journal carry the story however, has given me the feeling that in writing I am simply passing on to the reader what I have discovered about her."

Janice's familiarity with Savanna's journal may well have arisen from the sparse diary Catherine McGraw kept during her pioneering days as a young bride in western Arkansas. Janice had heard the stories repeated many times of the tiny, five-foot-one woman who journeyed across Arkansas in the 1870s aboard an iron horse, fifty years after the fictional Savanna covered the trail astride a lively horse; both to live in a log house, both to experience struggles in sparsely settled, rugged land.

Janice decided to take a break from writing during the latter part of July as the Arkansas heat was unbearable. "The house is comfortable, with air-conditioning," she wrote Ollie, "but we don't like being imprisoned and it amounts to that with the temperature around 100 each day. So, in view of the fact that I have done what I came here to do, the research and kicking the book off, we plan to go home shortly. Will let you know, of course, exactly when. My mother will go with us and continue to keep house for me until the book is finished. I'm in the stretch and it will write itself now." With a solid block of 450 pages behind her, Janice had "no fear of losing any momentum."

"Doing research and kicking off a book" with her mother keeping house was certainly a different perspective to Janice's exaggeration of the purpose and time spent in Fort Smith described in *Around Our House.* When *Savanna* appeared in print, it was dedicated: "To my mother, Lucy McGraw Holt, who made it easier for me to write this book." In a typescript copy of *Rode Hard and Put Up Wet: Autobiography of an Appalachian* written by Henry in 1966, he wrote: "We moved from Columbia back to the woods—Spout Springs in 1956. Twice since then we have been to Fort Smith, Arkansas to live indefinitely; maybe the rest of our lives, we told people. We could live with Janice's mother for as long as we wanted to do so. The first indefinite stay lasted three months; we came back with the springtime. And the second time we went to Fort Smith to live, that was it. We would probably live there forever, we said. And we had a good friend, Joe Spires, and his family move into our house. We're gone for good, this time.

"That time we did stay gone for nearly six months while Janice was writing a novel with an Oklahoma setting that was near Fort Smith. Then she finished her work, and a night or two later it came. (Although I was always ready at any time to return, I usually waited for Janice to make the decision to go home.) We talked and talked that night, then all at once Janice got to the point. Write Joe a card and tell him they will have to move. I've got to go home. That's the way it was for a while. Indefinitely between us doesn't mean much."

Whatever the circumstances regarding the stay in Fort Smith—whether Janice wanted to be near the research and region about which she was writing, whether she needed to help her mother, whether Lucy Holt was needed to help her daughter, or whether one cold winter writing with her legs wrapped in a blanket, her eyes monitoring stove flues, and her hands so cold she could barely type in an uninsulated log house was enough. One thing was certain. Another book was nearing completion. Janice and Henry were going home and Lucy Holt was going with them "to continue to keep house" until the writing of *Savanna* was accomplished.

Ollie forwarded Janice a copy of a letter he had received from Paul Brooks concerning Houghton Mifflin's consideration of reprinting *The Enduring Hills, Miss Willie,* and *Tara's Healing* for a Piney Ridge trilogy. The final decision was that republication would not be a wise move at that time. Brooks added that he felt *Savanna* "may turn out to be the most salable book." "Certainly we hope," Brooks wrote Ollie, "that it will increase both her reputation and her market. As you know, building up a novelist in the book trade is a delicate business, and I think we should run some risk in confusing the situation with new editions of earlier works that, for all their quality, could not hope to have the same reception as her present writing." Time would prove Brooks wrong.

Savanna was "marching forward with no difficulties." Because Janice was totally involved in writing and her mother was with her, the grandsons did not visit during the summer of 1960. Her commitment paid off. "Light a firecracker and shoot it off right in the middle of Fifth Avenue! *Savanna* is finished! At two o'clock Sunday afternoon, August 28th."

Savanna Fowler may have had the physical characteristics of Libby Hancock, but growing up on the "muddy, sprawling Arkansas River, loving passionately the wild land," Savanna had the lust for life and the endurance of her creator. Throughout her experiences with the frontier army, Savanna faced whatever came with "a strong, resilient faith in herself and life. Difficulties, hardships, setbacks, had always been a challenge to her." Like Janice, it frightened Savanna "to think of going into debt. All her life she had been scared of debt. It held a dreadful terror for her. To be out of debt, to her, was always to be free." Savanna's plea was "By myself," the author penned. But "no one ever did things alone. Behind every move, every thought, every deed, every heartbeat, stood all the others, with friendship and love and faith and trust and hope, and forever shining over all the radiant miracle of God in his world. . . . She had had bitter experiences. They showed. . . . She had known transporting rapture. It showed. . . . She had known grief. She had known pain and harshness and worry and fear and trouble. She had known excitement and fun and laughter. They all showed. . . . But what showed most and dominated all else in the face across which the dying sun slanted was the essence of Savanna. And the essence was—valor."

Of *Savanna,* Janice revealed, "People who read the kind of books I write are for the most part sentimental and they like to get a lump in their throats in the end. They want a lesson taught and they write me by the hundreds about how their own courage is strengthened." Janice could write convincingly about "grief, pain, harshness, worry, fear and trouble, as well as excitement, fun, and laughter" because she had experienced each of those emotions. The word "endure" or some derivation of it often appears in her writing. She titled her first book *The Enduring Hills.* Her own endurance was taxed many times, but with courage and inner strength she persevered.

With *Savanna* completed by the end of August, Janice became involved in activities she had not experienced before. She declared that she and Henry had "never done more than vote" until the fall of 1960 when John Fitzgerald Kennedy became the Democratic candidate for the presidency. Even though Henry, a loyal Democrat, dolefully shook his head over Kennedy's chances, she responded with enthusiasm when Pete Walker, a young Adair County Democrat "rapidly forging ahead in state politics," asked her to do some writing for the State Committee. One thing led swiftly to another, and Janice became one of three State Democratic Regional Chairwomen.

For many years, Janice had waged a constant battle with high blood pressure in addition to her other health problems. Throwing caution to the wind, Janice became intensely involved in Kennedy's campaign. "It was one of the most exciting, thrilling, most rewarding experiences of my life," she said. She passionately wanted Kentucky for Kennedy and attended rallies in his support one after another. She was introduced to him in Bowling Green where she shared a platform with Franklin D. Roosevelt Jr., whom, Janice said, she knew immediately "because he looked so much like his father." When Roosevelt asked her how it was going in Kentucky, she hissed, "Religious issue," to which he replied, "Damn!"

Janice also met Lyndon and Lady Bird Johnson and most of the Kennedy sisters, but the greatest thrill was being in charge of a tea for Rose Kennedy at Hugh's Restaurant in Columbia on Sunday afternoon, September 25, 1960. Photographed with Mrs. Kennedy for the local newspaper, Janice was quoted as estimating that 750 to 1,000 persons from twenty counties had filed through the receiving line.

Heartsick that Kentucky did not go for Kennedy, Janice was ecstatic when he won the election November 8. "This darned politics gets in your blood," Janice wrote Joe Covington. "I'm just wondering when I'll ever have time to write another book! I never had such fun in my life and I hope I can be right in the big middle of it from now on. But it'll have to turn up a job for Henry so he can support me while I'm out politicking!" But when the excitement of the thrilling experience dissipated, Janice reconsidered her involvement and expressed a totally different attitude. "I had been made ill, we had spent far too much of our own money, and I was thrown dreadfully behind in finishing a book I had laid aside. Politics and writing didn't mix. Besides, my blood pressure wouldn't stand any more campaigning."

In December Janice completed and mailed the final copy of *Savanna* to Ollie and wrote that she was thinking of returning to a Kentucky setting in the next book, "with probably a Cartwright son steamboating on

Green River. There is some interesting history about it and some fascinating stories and legends. The time would be in the 1830s and 40s. I have a feeling I ought not stay away from Kentucky too long at a stretch, and it might be best to do this one next." But in early January, she mailed him an outline describing a narrative of a journey across the western prairies with an announcement that she intended to finish the writing before July. "You know I could not keep idle until next fall and you also know that I have done very little writing since last August, so am fully ready to begin a new book. And this book is so fully formed in my mind that I think it will not require the time *Savanna* did. I expect it will shape up rather like *The Believers* did."

In less than a month, Janice had steered her thoughts from steamboats plying the waters of Green River to wagon trains rumbling across the western prairies. For the first time, in the book "fully formed in her mind," Janice returned to fictional characters introduced in an earlier historical novel. Johnny Osage was not the central character of the new book, but his wife, Judith Fowler, was. The book "probes the heart of a woman" on an arduous ninety-day undertaking from Three Forks in Indian Territory across the Spanish Territory to Santa Fe, where Johnny was determined to set up trade. In *Voyage to Santa* Fe, Janice wanted to "explore what such a journey compelled a woman to have in the way of heart and courage and humor and endurance."

The route of the tedious journey was not the usual Santa Fe Trail but one that Johnny Fowler mapped out much farther south and followed the Jacob Fowler route of 1821. Janice was intrigued that her fictional name was coincidental to a historical traveler. Originally from New York, Jacob Fowler (1765-1850) moved to the northeastern Kentucky frontier while in his early twenties. In September 1821 he led a fur-trapping and hunting expedition from Fort Smith, Arkansas, to the southern Rockies. With his party of eighteen, Jacob Fowler continued the pioneer route along the Old Taos Trail into New Mexico and explored the upper Rio Grande. Johnny Fowler left Three Forks on April 30, 1824, with a train of four wagons, three of them loaded with freight, twenty men, forty-seven mules, thirty mustangs, and one woman, for the long haul to Santa Fe.

Janice described the heart of the story as "Judith's struggle with herself; to be always what she knows she must be; to keep a good heart and a strong faith; when she is scared witless, to remain calm; when she is ill, to keep going; when her faith in Johnny falters, to bolster it again; and, finally arrived at Santa Fe, and called on to make the one sacrifice she thought she could not bear to make, the loss of her first child through a miscarriage brought on by hardships, to rise from a dark hopelessness when she thinks she hates Johnny, again to light, to faith, to love, and once more to an acceptance of his man's necessities."

By the end of January 1961, Janice wrote Ollie that the first chapters of *Voyage to Santa Fe* had been revised and rewritten in third person. She was making progress, but not very rapidly. "I don't feel in any great hurry and am working rather slowly and sort of feeling my way into Judith."

When Janice received the galleys and learned that Paul Brooks "loved *Savanna,* and thought it extremely eloquent," she was elated and wrote a personal message to Ollie April 3: "I realize that you have dozens of clients who make more money for you than I do—and yet you have made me feel, for almost eleven years, as if my career and my future and my hopes, were more important to you than anything else. That's quite wonderful, do you know? I only wish I could make you richer for it, and so help me some day I will! If I have been selfish and used you, forgive me, but I do rely on you so much—that integrity which Betty mentioned. It's a strong prop on which I lean, ungratefully all too often, I'm afraid. Next to Henry I love you and even my Libby says that next to Nash you are the *most* gentle man she has ever known! That's not dollars and cents, but it's something, and we don't live solely on dollars and cents. Accept our thanks!"

Ollie's April 7 response expressed similar feelings: "I wish I could tell you, without sounding too sentimental, how very moved I have been by your letter. I can only say that it is my very earnest hope that you'll never have occasion to regret the confidence you have placed in us."

A most revealing personal letter was written to Joe Covington the next day. Beginning with a statement that she was feeling "puny," Janice continued: "I've suddenly developed abdominal aches and pains in various joints, glands and muscles, as well as a very uncertain stomach. Doctors are not adding to my morale any with their poking, probing and needling. I expect them to tell me, any minute, (a) that I am mortifying by inches and slowly disintegrating with some unheard of disease, probably from outer space (b) that finally I must lose all my teeth, (c) back to my old bland diet for that damnable duodenal ulcer. This is what comes of the combination of being a writer and fiftyish. Either is unhealthy and the two combined are probably fatal!

"I am also melancholy over my income tax and am seriously considering writing a book only about every three years and limiting my income purposely to a minimum of taxes. The trouble with that is that writing a book each year is all that has kept me sane these twelve years in Adair County and I might as well make a reservation in a mental institution as to do without some purposeful occupation. I sound like Job, don't I? Or the Preacher in Ecclesiastes! Woe, woe and vanity, vanity! Well, when I hurt, I hurt big—in my soul as well as my joints! But I'll bounce back (if spring ever comes). I'm very resilient."

At the end of May, Janice put *Voyage to Santa Fe* aside to prepare for the grandsons' arrival June 15. The summer of 1961 would be the first time Libby planned to stay the entire six weeks' visit, "to help with both the work and the responsibility," as she had decided the boys were too much work for her mother and Henry alone. To Ollie, Janice wrote, "I must admit that in addition to being very happy to have Libby for a longer visit, I think with considerable relief of not carrying the full burden of discipline and decisions. In addition, I have found a good housekeeper [Mary Lee Payne] who will help full time during the month they are here. So please have me off your mind. It will be an easy summer in comparison to some I have known."

The 1961 summer visit was a time of transition for the grandsons, ages thirteen, twelve, and eleven. Since their friends and activities were in Santa Fe, summers in Kentucky were beginning to lose much of their "charm and savor." Janice expressed her reaction to the change, "We understood, for we had always known this time must come, and though we missed them, what we actually missed was the past summers when they were such little fellows. Time does not stand still, however, and we knew they must grow up and move on into areas where we could not follow."

In November Janice was visited by an archivist from the University of Kentucky Libraries soliciting her manuscript materials. She had previously donated several manuscripts and the original jacket design for *Harbin's Ridge* and was considering the eventual gift of all her papers. "Not knowing they would value galleys," she had given several sets to various individuals. Explaining the request to Ollie, Janice wrote, "My research files are probably the only papers I have that are likely to be valuable. It isn't likely that I will ever have the stature that will make my correspondence valuable, but since they press for a complete collection I am inclined to let them have it all some day. I should like to name your firm literary executors, not that any of my unpublished manuscripts are likely to be any more publishable after my death than before, but only you would know. Henry and Libby would be lost and ought to have your wisdom to lean on."

While Janice was inclined to let the University of Kentucky have all of her papers "some day," ironically, researching the next historical novel would change the destination of the bulk of her manuscript collection. Janice often traveled to Bowling Green to use the Library Special Collections in the Kentucky Building on the campus of Western Kentucky University. Appreciative of their assistance, Janice made friends with librarian Elizabeth Coombs and director Mary Julia Neal. Julia Neal related the story of the change.

A short time after the call from the University of Kentucky, Janice also received a request from someone at Bowling Green State University, Bowling Green, Ohio, about depositing her materials in their archives. Confused, Janice telephoned the Kentucky Library. Miss Neal helped Janice understand the confusion of the two Bowling Greens and declared, "Why, Mrs. Giles, you *can't* let *them* have your papers!" and immediately encouraged Janice to think seriously about her manuscripts becoming a part of the holdings of the Kentucky Library.

A pleasant and gracious woman who was also a published authority on the Kentucky Shakers, Julia Neal was successful in persuading Janice to donate the remainder of her materials to Western Kentucky University. Janice wrote Julia Neal, "I am so pleased that the rest of my papers will be in your care at Western. My commitment with the University of Kentucky was entirely to Lawrence Thompson, so I feel wholly free to give the balance of the collection to Western—with whom the ties are much, much closer after all."

In reality, Janice had already achieved the stature that would make her collection valuable. John Beecroft now accepted historical novels by Janice Holt Giles without hesitation. *Voyage to Santa* Fe was an immediate book club success and outsold *Savanna by* almost 50,000 copies, with a sale of 325,598 hardcover copies. In ten years Janice had published twelve books: eleven novels and one nonfiction work, *40 Acres and No Mule.*

20
Running the River
1962-1963

In January 1962 Janice discussed the possibility with Ollie of doing a nonfiction book about the log house, as a kind of "tide-over thing" for the balance of winter and spring before beginning the next historical novel in the fall. Explaining her motivation, in part, Janice wrote, "We have had some rather shocking news lately concerning the upper Green River dam which, if appropriated and built, will condemn this entire valley. Our house would be under the lake water. I want to do the book before that occurs, while we're still in it, while it's still here, and while there is some sense of heartbreak concerning it.

"For several years there had been talk about the proposed dam, but somehow you never quite believe that sort of thing will happen. I know it's for flood control and is a part of a general conservation program. But it hits this valley very hard, especially the old, old homesteads. We aren't the Seneca Indians, but we certainly know how they feel! We all accept it, but acceptance doesn't keep an old man from walking over the land his father and grandfather worked before him with haunted eyes."

Of their own house and location, Janice lamented, "We have some high land on which we can build, or if practical move this log house to. Even so, when I think of the blood, sweat and tears we've spent on this house, and the specially sweet curves of the little creek around the house, and Henry's beloved fishing holes in the river, it is dreadfully hurting."

Janice was eager to begin writing the nonfiction book she tentatively titled *This Old House* and asked Ollie to query Houghton Mifflin. "I am almost inclined to go ahead with it, on my own," she informed him, "and if H.M. don't like the idea, let the University Press have it. Couldn't I do that without disrupting the arrangement with H.M.? Just one book? I would hope to do sketches to illustrate the book and I think it might be very charming. No money, naturally. But haven't I been a pretty good money-earner for H.M.? Just once couldn't they let me do something of my own, in my own way?"

Janice was more than a "pretty good" money earner for her publishers. *Johnny Osage* and *Savanna* rapidly became two of her most successful novels, selling hundreds of thousands, which placed Janice Holt Giles in the first rank of American historical novelists. Appreciation of that accomplishment is apparent in Ollie's return letter, "I'm happy to report that Houghton Mifflin are not only willing to have you undertake the nonfiction project but almost anxious for you to do so." Editor Anne Barrett had written him, "The sad fact that the log house is now doomed might give the book an added poignancy and force but whether it does or not, we want to publish because, clearly, it means a great deal to Janice."

Janice began work on the new book January 16 and felt it as "such a labor of love that I'm certain the writing will fly." She also announced that she and Henry had a new hobby—oil painting. They had purchased an easel, paints, brushes, and canvas boards as part of their Christmas. "Both of us are fascinated and spend many engrossing hours sketching and trying to paint. I find it so time-consuming that I will have to discipline myself rigidly with the new book, or else I'll never get another word written."

By the first week of February Janice reported, "The new book goes well—a very happy piece of writing for me. Henry is going to do several of the chapters, especially some of those dealing with the actual building and the many difficulties which only vaguely concerned me but which he had to overcome. You've seen enough of his writing to know that it is easy and flowing, with a special kind of tongue-in-cheek sense of fun. His suggestion for a title is indicative of it—*A Little Better than Plumb*, which is based on an anecdote of the building. We mean to keep pathos out of it and in general use a light touch."

In one of Henry's chapters, he relates the origin of the book's title. Lead carpenter Joe Spires and his helper were putting up some studding "which had to be exactly plumb. He told the his helper so. While the helper held the spirit level to the stud Joe nailed it securely in place. Finished, he asked, 'Are you sure it was plumb, Ab?'

"'Sure was,' Ab rejoined cheerfully. 'Fact is, Joe, hit was jist a little bit better'n plumb 'ccordin' to the level.' Joe checked for himself and sure enough it was—a little better than plumb."

A feature article by Joe Creason appeared in the March 18, 1962, Sunday magazine section of the *Courier-Journal*, headlined, "Authors Face Real-Life Plot: Tragedy at Spout Springs." Creason explained the effects of the approaching dam. "As things stand now, the Gileses are not of mind to try to salvage the log house, a massive 52-by-42-foot structure which represents four 'sets' of logs and a year of hard work. They will simply sell their house and land to the Government and move into Columbia, the nearest town of size. Or they might buy a piece of ground back in the knobs and build a brand-new home overlooking the lake."

Creason mentioned Janice was writing a book about the building of the log house and added, "What is more they also will do the sketches which will go into the book as illustrations. Neither currently rates as a latter-day Rembrandt. In fact, they've only been painting a few months as a hobby. But both swing a rather talented brush, and their kind of painting should fit well in the book."

Creason applauded Janice's literary success: "How financially profitable her books have been is shown in sales figures. By now 1,690,000 hard-cover copies of the first four of her six historical novels have been bought; *Osage* has sold more than 500,000 copies in the hard-cover edition, while *Savanna* now is in its third printing. All of her books except *40 Acres and No Mule, a* nonfictional work, have been Doubleday Book Club selections." Mentioning works in progress and projected books, Creason concluded, "They'll have to start constructing days with more than the conventional twenty-four hours if she's going to have time enough in one life span to set down on paper all the stories that are in her mind."

Janice mailed the completed manuscript of *A Little Better than Plumb* to Ollie on the last day of May. Separate from the manuscript, she sent a few sample pen-and-ink drawings for consideration to be used in the book, not from her own pen but that of Pansy Phillips's. Stating she very much wanted her friend's line drawings in the book, she implored Ollie, "If H.M. are willing, you must guide both Mrs. Phillips and ourselves concerning her compensation. Bless her, she is quite willing to do it for nothing, but I insist on compensation. I think she's fabulous, but even if she wasn't she is my closest and dearest friend and I *want* her in her share of this book. She was in on the building of our house and is very warmly a part of it. It's appropriate that she should be."

In June Janice learned from Paul Reynolds that Dollar Book Club had chosen *Voyage to Santa Fe* for the January selection. He informed her that, despite Paul Brooks's pleas, the Literary Guild would not take her latest novel but added, "I'll make you a wager that one of these days you're going to have The Guild."

When Ollie Swan and his wife, Betty, returned from a trip to London and Paris, they were extremely pleased to learn of the dedication in *Voyage to Santa Fe:* "To Oliver G. Swan who is honorable in his dealings, wise in his counsel and warm in his friendship." Humbly acknowledging the dedication as "overly generous," Ollie wrote Janice in mid-June that he had found *A Little Better than Plumb* "a very personal sort of book" that he thought would be of enormous interest to her loyal and growing audience. "Personally, I found it very rewarding and at times a very moving piece of writing and especially meaningful to me, having had the pleasure and privilege of both eating and sleeping under your roof."

With A *Little Better than Plumb* completed by the first of June, Janice was ready to take a break from writing. The grandsons arrived in mid-June for a six weeks' visit, which "made summer so busy and fascinating," she claimed, that "there hasn't been time or inclination to do anything but enjoy them."

In early August Janice and Henry spent several weeks in Bowling Green, the town where they had first met on a bus, to complete her research at the Kentucky Library for the next novel, which would deal with steamboat trade on the Barren and Green rivers at the outset of the Civil War. "It will certainly have a male protagonist," she wrote Ollie, "and I am quite excited about the possibilities. I have had precisely the kind of break from novel writing I badly needed and feel refreshed and eager to go now."

While in Bowling Green, "flitting about trying to dig up material on the Green River steamboat era which began in 1828 and ended in 1932," Janice praised her good fortune in being introduced to Frank J. Thomas, former master of the *Evansville,* the last passenger-carrying packet boat to run the Green River. The *Evansville* burned at the Bowling Green wharf in 1931, but thirty years later Captain Thomas was still most capable of recalling vivid memories of his experiences as a riverman. His wife, "Miss Beulah," the daughter of a tugboat pilot, was a valuable source of knowledge too. Janice credited her with illustrating "the coonjine the roustabouts used to do as they loaded cargo," and explaining "how the staterooms were arranged, how good the food was and in what state it was served in the palatial red and gold dining room."

Beulah Thomas introduced Janice to her ninety-year-old father, Captain J.E. Wallace, who was keenly insightful. Captain Wallace told Janice that, in order to pass the pilot's examination in the old steamboat days, it was necessary to "write the river" from memory. With great clarity of mind, he then described "every bend, every bar, every shoal." He mentally and verbally "wrote the river" from Evansville to Bowling Green for Janice. Her proficient secretarial skills allowed her to capture each word of the poignant descriptions that rolled forth from the old captain's recollections.

Janice's dedication to meticulous detail in her writing was never more manifest than in preparation for the river trade novel. She wrote Ollie, "My entire attention is focused on the steamboat book now. We are moving this weekend into the fishing camp of some friends who have offered it to us for as long as I feel the need to be directly on the river. Of course we'll be home on weekends. Henry probably will drive home several times a week for mail and to feed the dogs. I've been on the river a lot, of course, but not to the extent of knowing it at every hour of the day or in all its moods and stages."

Some of Janice's best experiences occurred during the research and prewriting activities for the river book. Not only did she *live* on the river, Joe Covington arranged a *trip* on the river for Janice and Pansy Phillips, who intended to do some sketching for possible use in the book. Reflecting on the excursion, Janice wrote Covington on September 25, 1962: "I can't begin to tell you how invaluable that trip downriver was for me, or to thank you for arranging it, because however much Warren Hines had to do with it, it was your intercession which made it possible. We had a ball, naturally. You should have seen us at five-thirty, barely daylight and foggier than any dew, being deposited on a pile of rocks on the bank of the Barren!"

Warren Hines, vice president of a marine towing company, had arranged for the ladies to board the *Maple,* a diesel-powered towboat. "Oh, Joe, if Mr. Hines had looked all the rivers in the world over for two men to send me downriver with, two perfect men, he couldn't have found two better than the Nasbitts, father and son," Janice wrote. "They were not only wonderfully nice, they had a great sense of fun, much understanding of my needs, they were hospitable, they tried in every way to be helpful, and when we de-barked at Rochester, and I tried to thank them, they would have none of it. Instead, we had done them an honor—we had made an otherwise routine trip a pleasure.

"The last service those blessed men did for me was to give me a title for the book. Ashore once more, I shook hands with Jim Nasbitt, the owner, and he said, 'Well, now, you've run you a river, haven't you?'

"Isn't that fabulous? *Run Me a River!* How much I owe to them, and you and to Warren Hines there aren't words to tell! Just know how deep my feeling of gratitude goes!" Janice had long had her story, now the research was over, and she had the feeling of the river. She took great pains with descriptive passages in her writing as she strongly believed the character of the land determined to a very great extent the character of the people who lived in that land.

By the end of October Janice had rewritten the two opening chapters of the river book ten times because she did not want to settle for anything less than the precise word. "Why is each book harder?" she pondered. "Is it true that I improve with each? Is it that I have to 'top' myself? All I know is that I can remember some books that were a lot easier than the last four have been."

Run Me a River is the story of a five-day venture aboard the *Rambler,* a ramshackle steamboat that plied its trade from Bowling Green,

Kentucky, to Evansville, Indiana. Early in the *Rambler*'s 184-mile run, twenty-six-year-old Captain Bohannon Cartwright and his crew, Foss, Tobe, Luke, Jonah, Boone, and Catfish, overrun a skiff in a squall and have to pull two passengers aboard: Sir Henry Cole, "the great Shakespearean actor, late of London and New York," and his granddaughter, Phoebe Cole, age sixteen. Of Sir Henry, Janice remarked, "I didn't plan that old Shakespearean actor. He almost cost me my mind. He knew more Shakespeare than I did. All at once here comes a side character that just takes over and runs the book. He never quoted straight. It would start out and get all mixed up with the Book of Common Prayer and the Bible."

Sir Henry Cole may well have received his "knighthood" in the manner of Janice's father, Sir John, and been infused with husband Henry's humor. Sir Henry, a tent show ham who plunked a guitar like Henry and played a fiddle as did John Holt, expounded to Bo Cartwright: "Upon my word, sir, you have a great plenty of horse towns in Kentucky! We closed the show three nights ago at a place called Horse Branch and played at Horse Cave, Horse Hill, and Horse's Neck, until I began to wonder if propriety had deterred the people from conferring the opposite end of the animal upon some hapless community."

As for Phoebe's place in the novel, Janice said, "I don't enjoy writing about young love. It is long in my past. But you have to have a love interest to sell a book." In a *Courier-Journal* interview about the writing of *Run Me a River*, Shirley Williams quoted Janice as saying, "I was fifty-five when I wrote that book. You pull it all out of your brain and you just use yourself up. Every book takes something out of you, every page takes something out of you. I'm not richer, I'm poorer physically. I hope the reading public is richer by sixteen books. . . . I felt as tired when I got through with *Voyage to Santa Fe* as if I had pulled that wagon. Tired the whole time dragging that wagon train. I felt drowned as if my head had been under water the whole year when I finished writing *Run Me a River*. It is hard to realize that I'm Janice Holt Giles, that Henry Giles is my husband, and I've got supper to cook."

By the first week of November Janice had written fifty "good pages" of *Run Me a River*. The novel, begun with great excitement, was interrupted in grave concern. Janice received word from her brother that their mother had suffered a massive coronary thrombosis and was critically ill. She and Henry left Kentucky at 3:30 A.M. and drove the six hundred miles to be at Lucy Holt's bedside, greatly fearing she would be gone before their arrival.

For two weeks "it was a very delicate balance," Janice wrote, "but when she did begin to recover, it was with all her usual fire and spirit."

Lucy spent five weeks in the hospital while her children took turns attending her. Janice and Henry remained with her when John and Mary returned to their respective homes and businesses in Fort Smith and Fayetteville.

The novelist hovered over the cookstove a considerable amount, but with good help she managed successfully to serve eighteen of Lucy Holt's offspring for dinner on Christmas eve. The number included three children and their spouses, four of the five grandchildren and their spouses, and five great-grandchildren.

On January 4 Janice and Henry departed for Kentucky and left Lucy Holt, according to her doctor, "in the best physical condition she has been in for five years, and in excellent hands." Lucy wanted to continue to live in her own home, so Janice and Henry did their best to make it possible. They arranged for a man and his wife to live with her. Janice felt reluctant to leave her mother but sensed an even greater urgency to return to writing the novel that might well be necessary to support her care.

21
Pain of Parting
1963-1964

Weeks passed before Janice could return to work on the steamboat book. She had lost all momentum during the stress of her mother's illness and the weeks spent in Arkansas. She felt she would have to practically begin anew but had no complaints, declaring, "Mother lived and I can do what I have to do." Constantly concerned about her mother, Janice was elated to learn that she and Henry would soon have a telephone; the neighbors had been connected while they were away.

In mid-February Janice informed Ollie that she had about a third of *Run Me a River* written. She thought it was going extremely well and added, "It's going to be a good book, if I know the signs." Janice also extended an invitation to Ollie and his wife to the "big affair" that was being planned for Saturday, March 16, by the Greensburg Art Club for Pansy Phillips, founder of the group and illustrator of *A Little Better than Plumb.* They were hosting an autograph party at the log house for the book's March 14 release and a "Clothesline Fair" to exhibit the works of the Art Club.

Janice wrote Ollie that Anne Barrett would be arriving from Boston on the fifteenth and that his and Betty's presence was all that was needed to "make it perfect." Ollie had to send their regrets; Paul Reynolds was on an extended trip abroad and he would have to remain in the office.

A week after the successful open house, Janice mailed the first 105 pages of *Run Me a River.* Feeling she should have the book two-thirds finished by then, she was distressed that there had been so many interruptions. At the time she sent the material to Ollie, she and Henry were struggling to recover from the flu.

Janice had completed about three-quarters of *Run Me a River* in mid-April when she received a call from her brother that the couple caring for their mother was not working out and that Lucy Holt wanted to come to her home. Janice's sister, Mary, and her husband would drive her to Kentucky. Upon their arrival, Janice was appalled at her mother's condition. Within a few days Lucy was homesick and wanted to return to Arkansas, but she was bedfast and in great pain, and Janice felt it best to have her admitted to the hospital. "This may be terminal," she told Ollie, "but she may pull another miracle out of the hat. For the time being, of course, I do nothing but trundle back and forth. We have decided if she comes out of this to place her in a good nursing home. She no longer knows us and she needs full nursing care. On the surface, it looks foolish to have brought her here. But she did get to do once more the thing she most loves to do—have a trip—and she did get to have one happy week here with us."

When the crisis passed, Lucy returned from the hospital to Spout Springs. Janice had Mary Lee Payne as her housekeeper and hired Mary Ann Gaskins, a practical nurse, to care for her mother during the daytime. She and Henry shared night duty, but Lucy received "a shot for sleeping," so the nights were not often interrupted. "I know you think I'm a 'patsy' for everybody in the family," Janice wrote Ollie, "Henry's as well as mine, and perhaps I am. But I wouldn't be me otherwise—and perhaps something of that has helped to create the very loyal and warm following. Maybe it gets, a little, into the books and makes people love the characters."

With help in the house, Janice returned to writing and on May 13 mailed Ollie the next hundred pages of the river novel, asking him to "watch very closely to see if this section holds up. Most of it has been written under pressure. I can't allow the book to let down. I will welcome your honest appraisal. It's too good a book to fool with—and I will willingly rewrite this entire section rather than have it let down from the start. I can't tell. I feel that it held up, but I just don't know." Janice also told Ollie her brother had come the day before and had taken her mother, by air ambulance, back to Fort Smith. She added, "We have arranged to enter her at Sparks Manor, horribly expensive, but the only place to take her. We plan to sell her home to meet her expenses as long as possible, if we can get a decent price for it. It is such a tremendous relief to know she is going to be well cared for."

Janice continued working on her novel and was delighted in June with the sale of *Voyage to Santa Fe* to a French publisher. She felt it had come at a good time "psychologically" and, while the money would be welcome, more important was the recognition. "For several years I've had to fight a feeling that I was standing still, getting nowhere," she wrote Ollie. "It's been difficult to keep working with any sense of worth when such books as *Johnny Osage* and *Savanna* got no farther than any other books. Perhaps the author is the poorest judge of his work, but it seemed to me the western books were very good." Prophetically, she added, "I wish someone would pick up the entire historical series, and perhaps it will be done some day."

The rough draft of *Run Me a River* was completed on July 5. Libby and the grandsons arrived on the twelfth for what would be the last summer visit they would all share together. As teenagers, their trips to Kentucky would be more sporadic. Janice did not get the manuscript retyped before their arrival and did not even attempt to work on it during their active, happy visit. She wrote Ollie on August 5 that Libby and the boys had left on the third and that in the quiet left behind she had been typing ever since, hoping to mail the manuscript on the sixth.

Lucy Holt was transferred August 5 from the nursing home in Charleston to the nearest hospital, located just a few miles north across the Arkansas River in Ozark. Her life had gone full circle. Catherine McGraw had given birth to her in Ozark almost eighty-two years earlier. Born October 6, 1881, Lucy slipped away in her sleep at 5:40 A.M. on August 7, 1963, in the Turner Hospital. The certificate of death cited congestive heart failure and hypertensive cardiovascular disease. The funeral was at Fentress Mortuary in Fort Smith with burial beside her husband in the Rose Lawn Cemetery. "Thirty-five years of teaching in the city made the funeral one of the largest I've ever seen, with all its attendant obligations on the family," Janice wrote Anne Barrett. "I felt precisely like a puppet on a string and only after returning home came out of the numb and catatonic state. Then such grief and dreadful sense of loss and such sense of guilt that I did not go oftener and be with her. Well—one lives through it. I am so grateful that there is always the next book."

Anne Barrett immediately returned a handwritten note: "Just to give you my love and tell you how sorry I am about your mother. You must be utterly spent. But I think that the demands and the confusion of such a funeral are in their way a mercy. As for the sense of guilt, I think every human being has that. Which of us has done as much as he wishes he had for any of the people he loved? And the relationship of a child to a parent is perhaps the hardest of all. I remember the guilt I felt when mother died and am sure my children will reproach themselves over my grave. Of course it is nonsense to feel this way. We do the best we can, within the limitations set by circumstances and our own natures. But somehow it is never enough, on our own estimation. . . . I'll write you about the book tomorrow. This is only an attempt to express the sympathy I feel."

Soon after returning from Arkansas, Janice telephoned Ollie to discuss her novel, after which he wrote, "I think *Run Me a River* is one of the finest things you've ever done," and he suggested only minor changes. Janice was elated that he liked the book and responded that she was thinking ahead to the next Green River story, which she hoped to begin by the first of October. Her previous plans had been to go to Fort Smith in the autumn to do her "share" for her mother but as "circumstances" had given her the time free, she was ready to "get on with it." She needed to complete her research but wanted to wait until the summer heat was over and she had preserved all Henry's good garden things, "but I don't know, when I'm seized with a book there's not much I can do about it but get to work!"

In mid-September Janice and Mary Lee Payne were cleaning the attic of the log house and found the courtship letters Henry had written to Janice during his military service. She had kept the material through the years with the knowledge that some day, when she had time, there was a good book in them. She wrote Ollie that she wanted to use the material for the next book and call it *G.I. Journal.* "It is more than the usual repetitious diary entry of the average soldier, for Henry was older and more mature and much more thoughtful and observing. I think it can be excitingly different and I think my faithful following will love it. Through *40 Acres* and *Plumb* they have come to know Henry very well and the *G.I. Journal of Henry Giles*, edited by Janice Holt Giles, will have meaning for them. And it will not delay the next novel, for I often have to spend the fall months completing research to begin writing around the end of the year." Ollie responded that he was reasonably sure Houghton Mifflin would be interested in the *G.I. Journal* just as they were in *A Little Better than Plumb.*

By November 21 Janice had completed one-third of the *Journal* and was in touch with half a dozen men of Company A. If she received something useful from them, as she had from Jeff Elliott, she planned to insert it with Henry's record. She explained to Ollie that she had excerpted freely from Henry's letters and slid them in his purported "Journal" at the right dates and places and saw no need to make any distinction. However, there is no journal included with Henry's letters and Janice's World War II research notes in her manuscript collection. Janice remarked to Ollie, "I remember your being a little uneasy about the personal element in this book. I have cut it as much as Henry will allow. He says I was not only a part of his war but I was a damned important part of it and to take me out except for occasional and casual mention would leave it as unrealistic as taking out the artillery fire, the bombings, the Battle of the Bulge and the Bailey bridges. He says this was true of all the boys, no matter what their antics, and that mail call was to be emphasized because to the last man it was the most important thing in the world to them. And the longer they were in Europe the more important it got, as the reality of home and any kind of life back there, slowly faded. They felt almost desperate about their letters. Furthermore, we both believe that since my readers have followed us through *40 Acres* and *Plumb* they will like the thread of love in this book, as it shines rather beautifully through."

By the first of December Ollie told Janice that he had read every word of the *G.I. Journal* "with considerable personal interest" but was a little doubtful whether Houghton Mifflin would find it publishable, "much as they like you and Henry. It reveals to me a side of Henry that I'd never suspected and while I daresay his reactions were typical of thousands of G.I.s he doesn't make his experiences so unusual or so distinctive to have very much meaning for the general audience of book readers. I'm sure I don't have to tell you that I could be quite wrong about this but I honestly think we ought to consult Houghton Mifflin or show them the partial manuscript at this point so that you don't spend too much time on what might prove to be an unrewarding task. I'm sorry not to exude more enthusiasm but that's the way I feel."

Janice was sorry Ollie was not enthusiastic about the war diary. "Diary is rather low-key, I admit. Henry was and still is low-key as you know. He was regular army, besides, and had four years in the army by 1944. Very little shocked him and he wasn't given to rages and angers and feelings of injustice. He chronicles the jobs, some of the talks, some of the dangers, many of his own feelings, and unlike you, I think most of our readers will like his war story. So, nothing is wasted by going ahead with it. In fact, I have to be doing something or go out of my mind from boredom! If H.M. don't like it in the end, it's been a good project for me, and nothing else can be forthcoming anyway."

Unlike the excitement of the previous Christmas when all the family gathered in Janice's mother's home, 1963 ended sadly a few short months after Lucy Holt's death. The absence of the warm, fun-loving matriarch, whose temperament could lash with fire one moment and peal in high-spirited laughter the next, was keenly felt. Lucy Elizabeth, the mother whose zest for life kindled Janice's own, was always eager to go, to do, to see, and carried an abiding aura of security with her. Strong-willed since childhood and armored with fortitude, she bravely tackled every task and refused to accept defeat. Wherever it was, Lucy Holt made her home a source of delight with rocklike security—in Indian Territory, a campsite tent, the back of a covered wagon, or her house in Fort Smith.

Janice may have felt a sense of relief to have the long ordeal of her mother's illness behind her, but the pain of physical parting was nonetheless anguishing. So alike in temperament, their personalities had often clashed during Janice's maturing years, but those feelings had long given way to mutual love and great respect. Following her mother's demise, with both parents of her deceased, Janice assumed a new role—the generation next to death. The indomitable Lucy had stood protectively between her children and their own mortality.

At age fifty-eight Janice no longer had a parent to enjoy the presence of or to pick up a telephone and call to share life's struggles and joys. Libby was miles away in Santa Fe with teenage sons and a dizzyingly active household. Just before Christmas Janice wrote her, "We went in town yesterday a while to do a little Christmas shopping, for Henry's folks mostly. Our shopping has dwindled so, we only give to Pansy and Russell among friends now, the rest get Christmas cards. Several years ago we quit giving in the family except to Lucy—now, no Lucy. So, just Miss Bessie, Robert and Mr. Frank, and the Hancocks. Sometimes we think of a gift for each other, or for the house, sometimes we don't. We seem, anymore, to need so little."

22
Lump in the Throat
1964

The New Year began with the good news that, in spite of John Beecroft's retirement and his successor's not taking it for the Dollar Book Club, prepublication sales for *Run Me a River* of 7,300 exceeded the advance in earnings. Houghton Mifflin supported the novel with the greatest promotional effort they had ever done for a work by Janice Holt Giles, including a full-page advertisement in the February issue of *The American News of Books.* Delighted with her publisher's actions, Janice was ecstatic with the "most distinguished jacket" she felt any of her books had ever had. She was "in love with the white background and the sketch of the *Rambler.*"

With publication day set for February 20, 1964, Janice's elation with the success of her new novel may have influenced the somewhat facetious response to an invitation by Albert Stewart of Morehead State College. On February 16, she wrote, "I know I promised to give consideration to serving in your Writers' Workshop this summer, but I think it would be best if I didn't. I think I would be a misfit there and would be shockingly disappointing to you and to the participants.

"The truth is I am simply a storyteller, a rather old-fashioned one. I don't know a thing about writing. I don't even know the vocabulary. Writing to me is a job, like any other job. I don't think of myself as an artist nor do I consider my work art. I happen to have a facility for telling a story pretty well, which it is to my good fortune people like to read. I have the ability to sit down at my typewriter with a general story in mind and keep sitting there until the story is told. For this I am extremely well paid and that's all it amounts to.

"I did one of these things once, very reluctantly, for the University of Kentucky. All 300 people in the sessions knew infinitely more about writing than I did. I was asked dozens of questions, not one of which I knew the answer to. Technique? I haven't the vaguest idea what my technique is, nor anybody's else's. Style? If I have a style I am not aware of it. How do I use mood? I don't. Or if I do, I don't know it. I was asked how I can use first person in one book and shift to third in the next. I don't know. I

was asked how, as a woman, I could write a tough man's book like *Johnny Osage* or my new novel *Run Me a River.* I don't know. My editor, Paul Brooks of Houghton Mifflin, said when he read this last manuscript that I was the only woman writing today who could write convincingly from a man's point of view. How do you do it? he asked. I don't know. You see how disappointing I would be? How little help?

"I don't know anything at all about writing. I just write. I am either a freak, or a natural born writer without knowing why. I've never been to a workshop in my life and I have only a high school education. I do not know any writers, have never discussed writing with anyone, never discuss work in process even with my husband.

"I don't believe you would really want someone like me in your group who, if asked why I write, would in all honesty have to say because it comes easily, it takes only three hours a day, and it earns me $15,000 a year! The rest of my time is free. How upsetting to your young people it would be to learn that I wrote my first book to make some extra money because my husband and I were having a hard time—and how, further, that first book was accepted by the first publisher I sent it to.

"I would be the worst applecart upsetter you ever had in your midst! So, please excuse me."

It was true the first book was written "to earn some extra money" as well as the earnings becoming a necessity for the books that followed, but the writing certainly demanded more than three hours a day and did not always come so easily. Ironically, on the second page of the letter to Albert Stewart, turned upside down, Janice had scrawled in pencil:

Farm—1963
Income—1962 crop - 1963 crop $ 210.18

In a lengthy discussion, Janice updated her editor with the progress of the *G.I. Journal.* She had finished all she could do with her part of the book and was waiting for the stories from as many of Henry's unit as would respond. Janice had written Col. Ken Hechler, author of *The Bridge at Remagen,* for permission to use quotes about the 291st from his book and explained her difficulty in locating the men. Hechler, then a congressman, asked Janice to send him a list of the men and he would cut through all the military red tape to help her find them.

"It is strangely moving when we reach them by telephone," Janice wrote Anne Barrett. "Neither the men nor Henry can make much sense for a little while. They get all choked up as Sgt. Giles trained most of them as rookies in Texas. Henry does his opening so Henryly! He barks an order at them. You can hear a gasp usually, then a silence, then Sgt. Giles? Really, Sgt. Giles? They sometimes cry and Henry cries. That Company loved each other like brothers, or perhaps better than brothers, and I can't help believing they specially loved Henry. Last night the telephone company found Paul Hinkel, Henry's closest friend for several years, I couldn't even stay in the room. I was crying just as hard as they were!"

Writing to Anne in mid-February about her health, Janice said the doctor had given her a clean bill. She had been "a good girl, with good results" and no longer had a limit on hours of work or writing. On the same date, she wrote Libby a lengthy letter and discussed "heredity influences in bio-chemistry and the nervous system." She mentioned that Dr. Todd Jeffries had done a "wonderful thing" for her. He had prescribed the tranquilizer, Librium. To Libby she wrote: "I have long known that the nerves in the entire digestive tract were connected and were all affected when any part was affected. My nervous problem began with colitis. Five years later began the lump in the throat and congestion in the esophagus generally, and more indigestion that I enjoyed. Well, this Librium has totally eased all of it. The colitis has disappeared, for the first time in eighteen years, the indigestion has stopped and the lump in the throat is easy. I wouldn't take it at first, as you know. Didn't have any faith in it, didn't think I needed it, but Todd scared me, so I took it as directed for one week, then eased it off to two capsules a day—one morning, one night. It doesn't make me feel logy or dull, it doesn't make me feel any special way, (except full of energy), no tensions, just wonderfully well. Tranquilizers, of course, are like taking aspirin for the toothache when you need to see a dentist. But since there are no dentists for nerves—by golly, this stuff I intend to keep on hand the rest of my life."

In March Janice asked Anne the projected publication date for the *G.I. Journal,* expressing her desire to get as many of the 291st men as possible to come to Spout Springs. She had contacted Henry's Battalion Commander, Col. David Pergrin, and he was very interested in the *G.I. Journal.* Colonel Pergrin told Janice he would do a story for the section on the Battle of the Bulge and also help her understand what had occurred. During his unit's involvement in the Bulge, Henry was in a Replacement Center in Liege with infected ears.

On April 5 a 291st buddy of Henry's, Bob Billington and his wife, Rosemary, arrived at Spout Springs from Harrisburg, Pennsylvania, for a three-day visit. Billington was the first of the 291st outfit Henry had seen since the unit's dispersement, and, to celebrate, he laid in a store of beer and bourbon. After their departure Janice wrote Joe Covington, "They refit the war—and I haven't laughed so hard in years. The mellower they got the wilder grew the tales. I drank coffee, only, so I could absorb it like a sponge! Unfortunately and alas, most of the stories were a little unprintable! I am now fully convinced the 291st, singlehandedly, won the war!"

In spite of Janice's seeming gaiety, she typed a six-page letter to Dr. Franklin Jelsma, a neurosurgeon in Louisville, toward the end of May in which she said she was writing instead of calling for an appointment "because in the present crisis of my nervous problem riding in a car is practically an impossibility for me. In order to reach you by car I would have to have heavy sedation and I cannot see how under those circumstances I could possibly be coherent with you."

Identifying herself as a novelist, she explained to Jelsma that for fourteen years she had what her local physician "kindly calls esophageal constriction" and remarked, "after fourteen years of it, believe me I know how one must fight the tendency toward hysteria." Feeling that he would want to know her family history, she related that she had an uncle and two aunts with nervous disorders. Her uncle was a World War II veteran and one of the aunts had been trained as a concert pianist.

Janice explained that her own history of nervous tension began when she was twenty-three and her first husband lost his job during the Depression and she was very much worried about the support of their young daughter who was beginning school. Three or four years of anxiety took their toll on her husband, who became an alcoholic. By 1937 he would not face or attempt to do anything about his problems, and she was carrying almost the total load of their living expenses. She decided divorce was the only answer and, during the proceedings, began having trouble with her throat. She experienced a compulsion to swallow and at the same time a fear of swallowing. When the divorce was final and she knew she could manage the support of herself and her daughter, she had "several years of joyous freedom from any form of nervous tension."

Janice wrote Jelsma of her move to Kentucky and position at the Presbyterian Seminary. She also described the bus trip meeting with Henry Giles, who had "enlisted in the regular army in 1937 as a way out of the deep Depression still existing with small farmers." She explained the difficulties surrounding Henry's adjustment to civilian life after eight years in the army and twenty-nine years of bachelorhood, living in a city, and returning to school, and her own adjustments to being a wife again and trying to help him, and told Dr. Jelsma that the nausea and diarrhea had recurred. A complete gastrointestinal examination revealed "the same old story, nervous tension."

Indicating her determination, Janice explained to Jelsma, "I coped with it never missing a day of work, and it eventually passed off as my husband grew more accustomed to his life and problems. In the meantime, having always wanted to write, I began my first novel, writing at night after a day's work in the office." With the acceptance of the novel, Janice was willing to do "what Henry had been longing to do, buy a small farm and move to Adair County and leave the city."

Eventually, leaving the security of a regular paycheck and assuming the insecurity of a writer's life and a nonprofit farmer's wife, the anxieties reappeared and erupted violently during a Christmas holiday trip to Fort Smith and Santa Fe in a new car that had put them in debt, her greatest fear. Even though she believed they needed the automobile so they could travel comfortably to see her family, Janice had to be hospitalized and heavily sedated in January 1951, having gone ten days without food because of the throat constriction.

During the hospitalization Janice had psychiatric interviews in an attempt to get at the base of her problems. She explained to Jelsma, "Dr. McCool kept me in the hospital two weeks, then he dismissed me, saying that I was unusually perceptive, highly intelligent, that I fully understood my problem and should now be able to handle it. I left the hospital able to eat but with the new knowledge that neither medicine nor psychiatry had the answer, for neither insulin nor the muscle relaxant had relaxed the throat much. For fourteen years the lump in my throat has been there. Not for one day has it been absent. I have years when it is called 'tolerable.' That is, I can lead what appears on the surface to be a normal life. I can travel, go among people, enjoy life, carry on and manage my home. I have written fourteen books with the lump in my throat."

Janice reported to Dr. Jelsma that, since that first bad experience there had been dozens of minor flare-ups that were "fairly easy to conquer" and two bad ones, the first being her hysterectomy in 1958, after which she had fought her way back to what was normal for her. "The throat is never entirely relaxed," she wrote. "What wakens me every morning is the beginning of the constriction and I go to sleep each night trying to relax it."

The second major occurrence involved her mother's recent death, beginning with the call from her brother in November about her coronary. She and Henry went immediately to her mother's side and remained for two and a half months. Janice worried about the expensive care her mother would need and felt pressured to return to the book she was writing. "She died quite suddenly in August of last year," Janice wrote. "Again we started for Fort Smith. On the second day of the trip my throat exploded again. I don't know how I got through the funeral and the days of going through her personal effects, helping make decisions, etc. I remember only that I felt numb and I was struggling to appear normal and to do my part."

Janice thought when she returned to Kentucky the constriction would ease slowly but it had not. She had been able to "stay on top of it," begin and finish the next book, go to town, and visit friends; but in February, on a trip to town, her throat "suddenly went wild again." After one of those experiences, Janice explained, "it literally takes hundreds of times before I can feel easy again in a car."

Janice appealed to Dr. Jelsma for his help. "If, as a neurologist, you know of anything that would be helpful, I should so much appreciate your advice. Hospitalization is no use. Its relief is only temporary. When you leave, you are right back where you were—the same fight on your hands. I know researchers in nervous problems have made great strides and are beginning to understand that there is a bio-chemical problem and that they are hopeful of finding a corrective for the imbalance. But if tranquilizers, sedatives, shock treatments are still the only answer, then I'll simply have to fight this out once more again on my own—with sheer will power. Certainly nothing discovered yet has been of the slightest use to me."

Janice ended her letter to Dr. Jelsma, "I have written you a 'novel' haven't I, and you deserve a nice fee for reading it. Physically, I am not in bad shape except for being too thin again. The blood pressure is a little high, but not dangerously so. There is some neuritis in the left hand and occasionally in the left leg. But my local doctor tells me this is simply a part of the overall problem. Thank you for listening and do please send me a bill exactly as if I had had an interview with you."

Janice mailed a copy of her letter to Dr. Jelsma to Nash Hancock so that he might "more fully understand" her problem and added a bit of self-reflection: "I don't know whether I need a new environment or a whole new way of life. It's difficult for me to decide when the whole history of my life has been hopping around like a flea. I use up an environment very quickly. I'm like a sponge. I get it all very shortly, soak it up, then feel restless and bored, and move on to greener pastures (which are never greener). I don't know whether I'm simply bored with writing now, or whether when I feel better I'd rather keep on.

"It has seemed to me that I must at some place and some time settle down and accept things the way they are. I have moved Henry and me around so often and nothing was any better than right here in the end. And at least Henry is happy here. Perhaps as good a reason as any for my marrying Henry was that I was growing very bored with the Seminary. But when two people work very hard to make a marriage go, and do make it go, they come to be very close and love and affection grow. So, whatever I do now, whatever I finally decide has got to include Henry and not only include him but suit him, too. I have no right to decide arbitrarily that I am going to do this, that or the other.

"When Henry and I moved to the country, it intrigued me for a while. But I used it up within a year or so. By that time I had got all I needed for a dozen books, the background, the vernacular, the customs and habits. Dr. McCool told me that the very worst problem I had was that I was 'too smart.' He said the average person is able to persuade himself that what he is doing is important or necessary or useful. He told me I was never able to fool myself, that I could not objectively observe people, affairs, etc. but that I had to appraise myself, too.

"When I began writing I had all the confidence in the world that I had the talent, the skill and ability to write good and important books. I didn't really care about making a lot of money. What I wanted was to write books that would live in American Literature. Just as you have your own private goals and ambitions and feel discouraged when you don't achieve them, that was mine. It was the highest challenge I had ever faced. But my own literary tastes are so high, however, that it didn't take very many books or very many years for me to realize that at best I was just a good craftsman. My publicity has never fooled me for one minute. I know that I am just one of those durable hacks who keep publishers in business. It's difficult, under those circumstances, not to feel like you're on an assembly line.

"But there's been nothing I'd rather do than write and I still can't think of anything else. And when I get into a book, I do still hope. There are two books I'm very proud of. I myself would take them off a library shelf to read—*Johnny Osage* and *Run Me a River*—and *G.I. Journal* is a good book.

"So perhaps this is all just part of this nervous crisis and when I get back on top of the throat trouble everything will be all right. If not, then I will at least be able to do some straight thinking about it which isn't influenced by illness. Thank you for trying to be helpful. Nobody can. I just have to work this out for myself."

Dr. Jelsma responded to Janice's letter by return mail. "You write quite well," he wrote. "I can understand why you are a successful novelist." Praising her personal understanding of her troubles, Jelsma recommended what Janice had perceived in writing to her son-in-law: "Your treatment must come from within, and you, I think, must solve your problems yourself. It is unlikely that anybody can solve your problems that you hold within better than you can. Certainly, chemicals and drugs will not do it. They may aid you to feel better at times, and thru feeling better, you may yourself be able to cope with your problem better. They will not be a source of cure.

"You must realize that everybody has many problems, many troubles and, in most instances, most people have more trouble than you have, and more troubles than you have had in the past. The good Lord has given you a brain and a mind to overcome your problems, or to deal with them openly and solve them. It is necessary for you to realize you could have many, many troubles worse than you do have. I am sure you know this. Also, it is well for you to continue to think of good things, nice things in life, such as you are doing, and the things you are doing to help other people, and that you must be grateful and thankful for your part and for the place in life you are holding. Therefore, be good to yourself, help yourself and overcome your trouble." Dr. Jelsma told Janice his was not a professional letter, just a reply to her long and personal one, and consequently he would not render a fee for reading it. He hoped that she would find something in what he said to be helpful.

Janice wrote Libby on Sunday, June 21, thanking her for a warm and loving letter and expressing how helpful it was to know that she understood her "whole problem." She told Libby that, since she had to "leave off the Librium," she had gone back to using "a little whiskey when things are very bad," explaining: "Henry, himself, asked me to. I'm much afraid of it—afraid of leaning too much on it—but he says, with some bitterness and much reason for it, that he'd far rather live with a mildly tiddly wife than one who is moody and grim and joyless. That when I have some relief at least I am fun to be with, can laugh, enjoy life a little. It hurts him to watch me force myself through these everlasting choking spells. He's been through so much of it with me. Except that I've had some good years between, I really don't know how he has put up with me." Admitting to Libby that Lucy's death had affected her greatly, she wrote, "We had our ups and downs, but she was always there and like you when you turn to me, I could turn to her. We had some good times in Fort Smith with her and Uncle Fred when I was working on the western books. I miss her badly, and miss knowing there is no home—501 in the hands of the Sullivans is simply not the home place."

She also wrote Libby about a second thing she felt had caused her recent bout with anxiety: "I think I have been frightened less by the sense of financial troubles than by the fact that I'm afraid I've written myself out. For the first time, I have no idea for a book, and for the first time really don't want to write any more. What I really want to do, for the first time in my life is just quit—let Henry take over. There will be enough royalties from the back log, *Run Me a River* and *G.I. Journal* I think to see us through until I'm sixty-two—then there'll be Social Security as a base. Henry *can* make us a meager living. It won't amount to much—but that's why I've clung to the land so hard. With a simpler house that costs less to operate, the tobacco base, a cow and chickens and the gardens, we can manage. I've always thought of it as very far in the future—our real old age. But I know if it's necessary he can do it."

Janice was not concerned about what the government would pay them for their house when their property was condemned. She felt they would receive enough to rebuild a very small, simple home. "We aren't in any hopeless condition at all, except that I'm just tired, feel dragged out, feel moody and depressed a lot. And like you I loathe housework. I don't even like to cook, as you seem to. And making beds, washing dishes, mopping and dusting couldn't interest me less. I think a lot of my discouragement is simply self-pity. I feel sorry for myself because this has happened again when I truly didn't ever think it would. Why I didn't realize that a big emotional crisis, such as Lucy's death and long illness, couldn't send me into another tizzy I don't know. But it could be much worse. Something could happen to you—and if that ever happens, I could not live. I can't imagine even wanting to live unless you were somewhere in the world, too. When I try to think of nice things, as Dr. Jelsma advised, I think of you and what you're doing and how wonderful you are."

Janice shared with Libby that her local physician, Dr. Todd Jeffries, had told her to get more exercise, to get out and walk instead of, as was her custom, sitting at the desk all morning and reading in the afternoons. "So—I make the round up to the pond and back (and couldn't care less)."

Libby responded to her mother's letter on June 23, 1964, from Puerto Vallarta, Mexico, where she was vacationing with her three sons. "I have never felt so helpless about your present condition," she wrote. "Surely, you don't have to sweat this out in the country. I keep thinking if you would come to Santa Fe for a couple of weeks or so." She encouraged her mother to get out and be around people more. She was happy her mother was walking and encouraged her to keep trying to ride in the car as much as she could stand it. "I've thought of you so much while we've been down here. This thing that troubles you is so unreachable, no medicines, no psychiatry. I wish there was power in prayer and that I could stop say three times a day and say a prayer to dissolve the lump. What a comfort religion is."

Libby admonished her mother for continuing to feel guilty about Lucy being in a nursing home. "She was so sick—and nurses did tell you that when things are that bad they aren't happy anywhere. You were all trying to do what was best. Dwell on the good things. How about Lucy's mortgaging her house and going on another trip when she felt like it. Wasn't she fabulous? I'm so glad you included the chapters in A *Little Better than Plumb* that you included on her." Libby filled the remainder of her lengthy letter with descriptions of the boys' activities and her enjoyment of their vacation.

Four days later Libby wrote another six-page letter telling her mother she had been walking by the sea and thinking more about her problems. "It would be a concern to feel written out. You've talked about it a little bit the last two times we were there. It's difficult for all things when you are tired or don't feel well. Most writers travel. They all got ideas from people, places—and for the Oklahoma books, you traveled. We could go to Europe if we had the time. That would give you a new lease on life. Maybe you'd feel like developing several short stories this summer. Your stories are beautifully written—each letter to us is a composition. There has got to be a way out of this and I know any way that would help, Henry would be all for it. He's been so patient, so good all these years with all of us. We're all a bunch of characters!"

On July 4, Libby wrote that it was so good to receive a letter that her mother was feeling better. "I had a very desperate and helpless feeling about you. I was just about to tell Nash when I returned home that I'd need to get to Kentucky and do something. Drive you to a hospital for good food and a change or bring you home and let you rest in St. Vincents. I had planned to tell my friends you weren't well and couldn't receive visitors and that would have helped. I know when you are ill that's the last thing you want to do. I felt perhaps that much might help you." Relating more stories of the boys' antics, Libby concluded, "I hope all is well with you and that you don't miss too many meals."

On July 9 Paul Brooks wrote Janice that he could not be happier about *The G.I. Journal of Sergeant Giles*. "My guess is that this book will be read for a long time." Brooks scratched through "Yours," before his signature and wrote "Love." Janice responded on the twelfth: "Thank you—thank you—thank you, for your warm and truly loving letter about the *Journal*. You know, as well as I do, that I have tinkered with this material and blended it with a novelist's sure hand. But it is all true, all facts. All I did was take the facts and the color and blend them, invent some conversations which certainly Henry didn't put down but when he read it he said it was sure and right—it was the way they talked. I left out the obscenity and vulgarity, because Henry doesn't talk that way and I can't believe he did even then. He uses a lot of hells and damns but he doesn't ever descend to the lower levels of obscenity, and he says he never did."

Janice closed her letter to Brooks thanking him for crossing out his usual signature and making it "love" and commented, "I need all the love anyone can give me these days. Anne Barrett can tell you something of what I have been going through since my mother's death."

23
Reunion
1965

As far as her physical strength was concerned, Janice had bounced back into all her old energy and interest by mid-September 1964, but the throat constriction was still with her. "Some days it is fairly relaxed," she wrote Libby, "some days not so comfortable. I am still taking regularly the vitamin B complex and hormone tablets, but have not taken any of the bromide since you left. And of course no sleeping capsules since the second night I was home from the hospital. Since I only sleep about six hours a night, I stay up and either read or watch television until eleven or twelve."

The letter to Libby also provides insight to rumors that circulated in the local region that Janice was an alcoholic. "As far as the other complication is concerned there is yet no problem. Todd never mentions it (probably can't because of his office secretary and nurse) and when I talk to him, seems to be leaving it entirely to my will power and so far it has sufficed. By the way, did you read the Speaking Out column in last week's *Post*? It really threw the book at AA and in my opinion offered new hope to people with that particular problem. I agree with the doctor who wrote it, that one's doctor or psychiatrist offers the best help. I have never understood how AA *could* be helpful, at least to thinking people, with its dreadful reliance on God and its humiliating public confessional, etc. Just a lot of piousity and falseness. I was extremely fortunate, I think, to have caught this while it was relatively new. Of course we have both been 'Happy Hour-holics' for five or six years and it's very easy under pressure to slip from that into more need and use. Henry, of his own wish and accord and not because of me, is now limiting his evening drinks to two. He had gradually slipped into the need of three and sometimes four. Whatever he does, I have no difficulty sticking to a glass of orange juice or Seven-up, or a cup of Sanka."

On October 1 Anne Barrett wrote asking Janice if she wanted to compile an index for *The G.I. Journal of Sergeant Giles* or have Houghton Mifflin arrange to have it done for about $150. Janice responded that she could see the value of an index and would do it herself as she had "done many a one" for Dr. Sherrill's textbooks when she worked at the seminary.

Anne Ford, in charge of publicity, told Janice that Houghton Mifflin was interested in any ideas for promotion she might have for the book. Janice responded that they had heard from the battalion commander of Company A and nearly all of the key men of the unit, most of whom had contributed their stories, particularly about the Battle of the Bulge, and she wanted them to have publicity in their local newspapers. Janice enclosed a list of their names and suggested a reunion of the men themselves to be held prior to publication at Spout Springs. Anne Ford was most pleased with Janice's ideas and announced that March 23, 1965, would be the publication date. She instructed Janice that Houghton Mifflin would pay for "refreshments" and any additional expenses to the Gileses in hosting the party in their home, as well as supplying twenty-five books so each of the men could receive a gratis copy. Janice felt their offer to pick up the tab for refreshments was "very generous" and remarked, "If their capacity is anywhere near what it was during the war it's likely to be right sizeable."

By Thanksgiving, Janice was feeling much better, her old spunk and spirits returning. Most important, her fear of "writing herself out" had dissolved as a new novel was brewing. She wrote Libby: "I have found the thread that leads me through the maze of the fur trade and the western expansion for a new book! In all my background reading something kept nagging at me and I knew it was connected somehow with Captain Bonneville who got a two-year leave from his Army duties and went west for awhile. Then the other day I found it in DeVoto's *Across the Wide Missouri.*

"How beautifully it ties in with my central character, who is Savanna's brother, Manifee Fowler. He wouldn't have known Bonneville, but Savanna did. I can move Fowler into Bonneville's party, explore both California and the Columbia regions, interpret the western movement much more lucidly than through the eyes of one character."

Janice's bright mind, infused with research and sparked with creative talent, is most apparent in her excitement expressed in the letter to Libby: "The lovely part is that once again I have found that true history is stranger than fiction and can hang the book on facts, as I have been able to do with every one of the historical novels. Oh, there's real gold in those historical events! Endless, endless reading and searching through until you have absorbed all the facts, made the real people contemporaries of yourself, soaked yourself in the time and the vernacular until you are home with it and about that time, when you're back in 1832, you're jolted back inside yourself because it's time to get a meal, or someone comes, or the telephone rings and in a kind of foggy haze you come down to earth on Spout

Springs Branch again! Writing is frustrating enough when you deal with a contemporary period, but when you go back in time and spirit it's doubly frustrating for you have to live on two levels—the one you live in the book (and it's as real as your own environment, perhaps realer) and your current life. To get from one to the other takes time every day. I sometimes feel like a ghost."

In addition to the emotional stress she had endured since her mother's death, Janice, at age fifty-nine, was facing the extraction of all her teeth. She hoped to have the new lower plate before Christmas but did not plan to get the upper teeth extracted until after the holidays. Henry had found Dr. James Holloday very thorough with his work, so it was decided that he would do Janice's also. Henry's "fit well," she wrote Libby, "although after ten years of teeth which didn't fit too well he's gotten into the habit of going without them too much, even these he takes out the minute we get through in town and head for home, or the minute he finishes eating at home. I don't mind, he looks like Winston Churchill without them, but he's always being caught by strangers. I just hope I end up with something I can stand in my mouth!"

On the last day of November, Janice asked Ollie if he could obtain any royalties that were due in mid-December. "Everything from insurance to taxes seems to come due in November, and December 15 is a little late to see me through Christmas. By the way, Libby and her family will be with us. This will be the first time the grandsons have spent Christmas at Spout Springs and I do want it memorable."

Soon after the holidays, the ridge was buried under a six-inch blanket of snow, and temperatures dipped to twelve below. Janice wrote Libby on Sunday, January 31, 1965, that she had two upper molars extracted Thursday and spent most of Saturday watching Winston Churchill's funeral on television. Fascinated by the pomp and splendor, she declared Churchill "a really great man with a tremendous zest for life" and was glad she had "lived through the war years with him at the helm." Concluding her letter, Janice remarked, "My feet are freezing in this corner. The house is warm but our floors are cold with this kind of heat. Henry is here with the Sunday paper so I'll sit by the hearth for a while."

Janice received the first copy of *G.I. Journal* on February 25 and wrote Anne Barrett, "It is a beautiful book, fully living up to all we hoped for it in quality. Houghton Mifflin have never let me down in the production of a book, but of course you know this book was very, very special to me. I'm so glad it was decided to use the 'champagne happy' picture of Henry on the back cover. It is my favorite picture of him and it has been on my desk since 1944 when it came." Janice was also extremely pleased and deeply moved when she and Henry discovered the sergeant's chevron embossed on the front binding.

Work on the new novel was soon put on hold to make final preparations for the publication party in Spout Springs for the *G.I. Journal*. Libby was among the first to arrive on March 18. Out of 175 men of the 291st Combat Engineers, twelve had contributed to the book and were invited to the celebration. Only nine could attend, five of whom would bring their wives. Except for a visit by Bob Billington, Henry had not seen any of his comrades since they parted company in Europe in 1945. He and John Pink were so emotional after their initial greeting, they pulled up two chairs, faced each other, and unashamedly let the tears flow. There was much joy and whooping as each car drove up, with Colonel Pergrin the last to appear.

Around 4:30 P.M. Henry convoyed the men eighteen miles to a motel in Columbia to freshen up before dinner. He had alerted the city police in the small town, so when they saw his lead car turn onto the square, they stopped all traffic and paraded them twice around, then gave them a motorcycle escort to the motel.

The group reconvened at Spout Springs for cocktails and decided to form an honor guard for Colonel Pergrin. When he walked in and saw the men at strict attention, their company commander at their head, he saluted. Captain Gamble returned his salute. With great emotion, Colonel Pergrin marched down the line, inspecting his troops. After a late dinner, the old soldiers departed at 4:00 A.M. for a slow, slick ride into town through a three-inch snowfall.

Saturday was a day of comfortable freedom. The men hiked the hills, visiting the spring, the pond, the old schoolhouse, and the crossroads store. In the evening Henry brought out his guitar and began a songfest much like the ones they had enjoyed when bivouacked "in some dirty little German town with their looted mandolins and guitars." The favorite song was the official engineers song, "I'm a ramblin' wreck from Georgia Tech, a hell of an engineer." Janice had asked Colonel Pergrin to present the books on Saturday evening, with personal words to each man.

When the dust and excitement of the men's departure settled, Janice wrote Anne Barrett on March 28, "My pride suffers at having to tell you that as far as ready cash goes after the party, I am about flat broke." She was extremely pleased when, within days, she received a check for six hundred dollars. "You and Henry never come to Boston or New York," Anne wrote, "so we could not give you a party here. We are getting a lot of publicity out of your party, not only locally but in the cities where the men from the 291st live. It was really a publicity party for the book, as well as a celebration for a very special group and we are delighted that it went off so beautifully."

By mid-April Janice had written thirty pages of *The Great Adventure*, and aimed for three good pages a day. Near the end of May, she wrote Ollie that she would soon have the first several chapters of the new book ready for him to see and added, "I've been happily transplanted to the mountains with Joseph Manifee Fowler (Savanna's brother) hunting beaver the last few months." She wrote Libby in the same tone, "I do feel wonderful, am happy, and life is full and interesting, work is going well. I sent the first chapters of *The Great Adventure* off Thursday. Copies went to both Ollie and Anne Barrett. Naturally, I'm eager to hear what they think of it, but deep down inside I *know* its good—every word tight and intense, saying precisely what I mean. This book has been simmering, as far as absorption of land and climate and impressions is concerned for fifteen years—and how nice that I have seen New Mexico in every season, felt it and looked at it and like a sponge soaked it up. And the handwriting is on the wall—the western setting is just plain more popular. When the last royalties came, *Johnny Osage* was still outselling everything (except *G.I. Journal*, of course) even *Run Me a River*. So a man in the west is what people like best."

Paul Brooks responded that he was "enormously excited and impressed" with the work Janice had done on *The Great Adventure*. "I can't think of anyone since Benny DeVoto who could treat this subject with such gusto and understanding and feeling for the country and the people. I have an uneasy feeling that I am repeating myself when I say that you improve with every book, but I feel obliged to say it again. I'm writing Reynolds about a contract."

Ollie told Janice that the time had come to get a substantially larger advance from Houghton Mifflin, which he thought was entirely possible based on Paul Brooks's enthusiasm for the new book; he was prepared to ask for five thousand dollars. Janice told Ollie to do what he thought best about the advance, declaring, "I don't know a thing about such things and you're the boss."

By the end of July Janice was working at her desk until noon on *The Great Adventure* but admitted she was having some frustrating weeks. "More than anything I want to go into hibernation with this book. It's ready and I'm ready and it's of prime importance. But people keep coming and going. I write a dozen pages over a couple or three days. Then I must stop, get the house ready for guests, plan meals—I do it in a sort of blind rage at being interrupted, which isn't good. Everybody else is on vacation, of course, I tell myself to relax—let these weeks till September go, just count them lost and skip it. But that's impossible for me, with this book burning inside. So I dash to the typewriter, get something formed in my mind on paper so I won't lose it, then go back to meals and dishes and vacuuming. Well, it will end. Everybody will soon be settled back in jobs and school and the tourist season will be over, and I can get in four or five months of uninterrupted work."

Janice returned the signed contract for *The Great Adventure* to Ollie August 16, 1965, and by September 7, there finally materialized a good, long stretch of uninterrupted time. She had revised the first section by the beginning of October and had almost completed the second section. She felt confident she could complete the novel by January 1. "My trappers have moved into the mountains now, but for several weeks I was in Taos and Santa Fe," she wrote. And of course for months before, I was absorbing the country again through reading. So much, so very much reading and soaking up material, to show so little in a book! Months of reading, so a dozen pages can be right. But that's the only way I can do it and I think it's responsible for the comments of so many readers, I was right there—I could see the country—I was simply living every minute of it, etc. You've got to get a country so deep in your bones that all its history, its weather changes with sky and mountains and rivers and trees, etc. what's made its people, it's all got to be part of you before you ought even to write one word about it."

Inviting Joe Covington to join them along with her brother and his wife for Christmas, Janice remarked, "I am about worn out traipsing up and down these Rocky Mountains hunting beaver! Also my conversation is suffering. Between 'Wagh!' which expressed everything with mountain men, and 'Ugh!' which said it for the Arapahoes, I am beginning to feel uninspired. Henry says I hit an all-time low when I greeted him with 'Wugh!' the other morning. Do come and civilize me again."

24
Home to Come Home To
1965-1967

John and Evelyn Holt were the center of the 1965 Christmas celebration at Spout Springs. Soon after they departed for Arkansas on December 30, rain began. By New Year's Eve five inches had fallen, washing out the Green River earth dam. Repeatedly the old-timers had told the Corps of Engineers the earth fill was not deep enough or high enough and would not hold the unpredictable waters of the Green. Construction of the fill was completed the week before Christmas and the first big rain of the new year washed it out. Like most locals in their resentment of the dam, Janice and Henry chuckled over the washout and vowed not to turn the first shovel of dirt around their property until the dam was secure and the lake impounded. "The old Green is a wild river," Janice stated, "with hundreds of steep tributary streams just as wild. It may look like a little creek, but it can rage like the Colorado."

While Janice was well into writing about fur trappers and Arapahos in *The Great Adventure,* Henry moved his typewriter into the little tin toolshed to work on his own project. He returned there day after day and eventually appeared with a 204-page manuscript titled *Rode Hard and Put Up Wet: Autobiography of an Appalachian,* which he submitted to Houghton Mifflin. In thirty-two chapters he related stories from his childhood through adulthood in dry wit and humorous anecdotes, including the meeting of Janice Moore.

Houghton Mifflin did not accept *Rode Hard and Put Up Wet,* about which Janice commented to Anne Barrett: "I am glad you did not take Henry's recent manuscript in its present form. I was not asked for advice on it, and did not offer any. It is sometimes best to let things run their course, but it would have been a dreadful waste of some excellent material which could be developed in a somewhat different form. Few Appalachians (and Henry is one) are articulate enough to speak for themselves. With a little help, Henry is. No one, reared in the folk ways of this particular subculture, growing up in it, understanding it, as he does, has spoken—not in its defense particularly, but from the 'inside.'

"I am eager for him to do this and, having now learned that his particular approach of 'folk humor' is not very well understood outside of Appalachia, he is eager himself to do something a little different with the material. There are so many things, so many ways of looking at things that no one but an 'insider' knows. There will never be a better time for his own material to have relevance than now, with the whole Appalachian problem so much the focus of national attention.

"We have been much amused, and this is something which probably only we in the area can understand, at the disgruntlement of some of our less hilly and more affluent county neighbors who are not included in the Appalachian program! You would be amazed at the strings the county courthouse politicians have tried to pull. They'll gladly take the poverty taint to get the federal funds!"

During his 1959 presidential campaign, John F. Kennedy's astute observation of the deprivation and degradation that the poor had to endure filled him with great concern. President Kennedy and Lyndon B. Johnson made poverty their priority in the sixties and championed new ideas for reform designed to help the depressed states of the Appalachian range. The Area Redevelopment Administration was organized in 1961, with $300 million appropriated to those states, which included Kentucky. Many of Kennedy's plans served as the basis for Johnson's "War on Poverty," established in 1964 to provide assistance to eastern Kentuckians and other residents of Appalachia.

Numerous articles appeared in a wide range of publications addressing the plight and perils of poverty-stricken Appalachia. Janice, very much aware of the great number of sociological studies, submitted an article dealing with their religious conçepts to Ollie for placement. Explaining her intent and recognizing Ollie's sometimes seeming lack of interest in her short stories, Janice wrote, "I wish you could be sincerely aggressive in pushing this article. I wish you could feel it important. It is new. No one else has ever probed this area. And I know what I'm talking about."

Less than two weeks from his visit, Janice received word on January 9, 1966, that her brother had suffered a mild coronary attack and had been admitted to Sparks Memorial Hospital in Fort Smith. Doctors assured the family that his condition was stable, but they were greatly concerned because it was his second attack in five years. Janice feared the trip to Kentucky during the holidays had been too much for him. She and Henry left immediately for Fort Smith to be with John and also to spend some time with her sister Mary, who had purchased their mother's old home.

Back home in early spring, Janice was contacted by Gerald Piercey, a freshman in an advanced English course at Georgetown College, Georgetown, Kentucky, who was assigned to visit and write a paper about an author's life and work. Piercey, who had family members in the Columbia area, had read most of Janice's books. He telephoned her about his assignment, and she cordially invited him to visit the log house March 19, 1966.

Janice equipped herself with a pack of Salem cigarettes and a cup of coffee before the interview began. The young student was very impressed that she spent so much time with him and treated him like a newspaper reporter rather than a college freshman. Piercey said she seemed like just "plain folks" and was an excellent communicator. "She helped me ask her questions, and suggested things I could put in the report, so in some ways she was also a good teacher." Piercey took his camera, but Janice asked him not to photograph her as she was having all her teeth extracted and dentures made, but she gave him a photograph of herself and a copy of an autobiographical sketch. She also allowed him to take interior as well as exterior photographs of her home.

Janice spoke briefly about each of her books, describing the nonfiction books as "breathers" and explaining that, when she tired of the historical series, she wrote nonfiction. She told him she was nearing completion of *The Great Adventure,* scheduled to be released in September.

By the first of April 1966, Janice was amazed to learn that, of her books, *The Believers* topped all others in sales figures with an impressive total of 504,759; *Johnny Osage* was next with 463,012 and *A Little Better than Plumb* sold the fewest. The grand total of books sold, including book clubs and reprints, was 3,964,363. "Henry has teased me unmercifully," Janice wrote Libby. "*The Believers* is the sexiest book I ever wrote (in a nice sort of way you never get far away from sex in it) and *Johnny Osage* and *The Great Adventure* are both about lusty he-men with Indian squaws. You still gotta get a guy in bed with a gal for a book to sell. Or keep him out, as I did in *The Believers* and emphasize the 'starvation.'

"It sounds as if I should be rolling in wealth, but it doesn't work that way because 90% of that total is book club circulation, on which royalties are considerably lower, and of which Houghton Mifflin take 50%. But according to other statistics, I have been among the few lucky ones able to even earn a living writing. Generally, a writer must make his living teaching or lecturing, and write on the side. It never once occurred to me I couldn't make a living writing, and it didn't surprise me when I did. How really naive I was! The biggest financial loss to me, and through me to Houghton Mifflin was when Mr. Beecroft retired as editor of the Doubleday bookclub dynasty. That has cost me at least $5,000 a year."

Ollie asked Janice in mid-February to send him a copy of *40 Acres and No Mule* as Houghton Mifflin was interested in reissuing it. She later thanked him for bringing her up to date on the status of her article on Appalachia and instructed him, "When it comes back from *Harper's* I think it would be as well to withdraw it. I have adapted it for use as a Foreword in the new edition of *40 Acres* and perhaps that is, after all, the best place for it."

In addition to the reissue of *40 Acres and No Mule,* Janice learned that Houghton Mifflin had made arrangements with Paperback Library to reprint the nine titles of the Frontier Series, including *The Great Adventure.* She would receive an advance of fifteen hundred dollars per title against a royalty of 6 percent on the first 150,000 and 8 percent thereafter. Paperback Library would begin with *The Kentuckians* in February 1967 and release one title a month through September. Janice wrote Ollie, "The money is welcome of course, but even more important to me is having the full series available."

On August 9, 1966, Nash Hancock's father, Bartlett N. Hancock, passed away in Finchville, Kentucky. Shortly after the funeral, Janice wrote Libby an insightful letter concerning her continued dealing with her own mother's death: "I wish there was something comforting to say to Nash just now, but I know from my own experience that there isn't. Death comes for a parent, usually, at a time in our own lives when we are at low ebb, facing our own older age, feeling, perhaps, already depressed, already failed—and the loss simply sinks us further into depression. But it does not last—I can tell Nash that much, at least. However futile the day's round seems to be, it has to be made, and the very habit of making it, of hanging on, lifts finally into something hopeful again. But there is that time, long or short, of asking one's self what it's all about, what's the purpose, what's the use. And for me there was the gray, bleak facing of the fact that I could not achieve what I had most dreamed of achieving, because I simply was not as good as I had hoped I could be. Being second best is hard—having to accept the fact that that's all you are, that's all you're capable of being is most depressing. Being totally honest with one's self is very painful. But I have come out on the other side, rather gay and unworried about it. I think I can grow old gracefully now. And if I have failed to achieve what I most wanted to achieve, well, I have still done some worthwhile things. I think it's well to have the dream and struggle toward it—but perhaps it's merciful that we don't realize the common human fate of failure."

Janice Holt Giles had not failed. She may not have achieved the literary recognition of Cather, Hemingway, Steinbeck, or Fitzgerald, but her publishing success was commendable. The recent news that Paperback

Library would reissue ten of her books was an impressive accomplishment in addition to numerous other forms of recognition continually acknowledging her work.

The Five Civilized Tribes Indian Museum, which opened in Muskogee, Oklahoma, in 1966, housed library facilities with a section honoring Janice Holt Giles. She was entitled to the honor not because she was reared in Oklahoma or portrayed the settlement in her books but because she was one-thirty-second Cherokee. Only people with blood of one of the five civilized tribes were eligible to be represented in the museum. Searching for personal mementos to donate to the museum, Janice found two books that had been hers as a child. *The Sunbonnet Babes* and *Black Beauty* had been Christmas gifts from her father. As *The Sunbonnet Babes* was her very first book, she sent the museum her copy of *Black Beauty*, which she had received in 1916.

Several months after Nash's father's death, he and Libby briefly considered returning to Kentucky to live on the Hancock family's farm in Finchville. Concerning that decision, Janice wrote her daughter: "Of course, selfishly I'd love to see you come back to Kentucky. You'd be just a whoop and a holler from Spout Springs. Twenty-two years without the joy of your presence has been a deep deprivation for me. Nothing has made up for it and it can never be recovered. But a parent can't hang onto a child and say this for me, I've loved you open-handedly." In comparing the "provinciality of Shelby County, practically a suburb of Louisville," versus Libby's active social life in Santa Fe, Janice remarked: "Any thinking person must make himself an interior life. Otherwise, all you do is serve time to the end of your days—and how you do it isn't terribly important. You can make a million dollars and you can write it off. You can cook a hundred thousand dinners and wash ten million dishes. It amounts to the same in the end. Do you know what is really important? The memories your children, your family, your friends have of you—your humor, your joy, your loyalty, your goodness—the life you brought to life. What you did, in the end fades out. But what you were is immortal."

At the end of summer, Janice looked forward to a trip to Arkansas and Santa Fe. "We are going to be delayed a little in leaving," she wrote Libby, "but it's only a delay. If it 'harelips Rachel' we'll get there!" While in Arkansas, Janice wanted to "wander around Kinta as nearly alone as possible, to soak up the look of the prairie, talk quietly with some of the older people there and go very deeply into its past and what formed it" in preparation for the book she planned to write about her early childhood years.

When Janice's first copy of *The Great Adventure* arrived, she wrote to Libby, "I am so happy with the book. Houghton Mifflin has made it so beautiful. The jacket is exquisitely done, the binding is excellent—the paper is good—the type clean and clear and uncrowded. Somebody up there likes me. Any author looking at it would envy me, it's so handsome. But a durable old workhorse like me is something all publishers appreciate. Houghton Mifflin are grateful for the stream of books which have made some money for both of us."

Ollie informed Janice that he was trying to interest the Paperback Library people in buying the Piney Ridge books and asked her to send a copy of *The Enduring Hills*. "Apparently he had no copy," Janice remarked. "They're scarcer than hen's teeth." She mailed him a copy and commented, "If they decide to buy the trilogy, I wish to heaven we could drop that asinine title, *Tara's Healing*. I think my title was *Scarlet Ribbon*. You remember it was Mr. Beecroft who dreamed up the final title."

In late October the Corps of Engineers appraisers were working with the Gileses regarding their property. Janice had great hopes that they would be finished by Christmas because she and Henry still wanted to make a trip west.

Almost every Sunday, without fail, Janice sat down at her typewriter and wrote Libby a loving, lengthy letter filled with news of happenings at Spout Springs. Libby, in turn, wrote a weekly letter to her mother, adding a little almost every day, like a diary. "Nash and I have always enjoyed your letters," Libby told her mother. "Through these years we have felt privileged to have a mother, so intelligent, always questing with a deep sense of humor. The letters' influence has been felt by us thru the years and I frankly think you've kept us on top many times—renewed our interest when we would have bogged down in the family-business rut—quite a contribution, Toots! Dorothy has chastised me for not preserving each and every one for a compilation—and I am a thoughtless, careless creature."

On November 9, 1966, the *Adair County News* announced the release of *The Great Adventure*, Janice's ninth book in her projected series of ten dealing with the American Frontier, and reported that Paperback Library would reprint the entire set. The article also revealed that *Hannah Fowler* was published in Sweden in 1958, that three Giles titles were bought by a publisher in France in 1965, and that Houghton Mifflin would reissue *40 Acres and No Mule* in February 1967.

Janice and Henry were too involved with "the government people" concerning their property to leave for Santa Fe for Christmas. Janice related that one of the real estate negotiators who had worked on every one of the Green River dams said he had never run into such a bunch of hard nuts to crack. "These people in this area are really tough. That's us Appalachians! They hadn't run into anyone like us until they hit Adair County. An Appalachian is courteous and polite, but he will litigate at the drop of a hat! What a *book* can come out of all this!"

By the first of December Janice was happy to write Libby that her teeth were "simply perfect." They fit so nicely she did not even think about them and had no discomfort. "Dr. Holloday just shakes his head. He says he has never had a patient do as well. *Now,* he tells me, that privately he didn't believe for a minute I could wear them. Said he fully expected me to show up the next day with them in my hand." From the Kentucky Military Institute, eighteen-year-old Bart wrote on December 6, "Mother Janice, I'm so glad you like your teeth. I can't wait to see you with them."

Ending a mid-December letter to Libby, Janice remarked, "It's spitting snow and turning very cold. I have a pot roast cooking. Henry has gone to take the tobacco to market (Greensburg) and will be home soon starved. Three loaves of bread are ready to go in the oven and the fire in the fireplace needs a log or two. We have the nicest home to come *home* to!"

25
Up the Holler
1967-1968

At the beginning of 1967, "home" to the habitants of Knifley, Kentucky, was rapidly undergoing change. Families were being uprooted as farms in the rich bottomland of the Green River were abandoned to empty the lake site and make way for the $30.4 million Upper Green River Dam. Over eleven hundred families were vacating the low hills and shallow hollows of northern Adair County. Some families were leaving the area; others were just transplanting their houses to higher ground, leaving behind foundation stones and outbuildings. The post office and businesses that made up the small town at the intersection of Star Routes 76 and 551 lay in rubble. Old Knifley was a ghost town; New Knifley was relocated about two miles "up the road" where a new post office, church, and gas station had been built.

On March 3 Janice wrote Ollie that they were "on the verge of settling" with the government but that the payment for the property might take some time. In view of that, she explained, "Henry is anxious to get as much done on the new home as possible, and as early as possible, so can you please arrange to draw $1,000 against royalties right now? This would give him a little working fund for immediate needs."

A month later the Gileses were "in the middle of a free-for-all" with the government over the house and eight and one-half acres. The offer was shockingly low, seven thousand dollars less than they had in the house, and Janice and Henry were prepared to litigate. On Friday, April 26, 1967, however, they signed the agreement with the Department of the Army, for "barely what it cost us to build it." They got to keep the house, and it could be moved. They only had to sell two and one-half acres of land, so they planned to "shift the house about 300 yards up the holler" and had eight months, until December 31, to do it.

On April 28 Janice mailed Ollie a revised copy of *The Happy Pappy,* later titled *Shady Grove.* The book originated in the short story, "Tetch 'n Take," written twelve years earlier for *Kentucky Writing* and later developed into a novelette and submitted to Houghton Mifflin as *The Figuring Man*. (At that time Paul Brooks had felt the story inappropriate, and

Janice had withdrawn it.) With national focus on Appalachia in the 1960s, she felt social conditions were ripe for the book, so she revised the manuscript, brought it up to date by addressing the federal relief programs, and created a central character named Sudley Fowler.

Sud Fowler was "a good neighbor, a good family man and a good Christian, according to his lights," whose escapades in the hills of Kentucky drove visiting do-gooders to madness. His story is told through the eyes of a strong woman character, his "door neighbor cousin and mainstay in life," Dorcas Fowler. Janice allowed "Darkus," in broad Appalachian vernacular, to "proudly, aggressively, and angrily" refute every argument the news media had advanced against Appalachians generally. She made moonshining a most natural profession to follow, she made the orthodox missionaries in the region look like the insensitive people they usually were, she made the Appalachians' pride in outwitting the "fools" in Washington look precisely as it was and is to this day—political patronage that one has honorably, to their mind, earned. She portrayed Sudley's pride in getting thirty-eight members of his big Fowler clan on the welfare "draw" as a natural pride.

In a succession of humorous stories, Janice revealed through Darkus many of her own feelings about her husband's native region, just as she had in the previous characters of Frony and Miss Willie. "I can swear, if necessary, and as Frony would say 'on a stack of Bibles,' that not only did every incident in the book have its basis in truth, they happened mostly within the Giles clan," Janice said. "I myself was personally involved in some of them, and there is only the slightest exaggeration of any of them. Furthermore, I left out even wilder incidents, knowing they would be totally unbelievable." Janice's handling of the vernacular in *Shady Grove* is impeccable. Every word, every nuance, every handed-down phrase she had heard in twenty-two years of absorbing ridge life was skillfully and masterfully executed.

Anne Barrett inquired about the risk of libel in the book's characters, to which Janice replied, "There is only one person in the book drawn almost entirely from real life. Some of the incidents happened, more or less, but are fictionalized out of context. The greatest risk, as I see it, might be the 'preacher.' Any one of half a dozen preachers connected with several missions in the very general area of southern Appalachia might see themselves in the character." Janice said she raced through the book and had a world of fun with it. "Many of the stories I've heard through the years (and Miss Piney's way of telling them) are going into it and of course Henry drops Appalachianisms every day of his life." She was delighted Anne had so perfectly sensed the intention of the book and remarked, "It has been a while since readers have had a social and cultural document set in the framework of humor."

In mid-May Janice and Henry signed an agreement with Bob Daulton, of Daulton and Son moving company, Nancy, Kentucky, to move their log house. In light of the decisions and the work ahead related to their house, Janice wrote Libby an interesting commentary the day after Mother's Day 1967: "Oh, a pair of barn swallows have built a nest on one of the rafters of the pond porch. They came almost to the dividing of the ways over it. *He* wanted to build on one side of the rafter, *she* wanted to build on the other. And each began a nest of his own. You could almost hear him saying, '*This* is the only sensible place to build a nest and *I'm* going to build it here!' And her reply, 'You can build your nest anywhere you please, but *I'm* going to build mine right here!" You know what? She won. He quit and began helping her. It works, even with the birds and bees."

Janice ended her letter to Libby commenting on grandson Scott's long solitary walks to think and occasionally going off to do "dirty, grubbing work" to give himself a chance to be quiet inside: "I *know* how that feels, it's so necessary for me. There is a goodness about being very close to natural things, a sort of restoring of the soul. I am finishing this letter at 5:00 A.M. People came yesterday and I was interrupted. At 5:00 A.M. there's nobody in the world but you and either it's nothing, or it's a time of exulting joy at being alive in a world of beauty. Enjoy—enjoy! Life has got to provide joy, or it's nothing but drabness.

"Fog is lifting from the valley—the birds are noisy—the ducks are beginning to 'enjoy' and the new pup is tugging at my houseshoes and Henry is somewhere outside making sure the sun comes up. 'He leadeth me beside the still waters and restoreth my soul.' It's time to get breakfast. Much, much love, Mom."

The teenage grandsons did not spend the long summer visits at Spout Springs they once did but often sent cards and letters to "Mother Janice" and Henry. Away at school, Bart wrote, "There isn't much I wouldn't do to have a squirrel breakfast with biscuits and gravy and some of Miss Bessie's butter. Hell will freeze over before they put anything that good on our chow line. I've also been dreaming of fishing back there. I think I'd crawl through twenty miles of broken glass to catch a sunfish the size of my little finger, right now." All three grandsons were eager to hear all about the changes to the farm because of the dam.

Janice usually typed all her correspondence, but on Saturday morning, September 16, 1967, she composed a six-page handwritten letter to her sister about the house: "Hi there! Rejoice and give thanks unto the

Lord! The house is moved! And it was done, when it was finally done, so smoothly, so efficiently, so beautifully, that not even one piece of chinking was cracked! Nobody really believed this house could be moved (even Henry didn't much believe it) but me and Bob Daulton who moved it. (Nobody believed it could be built, to begin with, but me). Every gloomy gus in the neighborhood shook their heads—it's too heavy a house—it's the wrong shape to move—you can't move logs! Well, the truth is, that with its interlocking system, a log house is one of the strongest, staunchest structures ever designed. If it's put together right, it can withstand a hurricane.

"By 7:30, word had traveled like wildfire and the crowds were coming. I never again had time to think *or* feel. There were too many people and everybody was too excited. Newspaper reporters and photographers seemed to be all over the place and I never got out of that red-striped seersucker dress I had put on to get breakfast, never got to finish breakfast nor did I get another bite until after four in the afternoon.

"Before the movers left, Henry and I went through the house, then, making a thorough inspection. We aren't sure, but it's possible, that about six inches of the quarter round molding around the bathroom ceiling loosened about a quarter of an inch! That was the total extent of damage! And neither Henry nor I are sure that wasn't already loose before the moving. Two kerosene lamps Henry had been using after the current had been turned off, were forgotten and *did* ride safely during the move. They mean it when they say you could leave a full glass of water setting on a table and they wouldn't spill a drop."

Both the *Somerset Commonwealth-Journal* and the *Columbia Adair County News* featured stories and photographs, explaining how twenty-six tons of steel beams were slid under the seventy-five-ton house, which was then lifted with hydraulic and railroad jacks and lowered onto a twenty-six-wheeled dolly. A twenty-ton bulldozer slowly inched the log structure across a diverted creek and through a newly cleared field, a distance of twelve hundred feet.

Several days after the house was moved, Janice took time out from all the confusion to write a poignant letter to Libby: "Soon you'll be having another birthday. I hope it's a lovely one. You were born on a rather chilly night at 12:45 on the morning of September 30 [1924]. But for a long time it remained the night of September 29th to me, and since you were due on the 29th I took some pride in the way you kept your appointment so promptly. It wasn't a long labor nor was there anything unusual about it except that with not even an aspirin for an anesthetic it was rather painfully clear in all its details. You weighed nine pounds and were twenty-one inches long and had an amazing amount of coal black hair. It had to be cut within a day or two. You were perfect in every way and are to this day. There is nothing about you I would ever have had different. No daughter was ever a greater joy, and I have known few women who could compare with your goodness and fineness. Or your wisdom, for by instinct and educated growth you have become a very wise woman, in all the things that really count. Blow all your candles out, at least figuratively, and may what you wish come true. All my love, Mom." In another birthday letter to Libby Janice had written, "My feeling is that you are God's grace made perfect."

In November Janice apprised Joe Covington of the fact that they had moved back into their house on the twenty-fifth, "but that is not to say it was ready to receive us, or will be before Spring! I simply had all I could take of camping out in the schoolhouse. When my sense of humor began to fail, I knew I had to get into something resembling a decent structure with heat and lights and *cold* water. I had been so uncomfortable for so long I could no longer laugh at it. So yesterday morning, in spite of my Appalachian husband, I rounded up four husky men and moved in! Henry was frantic for a while, but when I didn't call on him for anything but to stay out of the way, he relaxed. He is rarely anything but relaxed, of course, but I took him by surprise."

Janice grieved that they would soon need to replace the hand-riven white oak shingles that Henry's father had split, but in a blowing rain the roof had begun to leak and was impossible to patch. She was delighted that Henry put in a window over her kitchen sink and declared that few things they had done had made such a difference. She enjoyed the light and air so much, she did not place a curtain on it.

The greatest change inside the house was when Colvin Hutcherson painted the entire interior Etruscan Ivory. Janice liked it so well she wished she had had the courage to do it sooner, but she had "hated to cover the beautiful old logs with paint." They "were beautiful" but they also made the house dark and on cloudy days the darkness was accentuated until she sometimes felt their home had "become a cave." Janice hung Log Cabin latticework linen sash curtains, handwoven at Berea College, throughout the house. "No draperies anywhere," she said, "just the soft, beautiful lacy look of the natural linen."

A few days after Christmas Janice wrote Ollie, "We are comfortably settled in the house again, thank heaven! I am ready to go to work again but keep your fingers crossed, the story hasn't really jelled yet. The period will be the late 1850s or early 60s, and it will deal with the first transcontinental transportation system and mails, the stage-coaching period.

The working title is *Six-Horse Hitch.* The setting will be a stretch of the Overland Mail which ran from Atchison, Kansas, to Salt Lake City.

"Henry groaned when I told him this book would be about stagecoaching and said, 'We had to chase Osages all over Oklahoma, we had to trace the Santa Fe Trail, you had to learn to pilot a steamboat and run the river, we had to climb all over the Rocky Mountains so you could learn fur-trapping now don't tell me we've got to make a stagecoach trip west!' I said no, just put up a rack in the barn I could hitch six reins to, so I could learn how it felt to handle a six-horse hitch. He was much relieved."

The old year was filled with changes and hard work at Spout Springs and the New Year would welcome more. In writing Libby about beginning a new book, Janice declared, "I mean to be ruthless about interruptions. I want Henry and me to do another book together about the Pond House. Then I want to do a semi-autobiography called *Kinta*. It's nice to have so many things to do!"

26
No Dreary Moments
1968-1969

Publication day for *Shady Grove,* January 16, 1968, heralded the New Year. Most appropriately, Janice's old political comrade during the Kennedy campaign, Pete Walker, reviewed the "social document" for the *Adair County News* and declared: "President Truman never took more pride in his Marshall Plan that rebuilt an economically devastated Europe after World War II than did Sudley Fowler of Broke Neck, Kentucky, in his ability to make use of the programs of the New Deal, the New Frontier, and the Great Society. The thing that makes Sud glow inside is his great talent for placing members of his family 'on the draw.' The Federal Government is his first choice, the Commonwealth of Kentucky a close second, and the county government a poor third."

Fifth District Congressman Dr. Tim Lee Carter wrote to Janice that he and Senator John Sherman Cooper had great fun circulating the book in various circles in Washington, D.C., which included a copy to the Office of Economic Opportunity (OEO) and one to Sargent Shriver. Congressman Carter remarked, "I wish I had a Sudley Fowler in every one of the twenty-four counties of my district!" to which Janice wrote Ollie, "The fake—he knows very well he *has*! For Adair is merely typical of all twenty-nine counties in Kentucky Appalachia!"

In a letter to her grandson, Mike, Janice explained the happenings in *Shady Grove*: "My first target, of course, was the established church, with its arrogance. The second was the news media and the last, because it's really of no importance to our people, the OEO program. Not even the naivest Appalachian is naive enough to believe these programs have any worth. They are simply useful to get the most one can get legitimately, and often illegitimately, out of. Sudley, and all the rest of Appalachia, knows how to go about doing this most profitably. This doesn't shock me or bother me, because I know how little of it ever trickles through the pockets of the politicians into Appalachia anyhow." Janice told Mike she often had to compromise in writing her books. She did not like to follow, book after book, a "rather stereotyped line," but she did it, first because she meant to be published and read. Second, because although in order to be read she must "hew to the line," she had yet to write a book in which she had not been able, here and there, to say something she felt was important, usually in the field of human relations.

"My mail tells me how worthwhile this is. I don't reach the Establishment in my writing. But I reach millions of plain people, and what I have to say about the human heart has been, at least my mail tells me so, effective. When a woman scheduled for critical surgery tells me that she read one of my books the night before and felt lifted up and strengthened, I know my compromise has been a good one. When a man writes me that after reading one of my books he had the courage, which nobody had been able to give him before, to bring his wife home from a mental institution after three years of treatment (doctors had been urging him to take her home for half that time) I can't doubt that some of the things I manage to say, within the limiting framework of the novel, are worthwhile. Take heart, dear. Life is too short to be unhappy even *one hour.*"

Janice began *Six-Horse Hitch* on New Year's Day and made a firm resolution not to take any weekdays off from writing so she could have it "over the hump before planting time." She did not have to worry about January interruptions. The first big snow of the season began falling December 27 with several more smaller accumulations to follow. By January 10 it had been warm enough only twice to thaw the least bit. Late in the evening on the twelfth, blizzard-like snows gripped Kentucky, reaching depths of fifteen inches and dropping to "deep-freeze" temperatures. Schools had not reopened since the Christmas holiday and would remain closed for days to come. With snow tires, Henry "crept into town" the morning of the fifteenth and made it home with "fresh stores of food, magazines, books, other essentials of life, including new typewriter ribbons" so Janice could continue work on *Six-Horse Hitch*.

As in all her carefully researched topics, Janice knew her subject well. She had just read Jack Schaefer's *First Blood,* which attracted her attention because it was about "a stage driver." As Schaefer was a productive author of western novels, Janice assumed he did meticulous research and knew every detail about the period. "But," she wrote Libby, "he had his stage driver gather up the reins of a six-horse hitch *in his left hand,* and with his right hand crack his long whip over the heads of the leaders. This is an impossibility. Later in the novel, Schaefer had his driver tromp hard on the brake, with his *left* foot! Another impossibility. A stage driver always sat on the right and all brakes were on the right of the driver. He would have had to be a contortionist to use the brake with his left foot.

Obviously, Schaefer never drove even so much as a one-horse buggy, (as I have done many times), but worse, didn't check any sources, or even look closely at photographs of the stages."

In mid-January, when Ollie shared with Janice that his wife, Betty, had lost her mother, Janice wrote, "I still find myself wanting to tell my mother something, or write to her on Sunday, or pick up the phone and call her. I can't yet quite believe she's gone. There's a hole, a big hole and one is forever after, I suppose, truly a motherless child. If my mother was near, the world was right. Nothing could happen to me if I could hold to her. My mother could defeat anything! And I felt pity for other boys and girls who didn't have her for a mother. I wore a crown of stars because I belonged to her, and I wouldn't have traded places with a princess of royal blood. In fact, I *was* of royal blood because I was her daughter."

Janice learned in a letter from her sister, Mary, that their mother's longtime friend, affectionately called "Aunt Annabelle," had passed away February 22, 1968. Janice wrote Annabelle's son, Robert, on the twenty-eighth: "If there is some Elysian field, Robert, I'll bet John and Annabelle Snodgrass and John and Lucy Holt have picked themselves out a pretty little stream and the men are pulling in bass and crappie as fast as they can drop their lines, and the girls have a campfire going and a big iron skillet of hot grease and are frying them by the platters. That would be their idea of heaven!"

In February Janice was "deep, deep in the new book" and had shifted the telling from third person to first, realizing that what she really wanted to do was write "a sort of fictionalized autobiography" or personal narrative. "Funny how simply shifting from 'he' to 'I' was what was needed. I never really think about how a story shall be told. It usually takes care of itself. I don't give it a conscious thought. It's such a fascinating period of history. But this thing wasn't going free and easy the way it should and not until I experimented with a couple of pages did I realize that what I was wanting was the freedom and space of autobiography. It was like undamming a river! Now it will be sheer joy to write. I wanted the 'loose hitch' movement of a stagecoach itself and the lusty, extremely masculine world of the drivers—the pace and speed and grace of the horses. Only a stage-driver could tell it and I, in the skin of one, have to do it that way. That 'he' was between me and the driver all the time!"

Following the paperback release of *The Kentuckians,* there were notices in *Saturday Review* and *Coronet* describing Janice Holt Giles as a "fine woman writer in a field usually monopolized by men" and linking her with Barbara Tuchman, who "has a strenuous, masculine mind." Janice had established an admirable reputation and an ever-increasing popularity for which she was both pleased and displeased. She lamented to Libby, "There are times when just the mail can complicate my life so much I get bogged down. The longer you write, the more recognition there is, the more obligations and responsibilities there are. I was thinking just the other day how *much* time I had when I first started writing. Some years I even did two books. I wasn't known, the tourists hadn't discovered me, there was no fan mail, and no telephone! Now my life is unbelievably complicated and I have to fight for time to write at all. My poor stagecoach is stalled out near the South Platte!"

On July 11 Janice wrote Ollie that she was working on the new novel and would soon be sending the first 250 pages of manuscript. To assist her, she told Ollie, "Henry is going to try to keep the public warded off. But you know, the sign 'Private' posted here and there doesn't mean a thing. They climb right over the fence, drive through the gates, and if we don't answer the door wander around taking their everlasting pictures and picking the flowers for souvenirs."

Janice mailed the first 250 pages of *Six-Horse Hitch* on August 9, 1968, and wrote that the best she could see there were five more chapters to do, about another 150 pages. "Say a prayer for me," she pleaded, "that I can have just *four* weeks of uninterrupted time! That's all I need."

Once Janice accepted the challenge of writing a new book, she forged ahead each day in steadfast pursuit. Her excitement is sensed through her correspondence as she discusses the intensity of her writing while working on *Six-Horse Hitch:* "Every time a driver began his run, his whole effort was toward that perfect performance which his skill, and with luck the uninterrupted cadence, and with luck the grace of the road, could bring off.

"And then what did it feel like? Where are the words to describe the exultation he must have felt? You want to make new words! You want the feeling to create the words! So you fail—there just isn't any way to do it.

"And about that time the telephone rings, or somebody drives up, or Henry comes in needing something and you wonder what in the world all this anguish is about anyway! The average reader couldn't care less and you've spent hours and hours and weeks and weeks, dissecting one motivation—which you are bound to fail to make real. You just have to do it, that's all. I suppose, in the last analysis, a writer actually writes for himself.

"I have come out of this week's work feeling wrung out. I just sort of opened the refrigerator door and caught what fell out for supper. It's always such a joy to me to turn to the plants and the garden and the pond—and to work other muscles after a brain-wrenching week."

At 3:50 P.M., September 14, 1968, *Six-Horse Hitch* was finished. Janice wrote to Libby, "The book had taken on a life so real, I had known all day that it might happen, but couldn't be sure until about 2:30. Even so, when the last word was written, and I knew it was the last word, I could hardly believe it. I sat here at the typewriter and looked at it and felt sort of empty. I rolled the paper out, put it on the stack, then fixed a glass of iced tea and went to sit with Henry on the porch and tell him. His eyes filled with tears and he came over to kiss me and pat my shoulder. He can never find words and neither can I—except on paper."

Janice described to Libby how company had interrupted one of the hardest pieces of writing in the book and she had been afraid it might take a week or more to recover it. When they left, "while changing beds, cleaning the bathroom, picking black-eyed peas, my mind was on that piece of work. Next morning I began to move into it, with the actual writing. It turned out to be a page and a half in length, and it took me a day and half to write it. I must have done it forty times and it was not until the second day that I found the key word. This is the time, the place, the precise moment when this boy grows up—and it is a moment foreordained, predestined before he was born, over which he has never had any control—and yet he must face and serve this necessity. Pure Greek—fated and tragic. It would have been easy to slop through it with easy words and facility, but it was a birth to do it as hard and tough as this boy was. It will read quite simply, but every word is right. Eight hours Thursday, another eight Friday, almost eight yesterday, and the book was in the bag. Tomorrow I'll begin the final typing of this last 250 pages. Then off she goes."

Ollie Swan's response to the manuscript was, "Well, you've done it again! I finished reading last night and deliberately didn't read quickly in order to savor almost literally every word. I think it's a magnificent job and for my money among your most impressive thus far. As you know, I'm usually pessimistic about Hollywood but it seems to me there is a whale of a picture in this one."

After signing the contract for *Six-Horse Hitch,* Janice decided she was going to do a "rather short book," which she hoped could be published on the twenty-fifth anniversary of the Battle of the Bulge, December 17, 1969. "This will be a respectable military account of the activities of the 291st Engineers in stopping the spearhead advance of the 1st S.S. Panzers at Malmedy, Stavelot, Trois Ponts and Habiemont—in the Ambleve, Lienne and Salm river network," she wrote Ollie. "I have been doing intensive research on it since 1964 and will begin the actual writing this fall. The date for publication is auspicious and I see no good reason why a novel and the 291st book can't come out in the same year." Janice explained further that she had accumulated "a rather formidable mass of documentation, including all pertinent American and German unit histories, After Action Reports, depositions, maps, military orders, etc. And unless somebody beats me to it before December 1969, I have a few 'firsts' in the military records. A Belgian Engineer officer has done a lot of the on-the-spot research for me. I am hopeful I can write a colorful, readable, popular book which is at the same time fully documented and absolutely authentic."

On October 14 Nash delivered Libby to her mother's door in Kentucky. Janice and Libby left the next day around noon for Washington, D.C., for Janice to do research in the military section of the National Archives. They spent their first night of an eleven-day research and sightseeing venture in Abingtou, Virginia, then went on to Oxford where Janice interviewed Arch Taylor, who was a lieutenant and platoon leader in A Company, 291st, to discuss the 3rd platoon's involvement in the Battle of the Bulge.

Henry spent the eleven days "batching" and gained a lot more respect for housewives. "I have put into practice all the good habits which most well housebroken husbands have," he wrote in his column, "but still the whole house has been against me. Every time I turn my back, it messes itself up again. There's dust; crumbs on the tables; spots on the floor; and clothes of mine where they have no business being. And one thing this country needs is some kind of good lard that won't pop and sizzle out of the skillet and all over the stove when you fry stuff." Before the travelers arrived, Ruth White had cleaned the house. Janice declared, "It looked so nice and so welcoming."

Once home, Janice was ready to settle down to work on the winter's writing. *Prepare to Defend* was her first working title, then *They Were There,* the "scrappy, rambunctious little book" about the 291st's involvement in the Battle of the Bulge. "It is half finished," she wrote Ollie January 12, "and the second half will race along. I've had an enormous amount of fun with the officers on this book, most of whom I've now met, or had much telephone conversation with. They're about as salty and sinewy today as they were in 1944. If any of them have any reservations about a woman doing their story, they haven't shown it. They seem to feel I'm about as tough an old 291ster as any of them."

In early February Janice sent Ollie the partial manuscript of the book she was then calling *A Handful of Engineers,* which he found to be a fascinating story and one that gave him a clear idea of what the Battle of the

Bulge was about. He was looking forward with interest to the balance of the book. The rough draft of the book was completed by the beginning of March.

To check its validity, Janice had Mark Smith, a former staff member of Supreme Headquarters, Allied Expeditionary Forces (SHEAF), who was also writing about his experiences, read the synthesis, and remarked, "I am up with the 'moon shot' this morning after a telephone call from him. He says what I have done in the way of fresh and original research is simply 'miraculous.'"

In corresponding with Anne Barrett about *A Handful of Engineers*, Janice wrote, "It's a lovely Sunday, clear, cold and crisp. Henry is happy with the sun again. But something wonderful has happened to me, once I got over my mother's death. Every day is lovely to me and all the hours are joyous and exciting. Good health, no doubt! And the realization that, short of family catastrophe, only I can allow myself to have a single dreary moment. Refusing, there are none."

On March 17 Paul Brooks wrote Janice that, before any announcement was sent to the press, he wanted to write her a personal note about his future plans. "When I took over the job of Director of the Trade Division in 1967 (after more than twenty years as Editor-in-Chief) I told my colleagues that it must be for two years only, in order to devote more time to my own writing and to work in conservation." Brooks planned to continue at Houghton Mifflin on a part-time basis, largely in an editorial capacity, an average of two days a week. He informed Janice that Craig Wylie would become director of the Trade Division; Richard McAdoo, editor-in-chief; and Dorothy de Santillana would continue as executive editor. Janice wrote Brooks that she felt a little sad that he was giving up his official duties at Houghton Mifflin but that she applauded his reasons and expected to see many good things from his pen.

When Janice and Henry purchased the Spout Springs farm from Etsel and Violet Spires in August 1957, there was excluded about a quarter of an acre that the Spires had deeded to their daughter, Rebecca, and her husband, Sam Giles, for a homesite. The young couple had started their house and had it framed and roofed but were transferred to Indiana before it was finished. In June 1969, Janice and Henry purchased the small structure that was near their home and dubbed it "the Becky house." The Becky house became and remained Henry's "little diggings of his own."

Publication day for *Six-Horse Hitch* was set for July 14, 1969. The excitement had barely settled from the appearance of the novel and already Janice's mind was probing the next book, with three ideas swirling and the decision to make as to which one she was most ready to do. "Kinta, that land of my childhood, haunts me increasingly and I have never done anything with it," she wrote Anne Barrett, "but I don't know if I'm good enough. I don't know if I can recover its mystery, and the Indians, and the prairie. I'm afraid of it and yet I feel compelled to try. Well, I can always dump it in the wastebasket, can't I?"

27
Research
1969-1970

Before Janice could begin writing *Kinta,* there were frustrations to deal with involving *The Damned Engineers,* the official title of the book about the Battle of the Bulge. With the skills of a lion stalking prey, Janice Holt Giles had begun her military research of World War II in 1964 in preparation for *The G.I. Journal of Sergeant Giles.* Prior to that, as a young woman in her mid-thirties, she had lived the war through media broadcasts, newspaper reports, magazine features, and the involvement of friends and family members. The war was foremost in the minds and hearts of every citizen during those turbulent years. The man she loved and intended to marry was a foot soldier, a member of the cadre that formed the 291st Engineers Combat battalion. Through the years her husband remained "a walking encyclopedia on 291st habits and ways, their lore and tradition."

The publication and autographing party for *The G.I. Journal of Sergeant Giles* fueled her intrigue with their performance and history. The entire three days were one long conference with the men, and one eight-hour session was recorded. While in her home, Colonel Pergrin had asked Janice to consider writing a book about the battalion and had assured her that he would furnish his personal records and private papers from its origination at Camp Swift, Texas, in January 1943, through Munich and the war's end. It was decided then that the book's focus would be the Battle of the Bulge, as that encounter was the battalion's finest hour. With the philosophy that "one does not live very long without owing a debt to the society which has nourished one and made possible all the richness of choice they inherit," Janice accepted the challenge to write an account of how a battalion of six hundred Americans led by their twenty-seven-year-old lieutenant colonel successfully overthrew the attack of a heavily armored German column several times its size under the relentless command of Jochen Peiper, by deciding wisely "which bridges to destroy and which locations to defend, where to assemble and when to move." The Battle of the Bulge is recognized as the greatest battle ever fought by the American army, and the 291st played an important role in defeating the

most daring, dangerous German offensive through their quick, decisive, and heroic action.

By 1967 Captain Andre Banneux of Liege, Belgium, had spent ten years doing research for a book he wanted to write about the battles along the Ambleve. A friend of his, an American engineer working in Liege, gave him a copy of *The G.I. Journal of Sergeant Giles,* which provided information on a wide gap in his research, the action of the 291st. Banneux was frustrated by Colonel Pergrin's After Action Reports and by the lack of historical information on the outfit. He was delighted to receive a copy of *The G.I. Journal* and to correspond with Janice through Houghton Mifflin, making remarks about the book and asking questions concerning the battalion.

"I had completed much of my research on the 291st by that time," Janice wrote Anne Barrett on August 5, 1969, "and instead of replying to his questions, I offered him everything I had. Apparently this was naive of me and totally unheard of. But I knew nothing of the jealous hoarding of materials among scholars, and you know me when it comes to the 291st. I wanted all the recognition possible for them in his book, my book, anybody else's book! Well, cast your bread upon the waters, Banneux was totally bowled over by what he considered great generosity and he responded with trust in me. Slowly this trust enlarged until he opened everything to me, and he enlisted his associates to the extent of obtaining their permission to be quoted or referred to in the book. Professors at the University of Liege, Jarbinet and Natalis, as well as Captain Banneux's father, were all Intelligence officers in the Resistance forces. They know these battles like nobody else. They served as liaison, guides and Intelligence forces for the Americans during them and they testified at Nuremberg and in the Malmedy trial." Janice told Anne that Banneux had accumulated the most formidable mass of infinitely more detailed documents outside the official archives, and they had never been opened to any American before.

Banneux had traveled to Germany in 1963 and interviewed Peiper, who allowed him to tape their discussion, and he sent a copy to Janice. Fortunately, English was their mutual language. Thus "what was heretofore a fog of unknown units and intentions" was cleared up by Peiper and available to Janice in her research. "None of this has ever been known before, much less published," she wrote Anne, "including a photograph taken by Peiper's men and a reproduction of Peiper's own route map, marked in his own handwriting, and sketches he made as he talked with Banneux, to illustrate the situation at Stavelot. The material is unique and enormously valuable—actually priceless."

On October 28 Anne sent Janice a copy of a letter Andre Banneux had written to the editor-in-chief of Houghton Mifflin seeking credit for his "collaboration to the History of the 291st Bon from the Normandy to the End of the war." He claimed that he was finishing his book, after more than ten years of research, in March 1968 and had stopped in May and June to rewrite 120 pages of his personal history of Peiper for Janice Holt Giles. When she asked him to draw maps, he requested a copy of her manuscript as he did not know which of the German movements she had used and desired to read what she had written about Peiper. "This part, based on my manuscript, is the most important for me because I fear personal interpretations, by M. Giles, in contradiction with what I have written. *It is very dangerous for me as I am the only Belgian historian to have metted Peiper and discussed his battle.*"

Banneux claimed that he had supplied Janice with the location of all the positions of the 291st before and during the battle which would have been impossible to ascertain with only her documents; that he had furnished copies of the movements of all the U.S., Belgian, and German units, the Peiper story that he alone had, and Belgian and French reports. He believed that without his help "M. Giles could not in eight months, resting in her house, without visiting Belgium, explain new facts never discovered by other writers!" In concluding his letter to Houghton Mifflin, Banneux wrote, "I have asked M. Giles to be reported on the first pages as co-worker!! As M. Giles do not answer, my collaboration must be forget. I return the documents received from M. Giles and in no way M. Giles *can not use* one information coming from me. A Belgian Editor shall be charged to verify the respect of my request following the international rules concerning the rights of authors. I regret! All had been very correct till the manuscripts."

Janice was extremely distressed by Banneux's accusations but considered "the whole thing providential." In a letter of defense, she expressed a different opinion to Anne of Banneux's material than in the August letter. "His credibility is totally destroyed with me. I have no documentation to prove he actually had any interviews claimed by him. Practically all of his military material is in the archives in Washington and Arlington. What he appeared to do beyond that was to confirm places and dates with Belgian witnesses. But as you know, I always do my own homework, all my own research in primary sources. I never rely on anybody else and I needed nothing of this sort from him. I thought his Belgians added color and was happy to use as many as I could. But perhaps I have been saved from a terrible mistake, simply through Banneux's own rage.

"I shall delete everything which comes *solely* from him, and I shall take care to cite my own sources in footnotes. Some of the photographs he sent originated in the U.S. Army Photographic Section. I shall use such of those as are necessary, but none which would have to be credited solely to Banneux.

"The only safe thing to do, from every standpoint, is to wipe him out. And thank heaven he blew his stack in plenty of time. I'll be entirely clean of him and there won't be one thing that doesn't come from my own sources and can be so documented from our own U.S. archives, or my 291sters.

"Henry is consoling. He says of course I was naive and trusting, but that is me and nobody who knows me would have me different. I'm sure I have a rather child-like faith that most people are good, because I've found them so. But how little he understands (and probably could never understand) what eighteen years of a warm, *trusting* relationship between us has founded. Many thanks for your backing, your faith and your warmth there."

In late October Janice shipped Anne all the material Banneux had sent to her for Houghton Mifflin editors to examine before returning it to him and included a lengthy letter of explanation. Banneux's cover letter, included in the first information he sent, was dated November 27, 1968, and reached her the first week of December, at which time she claimed her rough draft was completed but not retyped. She had pieced some of the "new and original material" into her manuscript.

The past April Janice had mailed her first draft, retyped, of over two hundred pages to Anne Barrett. In late May she began receiving Banneux's Peiper material, which she felt was "bound to be what he bases his claim that I wrote my book from his materials on. His statement that the book is based on his materials is absolutely ridiculous.

"It should be understood that all military records of World War II—that is, AARs, Service Journals, unit histories—both of the U.S. Army and the German, are now available to anybody, anywhere in the world. Credentials are not necessary, nor is it even necessary to go to Washington. All you have to do is know what you want, write the Records Center, and for the modest fee of ten cents per page it will be reproduced and sent to you. Therefore, there is nothing at all here uniquely Banneux's. It is open to the world."

Janice derived the title for *The Damned Engineers* from a comment made by a German commander in exasperation with the men of the 291st, "who wrecked his hope of a rapid thrust forward across the Meuse, during the Battle of the Bulge, when they put up their small roadblocks and blew bridges he so badly needed in his face." Just as he approached the

last bridge he would have to cross, it too, was blown. The commander "pounded his knees in helpless frustration and screamed, 'The damned engineers! The damned engineers!'"

Houghton Mifflin editor Jacques de Spoelberch was in awe of the extraordinary job Janice had done with "a vastly complex subject." He felt she had "impeccably researched and detailed recreation of the important Ambleve battles. The drama and excitement of the narrative itself sweep one along until one begins to 'see' most of the pivotal spots in one's mind's eye without having to refer to the maps. I consider *The Damned Engineers* topflight military history and an exceptionally readable narrative."

When Anne inquired if Janice would like to do the index for *The Damned Engineers,* her response was entirely different from that for *The G.I. Journal of Sergeant Giles.* "Please have the index made there. I hate doing them with a passion, and I'm not really professional and always am terrified I'll overlook something." Janice returned the signed contract for *The Damned Engineers* on August 30, 1969.

Because of Andre Banneux, there had been great anxiety with *The Damned Engineers,* but Janice's previous book was creating much excitement. On September 19, 1969, Ollie sent a copy of a letter from Evarts Ziegler in reference to *Six-Horse Hitch.* "Per our conversation I have quoted $7500.00 against $75,000 to Arnold Weisberger for the motion picture rights in the above title. He, as I told you, is representing Edward Meyers in this. Meyers was a co-producer last year of *The Man in the Glass Booth.* We won't have an immediate answer because Meyers is out of the country for about ten days."

In November there was more happiness for Janice. Mike Hancock, her middle grandson, arrived Sunday, November 2, for an extended visit during which time he planned to drive his grandmother to Boston and, after their return, take her to Oklahoma and Arkansas to do research for the autobiographical book, *Kinta.* They left for Boston November 9, stopping overnight in Harrisburg, Pennsylvania, before traveling on to Cambridge, Massachusetts, where they were dinner guests on November 11 of Anne Barrett, senior editor at Houghton Mifflin. The next evening, Janice was guest of honor at a cocktail party and buffet given by the Board of Directors in the home of Ben Tilghman, chairman of the board.

The most heartening evening was November 13 when, following a dinner hosted by editor-in-chief Richard McAdoo and his wife in the board of directors room at Houghton Mifflin, congratulations were offered for the achievement of the sale of movie rights to *Six-Horse Hitch.* It was also announced that *Six-Horse Hitch* had been sold to Fawcett Gold Medal Books for publication in paperback.

Janice remarked to Ollie that Fawcett's suggestion that the paperback reprint of *Six-Horse Hitch* be issued under the name "Holt Giles" because they didn't think people would buy a book about horses and the west written by a woman was "the funniest thing." She said, "At first I was inclined to feel a little affronted. Then I thought, what difference does it make on a paperback. And it certainly is true that a woman's name does not attract the readers a man's does, especially with this kind of book. It is simply a fact that there has never been a great woman writer, and probably never will be, because women just don't attract 'followership.' It doesn't really matter to me. I've done what I set out to do, had a modicum of success, have remained, most importantly, Mrs. Henry Giles, and that's my full cup and I'm quite satisfied with it."

The 1969 Christmas was a family gathering with all the Hancocks at Spout Springs. After much turkey and celebration, the Hancocks dispersed, except for Mike, who left with "Mother Janice" on January 1 for the Arkansas and Oklahoma research trip in preparation for the work on *Kinta.* They spent two weeks "one jump ahead of a snowstorm" and were "weathered in" twice, when it was impossible to travel because of hazardous roads. Janice praised Mike as being a "real trouper" in taking her where she needed to go and making photographs along the way, six of which were used in the publication of *The Kinta Years.* While doing the research with his grandmother, Mike, at age twenty-one, heard much family history. He said he learned a lot about his heritage and decided that it looked to him as if he "came from a long line of people who didn't know how to quit, who held it a matter of principle to finish what they started."

In reporting on the travelers to the readers of "Spout Springs Splashes," Henry wrote January 15: "My housekeeper and choreboy were hung up tight in twelve inches of snow in northern Arkansas. It should be recorded that things here in the Hollow are too frozen up to Splash much. Three degrees above zero on the hot side of the house. And down in and around the mini-barn were cold-footed and dry-throated ducks, cold-combed and hungry roosters and hens. It was a COLD day. The ducks didn't even mention leaving their pen for the pool, and the chickens liked it better inside than out. The mother dominecker clucked slower than usual to her little ones. I noticed the more clothes I put on, the farther away my overshoe buckles were."

Acknowledging that the galleys of *The Damned Engineers* had arrived, Janice wrote Anne on February 22, "The movie contracts finally came, too. Ollie's Hollywood agent and the producer's attorneys have been haggling all this time over television rights. Eventually the producer was granted them, but at an extra fee for me. My goodness, Anne, if a series

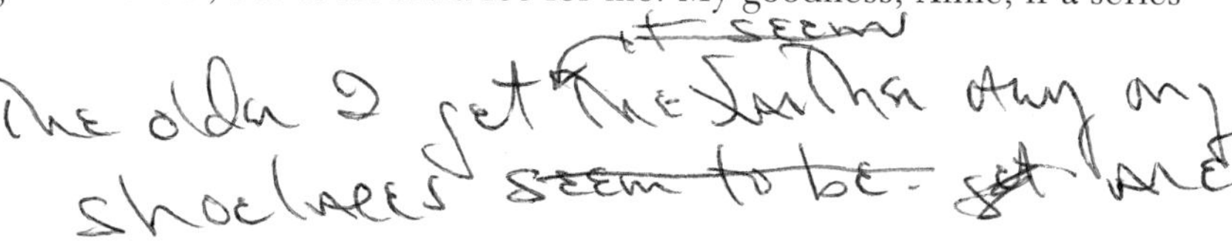

should be produced based on this book I wouldn't be able to count the money. Figures like that make my head whirl! But of course it isn't likely to happen."

At the end of April, Janice wrote Anne a three-page letter discussing her work and explaining her physical tolerance. "I hope you will not be too disappointed, but *Kinta* is only about half finished and Todd Jeffries won't allow me to work on it but two hours a day. Blood pressure again, and this time dangerously high. He knows it is worse to cut the work off completely, but he says I've done the work of ten men in the last three years, with two hard, major books, and altogether too much fun with the grandsons. Work really never hurts me. It's actually just that I'm into my 60s and high blood pressure is a family failing—too much good country food, perhaps an inherited nervous system that tightens up occasionally."

Janice told Anne that Dr. Jeffries thought working with autobiographical material was too emotional for her and too difficult to write at that particular time. Wanting to shift to something else, Janice rummaged in the attic through stored items of previous work and found a collection of letters written to the grandsons after their long summer visit when they were five, six, and seven years old to keep them in touch with the farm animals. She began a revision of the manuscript she had written years before using the letters and titled it *With Love, Grandma.* She hoped to have it completed in two or three weeks and then return to work on *Kinta* in the fall. "Thank you so much for reissuing *The Enduring Hills* and *Miss Willie,"* Janice wrote Anne. "I called Libby and we both shed a few sentimental tears. You do know, of course, that Mary and Hod are Henry and me—and that Miss Willie is based on my mother. Not the incidents, but the woman and her personality and character. And Mama did used to sit in a rocker and knit in her schoolroom, and she had a braided rag rug on the floor, a canary, flowers and goldfish and a phonograph. She played classical instrumental music while the kids worked math problems! The most imaginative teacher I ever knew. Or studied under myself."

In view of the distress surrounding *The Damned Engineers,* Janice was delighted to receive a letter dated May 4, 1970, from Maj. Gen. James M. Gavin, World War II commander of the 82nd Airborne Division, who had read the galleys. Gavin wrote, "I wanted to write and tell you what a fine book you have written. I am impressed by the tremendous amount of research that must have gone into it. I learned a great deal, also, that I did not know about the 291st Engineers Battalion as well as the movement of Peiper's column." In *The Damned Engineers,* Janice had described

the commander: "At thirty-seven, General Gavin was one of the youngest general officers in the Army. He had made quite a name for himself. He had fought in North Africa, Sicily and Italy. He had jumped with his men on June 5 into Normandy, and he had jumped with them in Holland only a short time before." In his two-page letter, Gavin told Janice, "You have written a fine book and Martin Blumenson has done an excellent foreword for you." After his signature, Gavin added in pen, "As a World War II veteran, thank you for writing this great book," which deeply touched Janice.

In June 1970, Janice received another accolade for *Six-Horse Hitch*; a plaque for excellence from the Western Writers of America was presented during their annual convention in North Platte, Nebraska. Alice Bullock, book editor of the *Santa Fe New Mexican* accepted the award for Janice, who was too ill to attend. The award is engraved: "Western Writers of America congratulates Janice Holt Giles SPUR NOMINEE—1969 for *Six-Horse Hitch* fine writing of the American West." On June 16, Janice responded to Anne Barrett's inquiry as to how she would feel about writing a foreword to two reprints of her earliest books. "Of course I will do a brief foreword for *The Enduring Hills* and *Miss Willie*. Be happy to. When do you need it?" Janice told Anne she was feeling better all the time and that the house was "quiet and peaceful."

Janice also informed Anne that her mother had kept a clipping file of all of her "Around Our House" columns for the *Campbellsville News-Journal* in the years 1954-56 and Henry's columns, which began in 1957. Her intentions were to edit those for a book titled *Around Our House*, "which would also answer the hundreds of questions concerning the fate of the log house, which *A Little Better than Plumb* left up in the air."

For the second time in two months, Janice was admitted to the hospital in July for a kidney infection. She was dismissed the sixteenth and wrote Anne of her receipt of the first copy of *The Damned Engineers* on June 22, 1970. "The book just came. Henry and I both were misty-eyed about it and handled it reverently. It's so beautiful, Anne. I quickly checked the maps and photographs, certain places where errors might have crept in. It's a beautiful job and everything is A-OK. Tell Sylvia she did a noble job making order out of all the chaos after Banneux blew up, and you, Anne. How can I ever thank you for your patience, the understanding, and above all your unflinching faith in my integrity and my determination this book should not be tainted by one little whiff of Banneux.

"I am feeling so much better, and all I needed to make me happy and well was my beautiful book today! It is the best medicine I could have."

Janice was momentarily feeling "much better," but the stress and anxiety associated with Andre Banneux had wreaked havoc on her emotional and mental health.

Twenty years had passed since the appearance of Janice Holt Giles's first book, *The Enduring Hills*, in 1950. Twenty years of dedicated work—researching, reading, long days of writing, endless correspondence, traveling—always focusing on the next story to tell. "I'm just a storyteller," she had said many times, but the road in the telling had been long, hard, and exhausting.

28
Green Bough in the Heart
1970-1971

By midsummer of 1970 Janice was beginning to feel much better and had been dismissed by her doctor. Whereas she had previously written for five or six hours a day, she was now working about two. "Even so," she declared, "I'll have another book ready by mid-winter."

On August 7 Janice responded to Anne concerning the sentiment shown to her by Houghton Mifflin friends. "Tell the Sales Department to cool down, but bless 'em for getting into a high dudgeon over that blasting review in *Library Journal.* And thank you and Dick for taking up the cudgels in my behalf. I don't think Mr. Newman's review is going to hurt sales at all, for I doubt if there are more than a dozen libraries in the United States who would accept a review in *Library Journal* over their own circulation figures. So, I don't think Mr. Newman did me any damage, but I am everlastingly grateful for Houghton Mifflin's anger. I have never yet written a critic or reviewer, so I don't think this is the time for me to begin. My readership following is solid and nothing can shake it unless I wrote a *Peyton Place* or *Valley of the Dolls,* which I certainly could *not* even if I wanted to, write. I don't even know the words!"

The review by William Newman, York University Library, Toronto, Canada, had appeared in the July 1970 *Library Journal.* Newman wrote, in part, "At this time, when the United States is involved in some of the most horrendous conflicts and decisions, both abroad (e.g., Indochina) and at home (e.g., Kent State), this reviewer finds himself at a loss as to what he should say about this book which is purportedly the history of the 291st Engineer Combat Battalion in World War II and in content and style is straight out of *Army Times.*" In addition to a few other critical remarks, he concluded, "It is a pity many trees had to be cut to produce the paper for this persiflage, which I find an insult to the dead and the living." Janice countered that Newman was "a Canadian who obviously took umbrage at her remarks about Field Marshal Sir Bernard Montgomery of the First Canadian Army."

After John Beecroft's retirement from the Doubleday Book Club system, Janice had been concerned that her readership would be lessened if her books were no longer book club selections. On August 17, she wrote Anne, "The best of my writing has come since then and sales figures would be around five or six million had Fitzgerald used them as consistently as Mr. Beecroft did. And without undue modesty, I think *The Great Adventure* and *Six-Horse Hitch* are far better books than many he has chosen, and he missed a big, big deal when he passed up *Shady Grove.* But that's the way things go. I got over my trauma on the book club deal long ago. I have actually made more money without them than before, because the split and modest prices for the books kept my tax percentage down to a lower level than our income is nowadays."

Janice was happy to tell Anne that she was feeling herself again, "all nervous weakness gone, ready to tackle lions (but not as a Christian martyr) if necessary!" She was also happy that she had arrived at a format for the next book, *Around Our House.* "It is to be divided in parts, as was *The Damned Engineers.* It actually is a sort of autobiography of a marriage, since it goes back to 1954 when I began writing my column, and brings us up to date in 1970. A lovely, lovely book, if I do say so myself."

The next day, Janice wrote another letter to Anne, beginning, "Just a note, since I wrote fully only yesterday." Janice needed to find out the precise date of the copyright on *The Damned Engineers,* giving the following explanation: "Professionally I am 61 years old, Anne, but actually I am 65. Our tax attorney tells me that earnings from all books with copyrights prior to my 65th birthday, March 28, 1970, are not considered earnings but royalties from preceding work and do not prejudice my Social Security standing. It would be with wicked glee I would file for my maximum S.S. rights, including monthly payments of $189.90, plus Medicare, retroactive to March 28, 1970, which would take care of most of that expensive hospitalization in Santa Fe.

"Our attorney tells me if my earnings from any book written since March 28, 1970 ever fall below $4,129.00 per year, they do not prejudice my S.S. rights, either. Heaven forbid they should fall that low. But since I never in my life expected to be able to collect a dime of that dreadful S.S. tax I have been paying (maximum annually) for twenty-five years, you can imagine how delighted I am at this unexpected bonus."

Janice's exact age had long been a mystery. Henry later told the story about when he learned the truth. He said, Janice entered the kitchen one morning while he was sitting at the table, drinking a cup of coffee. She poured herself a cup and sat down across from him. Looking up at him, she suddenly began sobbing. Henry said, "Honey, what in the world is the matter with you?"

Dabbing at her tears, Janice replied, "Henry, I have to tell you something."

"Well, it couldn't be *that* bad."

"But it is. I lied to you when we got married."

"You lied to me?"

"Yes."

"Well tell me what it is. I can't imagine what it could be that's so bad to cry over."

Sniffling, Janice said, "I'm older than what I told you. I lied to you about my age."

"How much older are you than what you said? I've lived with you all these years and it didn't matter. Why are you telling me now?"

"Because I'm eligible for Social Security!"

On August 20, publication day for *The Damned Engineers,* Anne telephoned Janice to tell her that prepublication sales lacked only eleven copies of selling out the first printing of five thousand. By that time Janice was typing Part I of *Around Our House,* which involved the editing, revising, and a little rewriting of the newspaper columns and supposedly her notebook, although one does not exist in her manuscript collection with the clippings. Regarding *Around Our House,* Janice wrote to Anne, "We do *not,* repeat *not,* want a contract this calendar year! We've got enough problems without adding another dime of income this year." She added, "I feel so wonderful that I have to pinch myself to believe I've been ill this spring and summer. Keep your fingers crossed."

Crossed fingers could not prevent the demons of professional jealousy that continued to attack Janice. Having achieved hard-earned recognition and success, it seemed she had become vultures' prey. Ellis Lucia, author of *Saga of Ben Holladay* [1959], claimed Ben Holladay, portrayed in *Six-Horse Hitch,* had been a forgotten figure until he wrote a biography about him, and he accused Janice of plagiarism, which in turn was causing major concern to Edward Meyers over the motion picture rights. Janice wrote Ollie, September 8, 1970, "Mr. Lucia's charges are absolutely ridiculous and totally unfounded."

In a three-page letter, Janice once again defended her research, which she had been doing in depth for twenty years for her frontier series. "Lucia does not own Ben Holladay simply because he wrote a biography of him. Far from being a forgotten figure, Ben Holladay strides like a giant across the pages of all western literature concerning the opening of the West, and especially of his epoch, the first mails and stagecoach transportation system. There are dozens of books and magazine articles and pamphlets, probably hundreds, in which Holladay is mentioned, briefly or lengthily, and if Lucia researched eight years to write his biography he knows how vast the literature is, for he was compelled to comb through it to get his book."

Janice said it was difficult to know when she began researching specifically for *Six-Horse Hitch* as the research constantly overlapped for the series, but as early as 1956 she was reading Bancroft and Reuben Thwaites, as well as other authors for her stagecoach book. She did not own Lucia's book, nor did she have it beside her when she wrote; his book was not in their regional library and had to be borrowed on an inter-library loan.

Without question, the portrait of Ben Holladay in her book was a composite of all she had ever read about him, but he was not the driving force of her novel. Janice listed an impressive bibliography in her letter to Ollie, citing twenty authors, some with several books that she had read specifically for *Six-Horse Hitch.* "I could go on and on, for the field is vast. As Bernard DeVoto used to say, 'the literature of the West is so vast as to be almost endless.' One reads hundreds and hundreds of books simply for the background and the feel of the period, and hopefully for just one more small fact." At the time, Janice Holt Giles had almost eight hundred titles in her personal library that lined the walls of the log house. Janice assured Ollie, "Had there been only one book about Ben Holladay, had he never been examined in dozens of books in literature, had that one book been Mr. Lucia's biography, he would have a case. As it is, his book provided a few more facts to the whole, enormous personality and portrait of the man. My book could have been written entirely without Lucia's book, and would have been if I hadn't found him listed in Ralph Moody's bibliography, 1967. I said plainly in the Author's Note in the front of the book that only the Fowler and Westmoreland families and the Indian, Popo, were fictional. All the other characters are real. This is a plain statement that this book is *history,* and that I was not trying to pass off any of the historical figures or events or facts as my own invention." She closed, "I hope this will satisfy Mr. Meyers' apprehensions."

During the height of her frustrations over Lucia's attack, Janice wrote her friend Joe Covington in Bowling Green, "Work is always my therapy, or has been, but how much longer I *can* write is always a question in my mind, and how many more books are there in me?" Janice invited Joe to come visit them soon and revealed, "I've not been too well lately. Hypertensive high blood pressure combined with a kidney infection have kept me dragged down. Physically I have been sort of crocky most of the summer."

In reference to *Six-Horse Hitch*, Ollie Swan mailed Janice a copy of a letter he received from L. Arnold Weissberger, Weissberger and Frosch, Counselors at Law, New York, New York, which stated, "While Miss Holt's letter is very persuasive, I am afraid that it does not help our situation. We are faced, it seems to me, with the inevitable prospect of a lawsuit. The existence of Mr. Lucia's claim and the possibility of a lawsuit would effectually prevent Mr. Meyers from financing a motion picture based on Miss Holt's book.

"I happen to represent the author of *The Great White Hope*, who is being sued for plagiarism by a writer whose claims are very much like Mr. Lucia's claims against Miss Holt, and Miss Holt's letter is, mutatis mutandis, a précis of the nature of my client's defense. We do not believe that the Plaintiff has any case, but that has not prevented him from suing. The Plaintiff's action was brought at a time when the motion picture was al ready far advanced, but I am certain that if the Plaintiff had made his claim before we entered into our contract with a motion picture company, we would not have been able to make the contract without first disposing of the claim.

"My point is that Miss Holt must persuade not us, but Mr. Lucia. Unless Mr. Lucia agrees in writing to withdraw his claim, Mr. Meyers has no recourse except to ask for rescission of the contract with Miss Holt, and a return of the $2,500 advance heretofore paid."

It is not surprising that Janice wrote Ollie September 22 that she had been back in the hospital, "with a *new* kind of kidney infection. Thinking it was the same old thing I took the medication prescribed for the other. It not only failed to work but did considerable damage so that I wound up with a temperature, the blood pressure up a little, and another series of tests to sweat out. How many different kinds are there? Anyhow, I came home yesterday and am so glad to be at home, but still feel pretty weak. I *loathe* hospitals!"

On the morning of October 2, 1970, Ollie called Janice with news she felt "simply too good to be true!" Ollie, himself "bubbling over with joy," informed Janice that *Reader's Digest* had taken *Six-Horse Hitch* for their spring 1971 condensed book club edition with twenty-five thousand dollars payable on signature, which was "about half what could be expected in the long run." Janice wrote Anne the same day, exclaiming, "I just can't take it in yet! You can imagine how I feel, after all these years of plugging along to finally hit the jackpot."

On October 5 Janice wrote Ollie that, since he thought it was a good idea to get a contract on *Around Our House*, she preferred to go ahead and take the advance. "The conditions on which I asked for deferment of payment have changed, and our income this year, Henry tells me, is low enough we can take that advance without materially affecting the income tax. It seems the checking account is unbelievably low and Henry was counting on Meyers' payment in September to see us through. So . . . Either we must have the advance on *Around Our House* or I must ask for an advance in royalties from Houghton Mifflin. If the *Reader's Digest* contract pays off anytime within the next three or four weeks, $2,000 of that would see us through. If it isn't one thing to worry me, it seems to be another, doesn't it?" She also told Ollie, "I have been so ill and so upset over this Lucia business that I couldn't even rejoice over the *Reader's Digest* deal until you called. Thank you so much for that telephone call, for it literally lifted me from despair into a new human being. I know you to be the soul of honor, and if you do not regard Lucia as a threat to the book club contract, then neither shall I. I shall simply rejoice over the whole thing."

With revisions enclosed for the manuscript of *Around Our House,* Janice concluded, "I am going to take a good long rest from writing, probably several months. I'm caught up and ahead and there is no point in pushing *Kinta,* or any other book just now. I have in mind much reading, some research for another novel, etc."

Anne responded that she hoped Janice really would rest and not push herself on *Kinta* or anything else. "We are certainly in no mood to push you. *The Damned Engineers* is going strong (we have just gone back to press) and we have the two reprint novels coming in February and *Around Our House* for the fall. So do relax and take it easy."

The year 1970 had been ravaging to Janice's spirit. In November Ollie regretfully informed her that Edward Meyers felt he could not go forward with the movie based on *Six-Horse Hitch.* Janice responded that no one regretted it more than she did. "I absolutely do not recognize the claim that has been made against the book, but apparently a valid claim does not have to be made for it to be legal for Mr. Meyers to ask for and receive a rescission of our contract. Under those circumstances I do hereby agree to that rescission and I will repay the $2500 advanced to me on March 25, 1970. This affair has been shocking and horrible to me. I am glad to have it concluded without further delay." Janice had long desired that one of her novels become a motion picture, and Ellis Lucia had destroyed all hopes for the production of *Six-Horse Hitch.* That the book was picked up by *Reader's Digest* was extremely gratifying, but a movie would have been the crowning success. Lucia was not successful in his lawsuit, but the damage to the soul of the one he accused was beyond monetary reimbursement.

In his December 17 column, Henry wrote, "On Sunday night of December 13th, I drove into Columbia to see Janice at the hospital. Going there and back the Christmas lights in and around many of the houses were truly something to see. While at the hospital some carolers marched through the corridors singing Christmas songs. They must certainly have lifted the spirits of patients there at the time. Janice and I thought so. The carolers' voices were subdued and beautiful." Janice's weary spirit needed lifting from all the cruel accusations in the year of 1970.

In "Spout Springs Splashes," Wednesday, February 16, 1971, Henry wrote of a confusing malady that had stricken him while he was riding his tractor down the hollow, dragging some logs to go around the tobacco bed. All of a sudden he felt like he was going to fall, not faint, just the feeling that he was going to fall. It happened several more times that day and the next, so he decided to see a doctor. The nurse checked his blood pressure, urine, and temperature; and while writing on his chart told him, "We're having a hard time finding anything wrong with you."

Henry then entered the doctor's office where the doctor told him simply but in a "highly professional, roundabout way, 'You're getting old.'" The doctor said that, after forty, certain things started happening. Henry said, "I wanted to tell him that after forty certain things STOP happening." The doctor prescribed some pills and told Henry to slow down some, and since then he had "not had a spell."

"Slow down, the good Doctor said. I hardly see how I can do that, because I am just naturally a slowed down person. I practice it daily. And if there is a need to quicken my pace, I merely get started earlier then go at my regular slowed down pace. But, if I should slow down much more in my daily goings about, I'd soon be going the other way." The article appeared five months before Henry's fifty-fifth birthday.

On April 5 Janice informed Anne, "I am home once again from the hospital but feeling far from myself. Each of the bouts takes a toll. This was both high blood pressure and a more serious kidney infection. The doctor says I am worrying because I can't work and that I *must* stop that. I shall do my best to try, but writing is not really a profession, you know, it's an obsession. You get hooked on it just as a drug addict gets hooked and not to get to that desk and typewriter every day gives me such a lost and useless feeling. But if I am ever to be healthy again I must do what he says.

"There was also this worry about the income tax. We ought not to have to need advances to take care of that. But Henry manages our finances and somehow or other nearly every year we come up short at income tax time! He *must* put aside enough of the enormous amounts that will be coming in this year to take care of it next year. I can't go on worrying about this kind of thing. Well, I shall do the best I can and hope it's good enough."

Anne, who had sent Henry fifteen hundred dollars while Janice was in the hospital, assured her by return mail that there was a lot more where that came from and insisted that she was not to worry about money. "Do take care of yourself," Anne remarked. "Perhaps the spring and the beauties of the countryside will be a help." Janice thanked her for her kindness and the burden of worry she had lifted. "When I was fretful over what I felt was some mismanagement of finances, I forgot that my doctor, medical and drug bills had been astronomical this year. And they must all be paid cash on the barrel head, naturally. Actually, nobody can afford, even with insurance, to be ill any more. We can't really afford to die!"

On April 10 Janice wrote Anne that her brother, John, had had open-heart surgery on April 2 at St. Luke's in Houston. "He is far from out of danger yet, but nothing terribly unusual or unexpected has come up. He should be out of the coronary care unit by tomorrow if all goes well. I have been uneasy, of course, but believe it or not the moment my doctor heard about John he made me come in for a blood pressure test and it was a nice, low 140! The medication he gives me is wonderful, I'm sure."

By the end of April, Dr. Todd Jeffries decided it would be wisest to let Janice write an hour or two a day rather than keep her from it altogether. "I know it is wiser," Janice declared. "No tension caused by the writing can possibly do me the harm the prohibition has done and it is very understanding of him finally to realize that." Janice picked up the *Kinta* manuscript again. "It will be slow going but perhaps it will be a better book for that. I have always written too fast."

In May Libby spent two weeks with her mother. Janice always looked forward to her May and October visits. "It was delightful to have her but such a lost feeling when she left last week," Janice told Anne. "However, I am so fortunate to see as much of her as I do. *Kinta is* coming slowly along. Libby read as much of it as is finished and loved it. I asked her to be quite objective and she said she was and that she found it too interesting to put down."

In addition to the German translation, Janice received a contract the first of August on the Spanish translation for their Reader's Digest Book Club. "It was a surprise to me," she wrote Paul Reynolds, "but perhaps shouldn't have been since Spain colonized New Mexico and had much to do with the opening of the West." Additional good news was announced in a letter from Anne on August 20, 1971. "I have been hoping that the sales for *Around Our House* would reach 6,000 by publication day and sure enough, they did."

In her letter of August 24, Janice thanked her friend Joe Covington for "such nice, appreciative words about the new book." Eight years after the death of Lucy Holt, she was continuing to commiserate with Joe over the loss of their mothers. "I still feel like a 'motherless child' occasionally—which of course we are once our mothers are gone," she wrote. "Somehow it never seems possible, even though we know they are reaching that age, that they can leave us. They are just so invincible that even death doesn't seem possible." Janice continued her letter, "Joe, this has been the roughest year of my life physically and I am truly glad to see the summer coming to an end with its trying heat. As you know, I have hypertension, which is enough of a trial. One day up, the next day down, with so much nervous tension. Then just recently I had a particularly vicious siege with a virus of some kind which put me in the hospital for ten days. I'm home again, obviously, and feeling fairly well, but mysterious viruses I can do without, particularly when they're gastric and keep me from eating. But perhaps the worst is over now. I do hope so.

"We will all get together again some day. There's an old Cherokee saying, 'Keep a green bough in your heart and a bird will sing.' I do try to keep that green bough and keep hoping the bird will soon sing again!"

29
Act of Contrition
1971-1973

In late August 1971, Janice wrote Anne Barrett, "You'll be glad to know that *Kinta* is nearly finished. Two or three more chapters is all I lack. I have taken so much time on it, but my interest in it has never flagged." Janice wondered if it would be better to call the book *The Kinta Years* as just *Kinta* had little meaning for the public. Anne was delighted with her progress and the new title for the book. She was also happy to tell Janice that *Around Our House* was very close to seven thousand in sales. Later in the month, Janice received the "wonderful news" that the Christian Herald Family Bookshelf had decided to take *The Enduring Hills.* She wondered if they would be interested in *Tara's Healing,* still bemoaning the "despised" title that had been suggested by John Beecroft.

In early fall Janice retyped *The Kinta Years* before writing the last two chapters. It had been so long since she started the book, she felt the familiarization in preparing the final copy would help her in composing the conclusion. Describing the book to Ollie, Janice said, "It deals with the six formative years of my life, from four to ten, when we lived in that small town in what had been the Choctaw Nation. It has one chapter on the history of the Choctaws, because the last Principal Chief of the Nation was still living when we moved there and his grandchildren were our closest playmates." Janice acknowledged "an immense debt of gratitude" to sisters Corinne Moore Rabon and Inez Moore Von Derau, her childhood playmates, for "willingness to help in reviving and reinforcing the old memories of the Kinta years." The completed manuscript was mailed at the end of November.

Anne Barrett informed Janice on December 20 that she and Ruth Hapgood had read *The Kinta Years* and that, while they both had had fun reading it and had found it a potentially "charming and touching story," they felt it was "not quite right" and needed more work. "There are wonderful moments, such as the child Janice climbing to the top of the barn and seeing the whole world spread out before her, but, curiously enough, that child (the real you) is not as clear to either Ruth or me as Katie in *The Plum Thicket* (the fictionalized you) was. We have wondered whether shifting the narration into the third person and fictionalizing the story to the extent of using more dialogue might make it more real to the reader, paradoxical as that may seem. We are not suggesting that you falsify anything. The little girl would still be Janice and she would still be you but writing about her in the third person might enable you to write more freely. It is a device that has been used before, sometimes with considerable success."

Janice was always appreciative of constructive criticism and, fueled by editorial suggestions, accepted the challenge to rewrite with an optimistic spirit; however, she felt repelled by the idea of shifting to third person and using false objectivity in the writing. Nonetheless, once the holidays were behind her she diligently "set to work" on *The Kinta Years*, inserting more conversations and a few livelier descriptions. "I think the book will be greatly helped," she wrote Ollie. "I just could not see putting it into third person. I recall how irritated I got when reading Jon and Rumer Godden's *Two Under the Indian Sun*, when they shifted constantly from third, talking about Jon and Rumer, into first as a family. And I should certainly have had to do that."

Janice explained that during most of the writing of the second half of *The Kinta Years* she was allowed to work only two hours a day by her doctor and was on medication most of the time. "I think some of my sluggishness during that period crept into that section. I want to do the rewriting carefully, but as you know I work rather swiftly, so it shouldn't be too long before it is finished. Henry picked up some kind of virus the Wednesday before Christmas and it rather spoiled the holidays for him (for me, too, because I do worry so when he isn't well!). He's well over it now, though."

Three weeks later Janice sent Anne the revised work saying, "I think I've now done my best on this book. It does read livelier and I hope Janice comes alive as you would like her to." Except for needing to make a few deletions to shorten the length, Anne was pleased with the rewrite. "I love the way you have brought your book full circle, beginning with the first meeting with Corinne and ending with the parting—an ending that brought a lump into my throat."

The author bio for *Six-Horse Hitch* in the *Reader's Digest* edition stated: "Slim and handsome, Janice Holt Giles is today one of the country's most respected and popular historical novelists. Many of her books, like *The Enduring Hills* and *The Believers*, are set in the Kentucky hills. Others, like *Johnny* Osage and *Six-Horse Hitch,* are set in the West that she knew as a child and which she often visits."

In addition to the German and Spanish translations of *Six-Horse Hitch,* Paul Reynolds announced in January that it would also appear in a French interpretation. On March 28, 1972, Janice's sixty-seventh birthday, Ollie mailed her an agreement to be signed for a Norwegian edition. She returned the contract telling him how pleased she was with the news. She added, "Winter is almost over, surely in New York as well as down here. But do take care, Ollie. You and Anne Barrett and I are all growing older together. And we must all take care. I can't do without either of you!"

Ollie sent more good news on March 31: Houghton Mifflin was preparing an advance of five thousand dollars for *The Kinta Years.* "I could hardly believe my eyes," Janice wrote when she saw the amount, as the only other time she had received that figure was for *Six-Horse Hitch.* The sizable advance reflected the confident editorial judgment of the talent and character recognized in her work. Ollie also informed Janice that Paperback Library was reissuing *The Kentuckians* and *Hannah Fowler* with new covers.

Houghton Mifflin sent Janice a gratis copy of *The Patton Papers* by Dr. Martin Blumenson. After reading the book, Janice wrote Dr. Blumenson a congratulatory note: "I know what an exciting challenge it must have been to you to have the Patton family ask you to edit these papers, how much hard work the editing required, but how much satisfaction the work gave you in the long run. Nothing makes a man so real, brings out his best and his worst, as his own letters and diaries. You have done *such* a good job with these papers. I feel as if I know Patton much better now—his good qualities show up so well, as well as some of his worst. There is no doubt the man truly loved war. Perhaps all generals do. Wasn't it Lee, watching from the heights of Fredericksburg who said, 'It is a good thing war is such hell. We should come to love it too much otherwise.' I want to tell you how very much I have liked your handling of the papers and to congratulate you on an extremely good book."

A few days after writing Dr. Blumenson, Janice sent Anne a copy of a complimentary letter she had received and remarked, "A letter like this makes writing, with all its hard work and tensions, well worthwhile, doesn't it? Of course not all my fan mail gives me such a nice feeling of having been helpful, but Anne, do you know that in my entire writing career I have never received an ugly or nasty letter? I get from twenty to thirty fan letters a week and they are all simply warm and generous thanks. That's something of a record I'm sure. Of course, popular success is considered mediocrity, but I'll take it and be grateful for it."

With *The Kinta Years* completed and thoughts turning to the next project, Janice inquired if Ollie would reexamine "that old book of mine written in 1957 called *Walk on the Water.*" She told him she wanted to revise the manuscript dealing with the rules of the Catholic church and change the title to *Act of Contrition.* When Janice had first submitted it, Ollie had discouraged her, feeling that the subject matter would antagonize John Beecroft and hurt her reputation. "I think we had better say nothing to Houghton Mifflin about this until you have seen it," she wrote. "I did not have, at the time of the first writing, the international reputation I now have, and while I might get a few rude fan letters, I think the book would sell well generally. By today's standards it *is* pretty innocuous and if I do say so myself it is a beautifully written book. I think, also, it might be very timely with the resentment among Catholics generally concerning divorce and marriage and with even priests willing to be excommunicated in order to marry."

Janice also shared another idea she had in mind for the forthcoming winter. She had a collection of some seventeen short stories and wanted to publish them in a book titled *The Gift.* Ollie responded that he would be happy to look again at "what seems to me to be a much better title, *Act of Contrition*" but was afraid he was a bit pessimistic about the proposed collection of short stories unless she could find "some sort of peg to hang them on or some central theme."

By July 15, 1972, Janice had revised *Act of Contrition* and mailed it to Ollie, stating, "It is a *good* book, the love scenes are very beautifully and delicately handled, and, as I said before, I think it would be very timely just now with the row over celibacy for priests and nuns, many of them leaving the church to marry." Janice was very optimistic about *Act of Contrition* and hoped, with the "barrier of Mr. Beecroft removed," it would have excellent sales.

The ensuing correspondence from the last of July 1972 to the end of December reflects a period of difficult months in Janice's physical health and emotional well-being. The correspondence, which largely addresses book proposals and finances, is less carefully typed and is, at times, somewhat incoherent. Janice was distressed with Ollie over financial matters because not since *The Great Adventure* had he included the clause that she need not take more than $20,000 per year in royalties, and she blamed him for their having to pay additional taxes to the IRS. In a letter to Craig Wylie dated July 22, Janice wrote, "I feel bitter about having to be a watchdog for Ollie, who is paid a commission to look after my affairs," and yet wrote Ollie on July 28, "Thank you for all your efforts. I do trust and have such faith in you."

Responding to a lack of interest in her most recent submission, Janice wrote Ollie in a most uncharacteristic manner on August 3: "If Mr. Wylie is not grateful enough for my performance for Houghton Mifflin all through the years, I must ask you, reluctantly, to take *Act of Contrition* to another publisher. I feel just that bitter about the situation and you can imagine what this whole thing has done to my blood pressure. My doctor is furious with you, with Houghton Mifflin, with the whole deal because he knows how hard I have worked, he knows how much I am entitled to, and that I have actually broken my health down to keep our heads above water."

A string of letters were written to Ollie in August with inquiries concerning a reprint of *The Plum Thicket*, a book of her letters to him and to Houghton Mifflin, a revision of *My Darling Daughter*, a book titled *Letters from Libby* based on her daughter's correspondence relating the growth and activities of the grandsons, a *Janice Holt Giles Reader* including her short stories and some of her early poetry, reprinting *Harbin's Ridge* using both her and Henry's names, and even reconsidering the old manuscript, *The Mill Wheel*. Ideally those titles could keep her published annually through 1977.

The perplexity of the correspondence is obvious in Ollie's response August 7, "This will acknowledge and thank you for your last four letters, two of which were dated August 3rd and the other two August 4th of which the earlier letter written August 3rd arrived Friday and the other three this morning." He tried to answer each of Janice's requests and suggestions including that he submit *Shady Grove* for a television series since *The Beverly Hillbillies* had just gone off the air.

Janice apologized August 9 for getting everything confused and, in her old, kind manner, told Ollie, "I just don't care one bit whether H.M. take *Act of Contrition* or not, and I have decided not to ask you to take it elsewhere. Nor do I care whether they take the *Janice Holt Giles Reader*. At my age, I have no fresh ideas and if they are willing to call it finished, so am I!" She also told him, "*The Mill Wheel* is dead. I had only written 115 pages of it and didn't know how to get any further with it. Besides, my doctor doesn't think I should do another novel. It's too great a strain and my hypertension is under beautiful control." In the second letter of the same date, Janice wrote, "I'm sorry if Houghton Mifflin don't like *Act of Contrition*. I had hoped to end my writing years with them, but I meant it when I said for you to take it elsewhere if they turned it down. Perhaps another publisher won't be so squeamish about it. I know they mean well, but you surely told them that Mr. Beecroft's death had made the difference and that I was prepared for the enmity of some Catholic people. I should probably get some rude letters and they can be thrown away."

Anne Barrett explained to Janice that, even though there was a new atmosphere of relaxation in the Catholic church and the story she wrote was true to life at the time she wrote it, the point was no longer a major issue. Janice responded in several letters defending her stance. She told Anne, "If it's the sex that bothers you about *Act of Contrition*, that is quite easily remedied. I would only have to rewrite three pages. But if it's the Catholicism thing, it's irremediable."

On August 16, Ollie attempted to answer another stream of letters explaining that *Shady Grove* had been submitted extensively in 1967 and that he would offer it again, that he was sorry *Act of Contrition* was not enthusiastically received by Houghton Mifflin, that he was still not entirely clear what she wanted to do about the income limitation clause for *Tara's Healing* and/or *The Kinta Years*, and that it was premature to discuss income clauses for *With Love, Grandma*, the *Janice Holt Giles Reader*, and *Yes, My Darling Daughter*.

Janice again changed her mind about *Act of Contrition* and told Anne she wanted Houghton Mifflin to let Dick McAdoo read it. "I think I would like him to know that I disagree with your decision. I don't see what earthly harm it could do to publish the book, whatever your opinions, so why not go ahead as I do so very much want it published. However, if you still decide you can't publish, I shan't take it elsewhere. As I said before, I'll stay with H.M. to the end, although I certainly do think it would be published by someone else."

Ollie Swan and Anne Barrett deeply respected their long-term client and were most kind to her in their responding letters during this difficult period. Ollie began his letter of August 23, "Many thanks for your three letters dated August 25th (although I suspect they were written on the 18th); also for the copy of your letter of the same date to Anne Barrett and most recently your letter received today dated August 28th (although once again I suspect that this was probably written on or about the 21st)."

In early September Janice wrote that she was glad to be back at work again. "I am going to try to finish the Cartwright's Mill novel first—then from there on I doubt there'll be any more novels. I don't have the first novel in mind." Through the years Janice had expressed a great fear of "writing herself out." Since the publication of her first book, *The Endur-*

ing Hills, in 1950, she had seen twenty-one additional titles appear in print, had received numerous honors and awards, and had established an international reputation. She was physically ill, but she was not ready to quit. The first week of September, she mailed Ollie the manuscript for the *Giles Reader*.

When she received the galleys for *The Kinta Years* on September 18, 1972, Janice wrote Anne, "I simply don't feel well enough any more to wade through them and make the corrections. So if you don't mind I'm just going to bundle the proofs back up. I know that what you wanted done is all right."

Learning that Janice was hospitalized again, Anne wrote October 5, "It is a great relief to know that your heart is all right" and cautioned her, "Take care of yourself and don't start doing too much too soon." She was delighted to inform Janice that Houghton Mifflin had decided to reissue *The Plum Thicket* and *Harbin's Ridge*.

On November 6, 1972, Janice wrote Anne, "I am at home again, and as well as I probably ever will be. But there is no doubt I have a crocky heart and must write less for a few months at least. Libby came to be with me when I came out of the hospital and we drove our new Ford LTD to Santa Fe where I spent almost three weeks regaining my strength. But Henry came after me Friday and I must say this old log house looked mighty good to me! It's so good to be able to be off the invalid list again! And fun to be writing to you and taking care of my own affairs once more."

On the same date she wrote Ollie that she was back and "ready to pick up my work on the new book. In the meantime I have been re-thinking the situation with regard to *Act of Contrition.* I think we can try it with several publishers and still keep me with H.M. by simply saying they have a prior option on my work. Do whatever you think best. Hope you are well. We all seem to be getting a little crocky as we grow older, but we have certainly had some beautiful years together."

Concerning *Act of Contrition,* Ollie wrote, "I'll do whatever you like although quite honestly my heart wouldn't be in it and I am still a little doubtful whether any really good publisher would want to take it on. On the other hand its publication might cause mild offense among some of your readers which I think would be unfortunate and which of course could be avoided if you were willing to have it published under a pseudonym." He did, however, submit the manuscript once more, to which Janice responded, "I have your note saying you have sent *Act of Contrition* to Doubleday. If they like it, go ahead and let them have an option. The book I am working on now is called *Dear Boys* and is the old book

Paul Brooks turned down years ago. If Doubleday like *Act of Contrition* and take it, then like *Dear Boys,* fine. Anne Barrett is having to retire next year and when she's gone I have no further dear ties with Houghton Mifflin and had just as soon be with any other publisher. My last dear link when Anne has retired is you. Wherever you want to take me, I'll willingly go. Just don't you retire on me! *That* day, I quit writing! For I can't do without you."

Janice wrote Richard McAdoo, editor-in-chief at Houghton Mifflin, November 21, 1972, that she received word that the Five Civilized Tribes Museum wanted to plan the premiere of *The Kinta Years.* "I plan to visit my brother, who has bought our old homeplace in Fort Smith, Arkansas, for a week at Christmas. It has occurred to me that if the book is ready we might jump the gun on its release for this occasion during my week in Arkansas. John, my brother, could drive me to Muskogee and I think I could promise that he and Phil Harris, City Editor of the *Muskogee Phoenix* would see to it that the party was well organized, that the autographing line was kept moving briskly, that I would have rest periods about every two hours. If so, my doctor would allow it. You may not have heard about my crocky heart, but the doctor had forbidden the autographing party, since obviously it would be an all-day affair unless it was extremely well organized. I think someone from Houghton Mifflin should also be present. Doubtless there will be a banquet or dinner that night. I think perhaps Mr. Wylie might be the proper person to fly down and speak for me at such an affair—or if there is no such dinner party, then simply be present to lend some prestige from the house to the affair."

Janice inquired of Ollie in late November as to how much her December royalties would be because she was thinking about buying a piece of investment property next door to her brother in Fort Smith, where she and Henry could spend the winter. Writing Anne, she said, "Have a nice Christmas dear. I'm going home! John has bought Mama's old place and it will be exactly like seeing her and Dad again. Henry will come after me." On December 7 Janice wrote, "I've got the flu or some sort of crud. Do hope it clears up so we can make our trip to Arkansas for Christmas! Feel much better today. The doctor has prescribed some sort of medicine and has told me my blood sugar is low and I must drink sherry! That is nice medicine, isn't it?"

On December 28 Janice wrote Anne, "I hope you had a lovely Christmas. It goes without saying that I did. The biggest surprise was that just before I left, Henry gave me a lovely new diamond ring. I had worn the one my first husband gave me all these years and he decided it was high time he gave me one himself. Needless to say I wear it with great pride. I don't think I shall be able to return for the publication of *The Kinta Years* in March. The doctor says no."

To begin the New Year 1973, Janice wrote Ollie on the second, "It is somehow appropriate that the first letter I write would be to you! How many, many letters we have exchanged over the twenty-three years of our relationship. Just let *Act of Contrition* go unless you really think it has a chance. I'm fairly convinced, now, that it is too dated and that H.M.'s judgment was right. You needn't even bother to return it. Just scrap it.

"I hope your holidays were great fun, that some of your family could be with you and that this new year brings all of us good health and continued prosperity."

30
Recognition
1973-1978

Sadly, the 1973 New Year did not bring Janice good health. In January she had a severe upper respiratory infection and suffered with angina. Her heart condition forced her to "be practically on bed rest," with doctor's orders to remain that way for some time.

Regrettably, Janice was unable to attend the presentation luncheon of *The Kinta Years: An Oklahoma Childhood* on February 10 at the Civic Center in Muskogee, Oklahoma. Her brother, John, and sister, Mary, were guests of honor. Remarks were made by Dr. Arrell M. Gibson, head of the Department of History, University of Oklahoma, after which Rev. Otway Rabon, husband of Janice's childhood friend, Corinne Moore Rabon, gave the benediction.

Janice wrote Libby, "There is a peculiar loneliness to being ill, when the whole world seems to be in good health all around you. You feel so left out of things. Your normal life, and all your control of it, suddenly is upset. It takes getting used to." Having been a strong, vibrant woman, inactivity was a very unnatural state for Janice that did indeed take some getting used to.

In early September 1973 Ollie submitted five Janice Holt Giles titles to Joanne Brough of CBS to consider for television motion pictures. Brough responded she personally found Giles's work delightful but, unfortunately, *The Believers, Shady Grove, Johnny Osage, Hannah Fowler,* and *The Kentuckians* did not fit their current program needs.

Janice received a letter from Suzanne Cassidy of Lexington, Kentucky, soliciting a manuscript for *The Bluegrass Woman,* a new quarterly she was editing. She responded in December that all her short stories and articles had been compiled into a book, *The Giles Reader,* to be published by Houghton Mifflin, but she did have some poems written when she and Henry were engaged and he was overseas. She hoped Cassidy might select one or two of the poems.

Included in the eleven untitled "Songs for Henry" was a poem expressing Janice's seeming self-content when she met Henry Giles:

I thought I had my life all planned,
So poised and sure was I.
You came along and touched my hand;
My plans began to die.
I thought I knew all that I wanted
Was work, and strength, and peace.
You smiled at me, and whispered,
And all my dreams have ceased.
"I am secure," my heart had cried,
"For me love has no part."
You kissed me once, and now, my dear,
A fire burns in my heart.

Janice's physical condition continued to dictate limited activity in 1973, and 1974 began with the prospects of the same. On February 9 she wrote Ollie that she was having more difficulty with her angina and had been taken temporarily off all work for a while. "The doctor says something about the tension and strain of getting into the characters affects me."

In addition to physical problems, Janice was burdened with grief. Her beloved brother, John Holt, had died February 21, 1974. "Because of my own crocky heart," Janice wrote Joe Covington, "my doctor wouldn't let me go to Fort Smith for the funeral. This was hard to bear, but he said I might wind up in the hospital myself and be a burden to everybody."

In May Ollie Swan sent Janice news that she had long dreaded. He and Paul Reynolds were retiring in July, although Paul would probably continue as a consultant. Ollie explained that he would become an associate of the Julian Bach Agency with an office in New York beginning July 1 and would be happy to continue representing her and her books should she so desire. He wanted to make it clear that the Reynolds office would also be delighted for her to remain their client, so the choice was up to her.

In late June Janice wrote she had been in the hospital six weeks and remarked, "I do so hate to lose you, but then I'm retired too. I can't type anymore without getting chest pains, and that was the very thing I was hospitalized for so, no more books." In an attitude reflective of her ill health, Janice added, "I take it Houghton Mifflin aren't going to publish the *Giles Reader.* I couldn't care less. I have *Dear Boys* which I'd like them to see, and *Yes, My Darling Daughter.* Then that's the end of Janice Holt Giles' career."

Indicative of their friendship and her appreciation of Janice's work, Anne Barrett wrote Ollie concerning *The Giles Reader.* "One point that worried me was that a few of the best pieces have been used—generally in slightly different form—in *Around Our House* and some of the other books. Ruth Hapgood suggested that we capitalize on this by saying in effect, 'This is how it started.' This seems well worth considering, but I am too rusty on the *Reader*'s contents to be sure how well it would work.

"The next step is to hole up with the whole lot and select the best and the ones that fit together so that the collection has some consistent theme. This shouldn't be hard. I'll get to it as soon as I can clear up the things I am now involved in and will let you know what results. But I feel fairly certain that a book of some sort will emerge."

Later, Anne wrote, "All that is needed is a title more descriptive of the book's theme, an updated introduction and how some of the short pieces were transmuted into books, which would also have the additional advantage of keeping the books themselves in the public eye." Anne felt they could expect only modest sales from the *Reader* but that it would appeal to the truly devoted admirers of Janice's books.

In his letter enclosed with *The Giles Reader* contract, Ollie asked Janice if she would feel up to doing the editorial work for the book. If not, Anne indicated that she would get it done and submit the results for her approval. A letter written by Henry dated September 27 responded, "Here are the signed contracts for *The Giles Reader*. Janice is in a nursing home again with a complication of ailments, so I took the contracts for her to sign. You can see by her signature that she is rather shaky. She didn't look over the contracts or ask what the advance was, or if there was an advance; but the advance is adequate.

"You tell Anne Barrett that Janice will not be able to do any editorial work on the manuscript. I am sure that Houghton Mifflin can handle it to our satisfaction. Thank you."

The first week of the New Year 1975, Anne shared her progress on *The Giles Reader* with Ollie, "After mulling over half a dozen unsatisfactory plans for providing a central theme for the collection, I have finally evolved one that seems to work fairly well. Since Janice is not well enough to edit this, I am drawing on her own books. At the beginning of each story or article I am putting a short passage from one of the books or memoirs to show how it relates to her life or her writing. A few of them may seem a bit strained but I think they will pass and I hope they will make the book seem more Janice's and less something concocted by her publisher. We will also have a short foreword to clue the reader in on what the book is. I am grouping the contents in three sections: Kinta, Kentucky, and Spout Springs." Ollie responded that he thought the plan was an excellent one.

A few weeks later Anne defined the progress in a letter to Janice. She explained how she divided the collection into three parts and added, "The only pieces not included in them are the ones on writing, which will come first, right after the foreword that Paul Brooks is going to write, and a poem which I think makes a perfect ending. It begins 'Life—so beautiful, and yet so fraught with tears.' Since the poem had no title and is placed at the end of the book, I simply put 'L'Envoi' before it. Except for the poem, each piece will be preceded by a quotation from one of your books. The idea is to show the relation of these selections to you and to what you have written."

In a reply, Janice expressed her enthusiasm for the work Anne had done and added, "I am feeling fine these days. Not even a headache and the woman Henry got to stay with me as nurse/companion is almost perfect. Her cooking is good, and her only flaw is that she loves soap operas in the afternoon. But I just go in the living room with a book and lie down and the time passes rather quickly. It was so good to hear from you and isn't it nice that my disastrous year is over finally!"

In March a member of the editorial staff at Houghton Mifflin suggested calling the book *Wellspring: A Janice Holt Giles Reader,* which Anne liked. Janice liked it too but could see no use in adding "A Janice Holt Giles Reader." She told Anne, "I am very superstitious about long titles, and think the shorter they are the better they are."

In mid-June Janice sent Ollie the manuscripts of *Dear Boys* and *Yes, My Darling Daughter* and remarked, "These may be the last I can write. As you know I spent a good many months in and out of hospitals last year and don't know whether I am up to writing any more books or not. Hope so, but will have to wait and see how my health does."

Toward the end of July, Janice thanked Ollie for his note with the good news that nine of the frontier series were purchased to be reprinted in paperback by Warner, with *Six-Horse Hitch* still in hardback. "At 70, I think I can be rather proud of my laurels, don't you?" Ollie responded, "Yes, you have every right to be proud of your laurels, and of course, I'm particularly happy that you're happy with the recent good news from Houghton Mifflin."

The decisions concerning *Yes, My Darling Daughter* and *Dear Boys* were not favorable. Receiving the news, Janice told Ollie that "it was worth a try" in submitting the manuscripts but she did not desire him to send them to any other publisher. "As I said before," she wrote, "I can rest on my laurels now."

In August Janice received a letter from Carroll Case of Thousand Oaks, California, inquiring about the motion picture/television status of *Six-Horse Hitch.* If the rights were still available, he wanted to know how much she was asking for an outright sale. He informed Janice that he was co-owner and producer of *Racket Squad* and *Public Defender.* He also produced the series *Frontier* and the first fourteen months of *Sugarfoot* for Warner Brothers. He had independently produced fourteen feature films, including a coproduction of *Two Mules for Sister Sara* with Clint Eastwood and Shirley MacLaine for Universal. Upon receipt of his letter, Janice responded that *Six-Horse Hitch* was "wide open for a movie or television series" but explained to Case the past negotiation with Ellis Lucia and, whether purposely or inadvertently, transposed his name to Lucas. At the end of her letter, Janice told Carroll Case, "If you aren't afraid of Lucas write my agent. I hope you aren't afraid of people and the book can be made into a movie. It would make an excellent one."

In October Janice received the pleasant news that pre-publication sales of *Wellspring* had reached 4,150, but disappointing word came in November that Carroll Case had lost his source of financing to purchase *Six-Horse Hitch.* In relating the news to Ollie, Janice remarked, "Well, I never really counted on it, so I'm not disappointed."

By that time Janice's literary success left little room for disappointment. In February 1957 a statement was made in *The Authors Guild Bulletin* that "In general, novel-writing as a career is just about as secure as betting on the horses. In the United States today there are about fifteen thousand professional writers; that means people who at one time or another have sold something they have written, maybe a four-line poem written for their local newspaper for a $2.50 fee. Of these fifteen thousand, anywhere from twelve to twenty are able to make a living functioning solely as novelists; the rest must pursue some perhaps less satisfying but more profitable writing activity. Or else take a job." In October 1959 John Fischer, editor-in-chief of *Harper's Magazine,* wrote, "The average novelist can rarely hope to earn as much per year as the linotypist who sets his books in type." By 1959 when the article appeared in *Harper's,* Janice Holt Giles had twelve books in print and in her impressive, self-supporting career would see twice that number published.

Ironically, *Six-Horse Hitch,* Janice's last work of fiction, would secure her prosperity. Not only did it receive the attention of movie producers, the *Reader's Digest* contracts were lucrative. In a special supplement, "Writing in America," published by *Harper's Magazine* in October 1959, it was noted that "the average hard-cover book published in this country doesn't sell enough copies to repay the publisher's investment in it." Publishers could only hope to sell their books to the large book clubs, with the largest by far being the Reader's Digest Condensed Book Club, which, in 1959, had two and a half million members and was known to guarantee as much as one hundred thousand dollars in royalties against future sales of a condensed book. The Book-of-the-Month Club, with nearly five hundred thousand members, regularly guaranteed twenty thousand to forty thousand dollars against expected sales. The article reported, "In 1958, 258 million paperback books for adults were sold as compared with 28.2 million hardcover adult 'trade books'—i.e. books of general interest as distinguished from texts. Most of the paperbacks were reprints from hardcover books and the royalties, split equally between the original publisher and the author, were an important source of income to both." Thirteen of Janice's novels were book club selections; *Six-Horse Hitch* was chosen by Reader's Digest Condensed Book Club and selected also for the German, Spanish, French, Norwegian, and Australian editions. The Piney Ridge trilogy and the nine novels in the frontier series were chosen to be reprinted by four paperback publishers: Warner, Fawcett, Avon, and Paperback Library.

The last new title to appear by Janice Holt Giles was *Wellspring* in 1975. On January 28, 1976, she acknowledged the excellent reviews of the book Anne had forwarded to her and added that she was thankful *Wellspring* was "getting any reviews at all as anthologies seldom do." Dr. Wade H. Hall, chairman of the humanities division at Bellarmine College, reviewed the book in the *Louisville Courier-Journal.* Dr. Hall describes the nineteen pieces in *Wellspring* that "span the world of Janice Holt Giles—the geography of her life and fiction, her interest and experiences, and each relates in some way to the twenty books she has hitherto published." He concludes, "Throughout the collection, Mrs. Giles employs her customary lean, spare style. And whether she's writing about religion in Appalachia or a tea for Rose Kennedy in Columbia, Kentucky, there is always a feeling of joy, of excitement. There is always the pulse of life in her words."

In early spring, Houghton Mifflin arranged with Avon for the reissue of the frontier series. With that impetus, Ollie Swan wrote Sharon Edwards of Universal Pictures on April 16, 1976, that he would like for her to explore the possibility of a television series based on the frontier novels by Janice Holt Giles, "which," he explained, "have been a staple backlist item on Houghton Mifflin's list for nearly twenty years and nine of which are being reissued (several for the second and third time) by Avon, starting in May with *The Kentuckians.* There's also another title of hers, which has been optioned to motion pictures on several occasions, although it is not related to the above, called *Six-Horse Hitch,* which I still think would make a wonderful picture."

In June Janice received word that Houghton Mifflin was going to reissue *Harbin's Ridge*. She was extremely pleased and informed Ollie that she would get busy and write the foreword when Anne announced the expected publication date.

On the back of a letter dated September 14 to Linda Glick, acknowledging that the proofs of the *Harbin's Ridge* preface were perfectly satisfactory, Janice had written in large letters: "Have had my breakfast J." The note had been left for Henry, for Janice's physical strength allowed little activity and, after breakfast, she usually returned to bed. After picking up the housekeeper in the mornings, Henry would make his rounds of checking on his parents and brother, stopping by the store to garner news and pass time with the locals, running errands in town, working a bit on the farm, or fooling around in the Becky house, where he had a shortwave radio. Throughout the day he looked in on Janice to see if she needed anything.

The first of November 1976, Anne Barrett sent Janice a copy of the jacket for *Harbin's Ridge* and informed her that she would be retiring at the end of February 1977 and added, "Don't think for a minute that I am planning to vanish into limbo next March. Even if I am no longer at 2 Park Street, I have no intention of losing touch with my friends." Ollie had informed Janice in May 1976 that he was terminating his association with the Julian Bach Agency on July 1 and would associate with a relatively new but enterprising literary agency, Collier Associates in New York. Ollie added, "I think it only fair to tell you that although I have no immediate plans, or target date, for retirement, that such a possibility in the indefinite future cannot be ruled out." How appropriate that the associates to whom Janice had once written, "I can't do without either of you," were reaching retirement near the same time as her own.

In 1966 when Janice received the news that Paperback Library had purchased the rights to reprint all nine of the frontier novels, she wrote Libby: "However much you tell yourself you've done worthwhile work—that your life's work has been and is worth doing—it is a wonderful thing to have others recognize it, too. I have long reached for the recognition that I was not only a novelist, but a historian and educator as well. When I began writing, simply to be a published novelist was grand and glorious to me. But if you grow at all, that comes eventually not to be enough. There has to be a reason for your work—a purpose in it, and the purpose has got to be worth as much as you can reach for, as much as you are capable of imagining and doing. To have it begin to be recognized while you are still living is a nice reward. It's been hard, hard work. Almost any writer who is a craftsman at all can turn out a book each year. But to stretch yourself to do a good book, better if possible than the book before, or all the books before, has some of the elements of crucifixion in it—and self-imposed at that. So it's very nice to have a publishing firm take a good long look at the whole body of work and say, 'This is worth a very wide circulation.'"

By 1978 Janice's health had so deteriorated that she found visitors exhausting and no longer granted interviews. But she was so pleased with her housekeeper, Mabel Daniels, she did not hesitate when Mabel asked if she would talk to her neighbor's daughter, Toni Shelton, a senior at Campbellsville College who needed to interview an author for an English course. Toni Shelton and her mother, Connie Dry, arrived at the log house on Wednesday, April 26, 1978. Janice greeted them warmly and invited them to sit down with her at the kitchen table. Dressed in a nightgown with a sweater around her shoulders, Janice sipped coffee as the young student asked questions about her writing. The following is a portion of the brief interview:

Q: What other kinds of books would you like to write?

A: Oh, nothing, I'm through. I don't have any more ideas for books and I've been ill. I don't know of another single book that I want to write.

Q: You don't have any other plans to write any more fiction or anything?

A: No more. No more books. No, I don't have any . . . I had one about half written [The Mill Wheel] and Houghton Mifflin wanted me to finish it and submit it and I found out when I sat down at the typewriter that I didn't have the energy for it. You know, Mabel works for me because I have been very, very ill. In fact, it was touch and go whether I would even live or not. My doctor thinks that all those years of writing a book every winter—I always wrote in the winter because Libby's little boys used to come in the summertime, and I would try to get through by the first of June because they came the minute their school was out. My doctor says all those years of writing were what caused my illness.

Q: If you had to do it over again, would you?

A: Oh, I sure would! I wouldn't take anything for those books! I mean—it's like a movie we saw on television last night—when you find out what you can do and do well, it gives you more satisfaction than anything in the world. If I had it to do over, I'd do it exactly the same way.

I could write. I really could, and I just discovered it accidentally. We were going to move to Adair County and I thought I'd better make sure we had some way to make a living besides farming.

31
Writing about Writing
1978-1979

Like many other authors, Janice Holt Giles explored the writing profession out of economic necessity and an interest inspired by a passionate love of books. She professed to have devoured an average of five books a week since her youth. "Reading, reading, reading," she declared. "Every writer is an omnivorous reader. Also he is a sponge soaking up impressions and nuances, absorbing everything he sees and hears, and like a pack rat, stores it all away to be pulled out and used later."

William James depicted "writing about writing" as "turning on a light to see the darkness," but Janice gave numerous insightful passages in her autobiographical books and manuscript materials explaining her development, challenges, and exasperations in becoming a novelist and described the craft as "the loneliest profession in the world." "It is accomplished only in solitude and a self-enforced solitude at that. As a writer, no matter what you may want to do, you have got to turn your back and every morning face that desk and typewriter for a given number of hours. You have got to pull out of yourself your philosophies, your emotions, your experiences, your very nervous system itself, the things that go into your book. You have got to create your people, make them believable, move them through a plot, and for nine months of the year live a schizophrenic life in which you are half the time immersed in the life of your book and the other half trying your best to cope with the necessities of being a wife, a housekeeper, a friend, a member of a community, a functioning human being. Most writers have ulcers from the effort. No one except other writers can know or understand the terrific shock to the nervous system and the wear and tear on the physical organs of the body itself which are involved in this long, solitary struggle which we put ourselves through, some of us each year, to write books. Believe me, the ink in any writer's fountain pen is blood, and the price for his appointment with destiny comes high."

For Janice, the most difficult time in writing a novel was just before a book began: "This is the time when I despair of ever breaking through, when I am ready to quit writing altogether, when I vow I will never put myself through such worry and fret and pain and anxiety again. When I tell myself it's not worth it. This is the time when I don't sleep well and when I burn the beans and when I only halfway know I've got a husband or a home or that there is such a thing as food or friends or anything else in the world except that hazy, weird, ghostly feeling of unborn people floating around in my mind, doing unformed things, going round and round and coming out nowhere. This is the time when I am quite capable of passing my friends on the street and never seeing them, of going off into space in the middle of a conversation and of feeling myself a gray ghost in a gray world.

"There does come a time, fortunately, or at least there always has, when with some semblance of certainty you can roll that first page of paper into the typewriter and type page one, Chapter one, on it and start. From then on it is a matter of discipline and sheer hard work. It is no life for the lazy. It is hard, hard work, exacting and nervewracking."

Almost twenty years had passed from the time Janice left Arkansas to begin her work at the Louisville Presbyterian Seminary when she was invited to speak to the Arkansas Library Association on "How One Writer Works." When asked "What are your goals?" she astutely responded: "Quite simply, a body of work which affirms my own faith in the splendor of man. At best one can only choose to do what he believes he can do best. For me, because I am an optimist, because I believe in man and his splendor, it has been to affirm his heroic qualities. And in that great valor of his, that great heart and courage, I base a renewed faith in the indestructibility of the positive values of life. This is what I write about. That is what I will always write about.

"Everything in my life, every radical and waking and known memory has led me along the road of faith and optimism. Every experience of my life, however hard and difficult at the time, has proven to me that life is splendid and that man is truly noble. There is nothing of the defeatist in me and I choose to write that affirmation of my own faith and belief. Like every novelist I have to keep remembering what I am, where I came from, and to use what I have with at least the greatest skill I can summon at that moment.

"Why, then, if writing is so lonely a business, if it takes such a terrific toll in nervous and physical well-being, do I persist in writing? I don't know. I have often wondered what the motive for other writers is. I have no idea what my own motive is, but I do know this—that no matter how frustrated and harassed I may be when I am working, no matter how ill it makes me occasionally, no matter what fatigue or nervous exhaustion I suffer, I am more vitally alive when a book is going than at any other time, and the three months of summer is the whole and entire length of time I can bear not to be at work. I have learned that writing a novel is, for me, a necessity; that between novels, which is never long, I am only half alive and feel an irritable and frustrating barrier between myself and the rest of the world.

"I think perhaps it is the knowledge that however many books have been written, no one else can do precisely what you want to do with a set of characters. They are yours, and in your hands they can say exactly what you want them to say, and you can create with them precisely the new object which has never been made before. One book looks very like another. One plot may greatly resemble many others. But the resemblance ends there. This book of yours is a creative achievement—it has come from your own soul and mind and heart, and it is therefore new, in the way a new-born child is new. Perhaps in our reason for writing lies also our greatest reward.

"What makes a human being keep on writing when it takes months of such hard work to begin with . . . then weeks of anxiety and tension? I don't know, but I have a theory. What made men want to climb Mount Everest? What makes a man choose to be a test pilot? What has sent men time after time to explore the Antarctic? I think it is the challenge and the adventure."

Early in her writing career, Janice recognized the extreme emotional and physical demands of her chosen profession. While working on *Hannah Fowler,* her eighth novel, she explained: "I am writing a good book and I know it. And now I know what it costs to write a *good* book. I know that I cannot ever again write anything less than my best and it may always cost me this division of body and mind and soul. I don't want to pay this price for writing, especially since I shall never be recognized as a literary writer. I shan't last in literature. But I must also face the fact that in spite of this knowledge it is too late to turn back. It is done. It is a fact of my life."

In a letter to Libby in 1965, Janice made some relevant observations about Willa Cather that would in time be apropos to her own life: "She was quite a person, I think. I have always had the feeling she would have written even better if she had ever married, but she believed there was no place for marriage in the 'artist's' life. I disagree there. The flaw in Cather's writing is that in one of the most important areas of life she was not experienced. Emotionally she was never roused and her books are cold in the area of love (except for family love). How a man or woman in love felt was incomprehensible to her, and the relationship between a man and woman was totally unexplored by her. Apparently she never so much as had a date in her life. She would have been unhappy in marriage, very likely—but unhappiness lends much depth to writing. But a genuine artist is enriched by all experience—unhappy as well as happy, and must risk it and make use of it. Cather's people are rarely involved with human relationships. They are involved with places, with things, with the artist's goals—the voice, religion, building and creating—she rarely makes them come to grips with the most urgent and compelling instinct in human nature. But nobody, absolutely nobody, evoked a scene as beautifully as she. You not only see it, you smell it and feel it and hear it and taste it. And she could do it without any waste of words. Perhaps of all American writers she used them the most sparingly and the most effectively. I wish she could have been happier at the end of her life. But she used herself up rather early and when that remarkable vigor and energy were gone, life lost its savor for her. She hadn't the ability, apparently, to use what was left of it more quietly and more contentedly. Well, it takes some doing. Here, also is where a husband could have helped enormously, and children. Cather was left first in nobody's heart when her parents died. When one has to face the shocking fact that the energy to work is beginning to taper off, it is immensely consoling to be able to turn to other creative things—making a home, growing things, and *being*, still, important to others."

Sadly, when Janice's "remarkable vigor and energy" for work tapered, her health did not allow the strength to turn to other creative things, and life began to "lose its savor." Janice's physical limitations caused a slack in her appearance. She didn't "feel good," therefore did not desire to be as attentive to her hair and dress as she always had. Not satisfied with her appearance, she did not wish to see people nor did she have the stamina to entertain.

From the early 1970s, medical problems continued to plague and depress Janice, ironically at a time when she could have enjoyed her success in great financial comfort without the pressing anxiety of having to provide the income. Libby was acutely attuned to her mother's needs, and tried to visit her often, as did the three grown, active grandsons. Because of illness, Janice could no longer travel the long distance to Santa Fe to the home of her only child.

Years before, Janice had acknowledged, "A writer is lost unless he is working. There is a deep inner misery which rides with him through every hour of every lost day. In the work, in it up to my neck, I can put aside everything else and then I am aware only of a certain motion of existence, a certain reality of joy and work and excitement." Without the challenge to her bright mind of researching and writing, Janice experienced dull, lifeless days, preferably alone. She spent them quietly, but without the desire for creativity, not always contentedly, experiencing what she had earlier described as "the dreadful loss of purpose and meaning."

In *The Kinta Years* Janice admitted, "Nobody wants to die. But now my feeling is more that I just don't want to leave this beautiful world and have things go on that I know nothing about. I want to keep my own identity and keep living in this exciting world and know what is happening." After being continually in and out of hospitals and nursing homes in her last years, life ended for Janice Holt Giles at dawn on Friday, June 1, 1979. She died of congestive heart failure in nearby Taylor County Hospital in Campbellsville, Kentucky, less than three months after celebrating her seventy-fourth birthday.

As the news of Janice Holt Giles's death spread throughout Adair County, flags were lowered to half mast in tribute to her life and works and remained there until her burial in the Caldwell Chapel Separate Baptist Church cemetery on June 4. Numerous proclamations appeared in newspapers throughout the region. Columnist Don Edwards of the *Lexington Herald Leader* recognized her as "successful in the best tradition of Kentucky writers of fiction" and acknowledged that Janice was an adopted daughter of the Commonwealth "who loved its land and people as much as any native daughter. She drew from the deep wellspring of Kentucky history for most of her books—which over the years gave her some title to the Green River and Cumberland Valley of Kentucky as her literary territory."

Several pages of the *Columbia Daily Statesman* and the *Adair County News* were filled with articles and photographs in homage to "a Great American." Adair County Judge Executive James C. Brock stated, "Our Nation, our State and especially our County, has suffered a tremendous loss. We will forever be grateful for the contributions she has made to History and our society."

Epilogue

Writing the story of a person's life is like taking a long journey on a road filled with hills and valleys and potholes. There are delightful views and thrilling encounters, and there are dangerous curves and lonely stretches. As I come to the end of my journey in writing Janice Holt Giles's biography, I vividly remember my first visit to her adopted and literary homeland, the ridge country of Adair County in south central Kentucky. Just out of curiosity, I was searching for the woman whose writing had so powerfully touched my heart. I wanted to see and experience her Kentucky home, the place where she had lived out her life and written her books.

On a bright spring Sunday morning in 1983, I left Bowling Green, and drove to Columbia, some seventy miles to the west. On the seat beside me I had a drawing that located the log house that she and her husband Henry had built and that she describes so vividly in *A Little Better than Plumb*. The air was cool as I headed down Highway 551 and wound my way over the narrow road to Knifley.

I passed the Lighthouse Tabernacle, the Plum Point Baptist Church, and the Egypt Christian Church, all with cars dotting their parking lots like so many spring flowers. As I drove along a sun-glistened stream, I scribbled notes on a piece of paper. I saw smoke curling from chimneys that topped small frame houses with tin roofs and long front porches. A large gentleman in bib overalls welcomed me with a friendly wave. I nodded to him and admired the butter-colored daffodils scattered around him in the yard. A little farther on, abandoned trucks and rusted cars competed with the natural beauty of the landscape. Then I spotted my turn-off. A friendly guide at a neighborhood store had given me directions. "Take Caldwell Ridge Road," he said, "and you can't miss their place."

As I drove along Ridge Road, I remembered Janice's words describing her first visit. "The first time I saw the ridge I couldn't believe it. . . . The beauty of the hills made me catch my breath. . . . " Like Janice, I was captivated by the land that she had moved to with Henry in 1949 and that she later called her home. As I traced the same path thirty-four years later, I was excited to actually see what she had seen and described so eloquently in her Piney Ridge Trilogy. I drove slowly, absorbing the region that had awakened and inspired the imagination of a woman who had made it her home and the locale of her life's work.

Before I saw where she lived, I wanted to see where she was laid to rest. I reached the Caldwell Chapel Separate Baptist Church as the service was ending. People were filing out of the simple white church and standing in small groups talking. I pulled into the tiny parking lot and got out of my car. I walked over to a kind-looking woman and introduced myself as a fan of Janice Holt Giles. "Can you tell me where her grave is?" I asked. She said she would be glad to show me and led me to the rear edge of the cemetery. "There," she said, pointing to a stone marker. As I read the words "Kentucky Author" inscribed on the stone, I was overcome with emotion. I thought, "I have found her."

As I stood there entranced, my guide asked, "Have you read *40 Acres and No Mule?* Do you know where that house is?" I said I had read the book but didn't know where the house was. She asked whether I would like to see it, I immediately replied, "Oh, yes!" She said I could follow her car to the house. "By the way," she added, "Helen and Johnnie Lee Giles live there now, and they would be glad to talk to you if you knock on their door."

We pulled out of the churchyard and drove only a short distance before my guide slowed down and pointed to Henry and Janice Holt Giles's first home on the ridge. My heart was racing as I turned into the driveway and walked along a tiny path through the grass to the open front door and knocked on the screen. Moments later, sitting on the porch with Helen Giles and her husband, I felt that Janice had come back to life. At that time, of course, I was but one of her millions of readers; I had no idea that I would someday write her biography. I just wanted to know more about her and see the places where she had lived. I had so many questions. That day with Helen and Henry's cousin, Johnnie Lee, was the beginning of a fourteen-year journey in search of answers.

When I returned to the ridge in May of 1997 with my friend, Jim Stuart, who would become my husband, I felt the same excitement at Janice's log house that I had experienced at her first ridge house. The spirit of her life lingers in the land and in her home. Jim felt it too. He and I have shared many conversations about her, and he has also come to share my passion for her. His bright mind and quiet understanding have helped me sort through many questions my reading and research have raised about her, her books, and her life on Giles Ridge. His wisdom and fresh insights have been indispensable to the completion of this book.

As Jim and I walked around the log house on that warm May day, the beauty of the surrounding hills still evoked their inspiring presence as an ideal place for Janice to write. The cold, crystal-clear water of Spout Springs still flowed down the hillside. The thick grass and tall trees surrounded the log house in shades of lush green. We looked for ginseng—the locals call it "sang"—and dug a bloodroot to examine its brilliant red rhizome. An indigo bunting flitted about the apple tree. The cellar house still held the haunting image of Janice's "fruit jars" filled with good things from Henry's vegetable gardens. These were the images that had been woven through the pattern of daily life for Janice Holt Giles. As we stood beside the lily-covered pond, I recalled Libby's poem, "Spout Springs," which brought her mother's presence even nearer.

> The foggy dew in the hollow,
> at first light,
> is ghost-like misty silence.
> An eerie scene over the pond.
>
> Then a rooster crows
> breaking the quiet.
> Insects flit on the surface of the pond
> silvering the water.
>
> The sun comes through, over the pond,
> Drying the mists and,
> Mama would say,
> "It's going to be another hot day."

As I traced the life of Janice Holt Giles, I had come to know a woman of great courage and determination, a woman of spirit and adventure. Standing there on that lovely spring day, however, I was still left with unanswered questions. Why did a bright woman, serving as the assistant to a dean at a theological seminary, marry a soldier eleven years her junior—a person she knew only from a 48-hour bus ride and 634 letters? And who was Henry Giles? What was his role in her writing? Was she happy in her adopted homeland? When the last book was written, was she happy during her remaining years?

Like a lot of women of her generation, Janice married a young soldier returning from World War II. She had idealized him as he fought a patriotic war thousands of miles from home and wrote her faithfully about his life and his love for her. Still he was a man she hardly knew. With the flair of a romantic novelist, she had first described her marriage to him as "a brilliant scarlet thread" in "the loom of her life"—a relationship that had "added excitement, adventure, love, and happiness." But from the beginning she admitted struggling with "the vast differences" in their temperaments and in their cultural backgrounds and interests.

Although they dealt with these differences in a variety of ways during the early years of their marriage, the situation reached crisis proportions during one of their visits with Janice's mother in Arkansas. When Henry left and went back to Kentucky, Janice at first considered this the end of their marriage. She went on to New Mexico for a planned visit with Libby and her family. But she soon realized that, despite the love and compatibility between mother and daughter, Libby had a family and life of her own. Trying unsuccessfully to concentrate on her writing in the midst of an active, young family, Janice realized that she could not write without Henry or, as she once wrote, "the comfortable knowledge of Henry's presence near me if not in the actual room, then somewhere within calling distance on the farm. As that kind of life becomes acceptable and pleasant, one grows to lean upon it."

Away from Henry in Santa Fe, she realized that there was more genuine happiness between them than she had admitted. Their marriage, she knew, was "basically good" with "sparkle and fun and a common meeting of minds." She finally accepted the fact that she would have to provide the income and that Henry would "always piddle along" but concluded that, in the last analysis, "marriage boils down to one thing—good companionship." Janice resolved to return to their Kentucky ridge and take her place by her husband's side. At that moment, she *committed* herself to her marriage to Henry Giles.

It was a commitment that would last until her death. Henry Giles was deeply rooted to the region of his birth, and he willingly shared that sense of place and security with her. Although she would continue to alternately love and despise the ridge, she was determined to plant herself there by Henry's side. She focused on the positive aspects of their relationship. In spite of her apparent deference to him, Henry allowed Janice to be herself. In spite of their wide differences, he provided her emotional security. While he hunted, fished, and visited his friends at the country store, he was giving her privacy and all the time and space she needed for writing. He was also her chauffeur, companion, and gatekeeper. Moreover, his quiet country folklife had provided her with the setting and subjects for much of her work as a writer.

Without question, Henry had a vital place in the development of his wife's writing career. The material for her Kentucky stories came from his boyhood experiences. Her first books, filled with Henry's rich folk culture, were the catalyst for all the works to come. Their marriage may have seemed impetuous and ill-advised, but it was the necessary component for the literary career that she created. In fact, the ridge and Kentucky generally played a decisive role in her writing. At first, it reflected the displacements of her own childhood and stimulated her as she and Henry moved from house to house and from city to country to city to country. It was this impermanence that led her to create permanent places in her fiction to which she could retreat.

As Janice aged, however, she began to crave "a certainty in life." While adventure and unpredictability had been challenging, she now had the desire for "at least one thing unchanging," her home. The time when she and Henry were building their log house beside a stream of water would come to represent one of the happiest periods of her life. At last she had a home of her own and of her own making.

The life of Janice Holt Giles validates the words of another displaced author, Marjorie Kinnan Rawlings, who wrote from her adopted Florida home: "Human happiness is radically related to place. For a person to find lasting happiness or fulfillment, it is essential for him to find a place with which his spirit can live in harmony, and for a person to live in a place where he is out of harmony with his surroundings would lead to a frustration amounting to a kind of death."

In *A Little Better than Plumb,* Janice explains that before her marriage to Henry and before they built their own house, she had been "as peripatetic a human being as ever lived," having moved "probably forty or fifty times." Constantly on the move, she was "like a homeless child" longing for something and knowing "no more than a child" what it was she wanted. She describes her new feeling when one late summer twilight Henry laid a fire in the new stone fireplace of their log house and lit it. "His eyes flicked at me," she remembers. "But that was what the lost child was looking for. That one brief glance which said I belonged someplace, belonged to *somebody.* This was home." To Janice, it was a moment "when you become real, when you know yourself in your environment, and know that you are forever. And I knew finally and forever the circle was completed."

At the ridge she had developed a deep sense of place that she was able to transfer to her books. This ability to evoke a sense of place in her fiction and nonfiction was one of her greatest gifts as a writer. Readers can experience even her made-up places as if they are real. In *Hannah Fowler* she eloquently expresses her own fondness and longing for a "houseplace." Hannah has escaped from her Indian captors and returns to her log cabin home: "There it was, just the way she had known it would be.

"The ridge looked just like she had known it would look, white all over with the blooms of the sarvis berries and the dogwood trees and the wild plums, with the Judas trees making a little sprinkling of red in between. It was the prettiest hill, the highest and the friendliest of all the hills about.

"The creek was shallow and clear and noisy in its chattering way over the rocks and stones. The meadow was green with rye grass and clover, and it stretched just as long down the valley, just as soft and plushy as it had always done. She felt as if she had been away a year . . . it was so known to her, so dear and so loved.

"The house . . . roomier, stouter even than the old one. She . . . walked all around it, touched it wonderingly. The logs were so bright and clean and sweet smelling. She put her foot on the old doorstone, felt its familiar smoothness through her moccasin. She felt like crying with her gladness. Oh, a house-place, a body's own house-place . . . it was the heart and the beat of a woman's life!"

But Janice was a woman with two homelands. She was a devoted partisan of her adopted state, praising Kentucky's beauty and extolling its heritage. Likewise, when she wrote about her native West, she was excited to be "going home." Kentucky was her new home, but it was the West that coursed through her veins. Even though she was sometimes ambivalent about Kentucky, I believe she cherished both identities. She loved the ridge country, which would become a principal setting for her fiction, and she loved its people who would become characters in it. At the same time, she was a resident outsider who paid lasting tributes to the place and the people in her books, but not in her social interaction with them. Whether through the solitude demanded by writing or her lack of interest in their lives, she withdrew from involvement with the people of the community. She preferred the company of her husband, her daughter, her grandsons, and a few close friends. Perhaps it was this separation from active community life that gave her the perspective and objectivity to preserve it in her fiction.

The hardest question for me has always been, "Was Janice Holt Giles happy at the end of her life?" I have strongly suspected that this master of writing happy endings spent a very sad and depressing existence in her last few years. As a novelist she wanted to leave her readers with a good feeling, as in her own existence she had often idealized her environment, her home, and her husband in the optimistic tenor with which she lived her life. Perhaps as a reaction to the unhappy or, at least, less-than-ideal events of her own life, she wanted to create an ideal place. Certainly, it is a trait of her fiction that has endeared her to millions of readers.

Writing is a solitary profession, and isolation is an occupational hazard, especially as one ages and suffers old-age disabilities. But had Janice, in her quest to become a successful novelist in the "loneliest profession in the world" narrowed her world in necessary and self-enforced solitude? In poor health, Janice's beloved house-place eventually became her prison.

Family members were dead or lived far away; she had few friends. As I neared the end of my journey of writing about the life and career of a person I so greatly admired, I became bogged down in the valleys. Suddenly these valleys seemed to overshadow the beautiful vistas that had charactizerized Janice's earlier life, and I didn't want to follow the road to its natural and inevitably tragic end. I stopped writing. Just as she had wished for a happy ending for her beloved Willa Cather, I also wished one for her. I wished she could have been happier at the end of her life. I wanted her to have used the remains of her life "more quietly and contentedly." I wanted her to have known the literary significance of her work. I wanted her to have had the health and energy to enjoy her financial success. I can never know, of course, but I hope she met her death with the joy and peace in her heart that she so lovingly gave to her characters.

Admired and honored in her lifetime, Janice Holt Giles and her work continue to gain attention and serious study. Her artistic achievement was the result not only of significant talent but of her "rock-ribbed determination," courage, ambition, and endurance in the face of adversity. In her books she portrays regions of the American past with a finely honed precision that preserves their characters forever. She has given the permanence of art to nature and folklife and imbued it with goodness, valor, and human triumph.

Mark Twain once defined literature as consisting of those books that gain immortality, a length of time he estimated to be "about 30 to 35 years." Almost fifty years after its publication in 1950, *The Enduring Hills* is still in print. Indeed, more than half of her books are available in new editions for new generations of readers. Her original editions bring premium prices and are cherished by collectors of America's heritage. In the Giles ridge country, a thing that lasts is "enduring." Something very old is "forever and enduring." In the books that she wrote from her heart of what she had seen and felt and believed, Janice Holt Giles has surely claimed her "forever and enduring" niche in American literature. Her books are her timeless legacy.

Selected Bibliography

Published Works

BOOKS BY JANICE HOLT GILES

✓ *The Enduring Hills.* Philadelphia: Westminster Press, 1950.
✓ *Miss Willie.* Philadelphia: Westminster Press, 1951.
✓ *Tara's Healing.* Philadelphia: Westminster Press, 1951.
Harbin's Ridge. Boston: Houghton Mifflin Co., 1951.
40 Acres and No Mule. Philadelphia: Westminster Press, 1952.
✓ *The Kentuckians.* Boston: Houghton Mifflin Co., 1953.
✓ *The Plum Thicket.* Boston: Houghton Mifflin Co., 1954.
Hill Man. New York: Pyramid Books, 1954.
✓ *Hannah Fowler.* Boston: Houghton Mifflin Co., 1956.
✓ *The Believers.* Boston: Houghton Mifflin Co., 1957.
The Land Beyond the Mountains. Boston: Houghton Mifflin Co., 1958.
✓ *Johnny Osage.* Boston: Houghton Mifflin Co., 1960.
✓ *Savanna.* Boston: Houghton Mifflin Co., 1961.
Voyage to Santa Fe. Boston: Houghton Mifflin Co., 1962.
A Little Better than Plumb. Boston: Houghton Mifflin Co., 1963.
Run Me a River. Boston: Houghton Mifflin Co., 1964.
The G.I. Journal of Sergeant Giles. Boston: Houghton Mifflin Co., 1965.
The Great Adventure. Boston: Houghton Mifflin Co., 1966.
Shady Grove. Boston: Houghton Mifflin Co., 1967.
Six-Horse Hitch. Boston: Houghton Mifflin Co., 1968.
The Damned Engineers. Boston: Houghton Mifflin Co., 1970.
Around Our House. Boston: Houghton Mifflin Co., 1971.
The Kinta Years. Boston: Houghton Mifflin Co., 1973.
Wellspring. Boston: Houghton Mifflin Co., 1975.

SHORT WORKS BY JANICE HOLT GILES

"100 Years: History of Warren Memorial Presbyterian Church, 1848-1948." Louisville, Ky., 1948.
"Portrait." *Publishers' Weekly* 175 (Jan. 14, 1950): 147.
"Hill Writer." *Writers' Digest* 31, 8 (Feb. 1951): 18-21.
"Viva la Fiesta." *Louisville (Ky.) Courier-Journal Magazine,* Sept. 27, 1953, pp. 20-22.
"Tetch 'n Take." *Kentucky Writing* (Morehead [Ky.] State College) vol. 1 (1954): 116-29.
"Shop Talk." *Louisville (Ky.) Courier-Journal Magazine,* June 12, 1955, p. 2.

"The Gift." *Good Housekeeping* 144 (Jan. 1957): 64-65, 128-32. Reprinted as "The Gift of Love." *Australian Women's Weekly* 26, 5 (Sydney: July 9, 1958): 24-25, 45. Incomplete data on reprinting in *Mother* in Great Britain and translations in Danish, Norwegian, and Swedish.

"What I Owe to Libraries." *Murray (Ky.) Ledger and Times*, April 12, 1957, p. 4.

"Adios, Miss Em." *McCalls* 85 (Feb. 1958): 38-39, 120, 123-24, 126-27. Reprinted as "Just for the Summer." *Wife and Home* (Great Britain: Sept. 1958): 18-20, 22, 43-44. Incomplete data on Scandinavian and Dutch translations.

"The Edge of the World." *Woman's Day* (Nov. 1958): 34-35, 98-100.

"Autobiography." *The Register of the Kentucky Historical Society* 57 (April 1959): 144-50.

"Autobiographical Sketch." *Kentucky Library Association Bulletin* 23 (Jan. 1959): 12-13.

"When the 'Lectric Comes to the Ridge." *Kentucky Writing* (Morehead [Ky.] State College) vol. 4 (1963): 71-81.

"We must build, but . . . carefully." *Louisville (Ky.) Courier-Journal Magazine*, May 28, 1967, 11-12.

SHORTER WORKS PUBLISHED UNDER HENRY E. GILES

"The Sheriff Went to Cincinnati." *Ellery Queen's Mystery Magazine* 17, 88 (March 1951): 65-78.

"He Hates Cats." *Louisville (Ky.) Courier-Journal Magazine*, August 31, 1952, p. 12.

"Safety Locks, Block & Barrel." *Louisville (Ky.) Courier-Journal Magazine*, April 14, 1957, pp. 58-60.

COLUMNS BY JANICE HOLT GILES

"The Bookshelf." *Campbellsville (Ky.) News Journal*, August 16, 1954 to January 19, 1956.

"Around Our House." *Campbellsville (Ky.) News Journal*, January 26 to November 29, 1956.

NEWSPAPER COLUMNS BY HENRY E. GILES

"Spout Springs Splashes." *Adair County (Ky.) News*, 1957 to 1970.

Unpublished Works

Library Special Collections, Western Kentucky University, Bowling Green, Kentucky, houses the bulk of the extensive Janice Holt Giles Collection. A *Guide to Janice Holt Giles Collection* was compiled and edited by Patricia M. Hodges, 1991. The earliest papers and a smaller collection of Giles's material is located in the Margaret I. King Library, Division of Special Collections, University of Kentucky, Lexington, Kentucky.

BOOK MANUSCRIPTS BY JANICE HOLT GILES

"Out of My Heart." 1943.
"Elizabeth - Libby." 1943.
"My Darling Daughter." 1950.
"Act of Contrition." 1957.
"With Love, Grandma," later titled "Dear Boys." n.d.
"This Old House." n.d.
"The Mill Wheel," later titled "Cartwright's Mill." n.d.

MANUSCRIPT BY HENRY GILES

"Rode Hard and Put Up Wet: Autobiography of an Appalachian." 1966.

SHORT WORKS BY JANICE HOLT GILES

"Tack for Sist," also titled "Thanks for the Last Time." 1958.
"Smitty and the Betsey Bug." 1958.
"Saturday Night." 1958.
"The Civilized Girl." n.d.
"Deadline." n.d.
"Himmie Keeps the Boys." n.d.
"The Little Man with Pink Wings." n.d.
"The Minor Miracle." n.d.
"Tobacco Man." n.d.
Untitled (Income Taxes). n.d.
"Thanks for the Last Time." n.d.
Unpublished poetry. 1943-45.

Interviews by author

Bair, Billie, Fort Smith Public Library, Fort Smith, Ark., March 20, 1991.
Brooks, Paul. Telephone. Lincoln Center, Mass., March 17, 1997.
Caudle, Eileen. Telephone. First Christian Church, Frankfort, Ky., February 4, 1994.
Cosner, Marcella. Telephone. Roland, Okla., December 12, 1993, January 14, 1994.
Davison, Peter. Telephone. Houghton Mifflin, Boston, Mass., December 21, 1993.
Dixon, Wayne and Nancy. Knifley, Ky., October 18, 1994.
Dry, Connie. Telephone. Columbia, Ky., November 7, 1996.
Dunbar, John and Mary. Knifley, Ky., February 17, 1992.
Courtemanche-Ellis, Anne. Telephone. Harrison, Ark., December 21, 1993.
Elwes, Carolyn. Telephone. Park College, Parkville, Mo., February 4, 1994.
England, Marjorie. Telephone. Somerset, Ky., October 11, 1996.
Fish, Janice. Telephone. Atherton High School, Louisville, Ky., January 4, 1994.
Giles, Clifford. Knifley, Ky., March 2, 1994, October 18, 1994.

Giles, Elvin. Knifley, Ky., January 7, 1993.
Giles, Geneva Waggoner. Columbia, Ky., May 11, 1992.
Giles, Helen and Johnnie Lee. Knifley, Ky., March 25, 1990.
Giles, Kenneth. Telephone. Saint Thomas, Pa., February 19, 1994.
Giles, Robert. Greensburg, Ky., August 1, 1990.
Grant, Leland. Knifley, Ky., March 17, 1994.
Greer, Sharon. Knifley, Ky., October 18, 1994.
Hancock, Elizabeth Moore. Santa Fe, N.Mex., March 21, 22, 1991; Bowling Green, Ky., June 15, 1992, October 28, 1993; Louisville, Ky., October 24, 1996.
Hancock, Bartlett Neal. Santa Fe, N.Mex., March 22, 1991.
Hancock, John Graham "Mike." Santa Fe, N.Mex., March 22, 1991.
Hancock, James Scott. Santa Fe, N.Mex., March 22, 1991.
Harmon, Lee Ann. Columbia, Ky., August 10, 1989.
Hendrickson, Mary Lee Payne. Columbia, Ky., July 12, 1993.
Holcomb, James. Knifley, Ky., May 11, 1992.
Leitchhardt, Mitchell. Bowling Green, Ky., March 21, 1992.
Lowe, William Marshall "Buddy." Greensburg, Ky., February 17, 1992.
McCloud, Dale. Columbia, Ky., October 18, 1994.
McCloud, Evelyn.Numerous interviews. Columbia, Ky., 1991-98.
Moseley, Senator Doug. Telephone. Columbia, Ky., August 23, 1993.
Neal, Mary Julia. Bowling Green, Ky., August 24, 1982.
Nelson, Rev. Arnold. Telephone. Pulaski Heights Christian Church, Little Rock, Ark., February 4, 1994.
Pelly, Don. Telephone. Harrodsburg, Ky., July 17, 1991.
Pollard, Maxine. Eminence, Ky., January 21, 1994.
Phelps, Richard. Columbia, Ky., October 18, 1994.
Rabun, Corinne and Otway. Kinta, Okla., March 19, 1991.
Rector, Cora Mae Giles. Winchester, Ky., December 5, 1992.
Roper, Sheila. Telephone. Fort Smith High School, Fort Smith, Ark., January 4, 1994.
Roy, Lana. Summit Manor, Columbia, Ky., March 18, 1994.
Sanders, Annie. Creston, Ky., March 17, 1994.
Scott, Irene Giles. Pulaski, Tenn., August 16, 1990.
Skotzke, Shirley. Pulaski, Tenn., August 16, 1990.
Smith, Marilyn. Telephone. Public Library, Harrison, Ark., January 4, 1994.
Spires, Anthony. Bowling Green, Ky., May 4, 1989.
Spires, Joe. Knifley, Ky., January 7, 1993.
Spires, Opal and Rondel. Knifley, Ky., October 17, 1994.
Spires, Velma and William. Knifley, Ky., April 7, 1989; July 26, 1989.
Stein, Jeannette (Mrs. Jennings). Telephone. Fort Smith, Ark., January 4, 1994.
Stotts, Rosetta. Columbia, Ky., August 8, 1996.
Streeval, Edith and Ernest. Knifley, Ky., March 16, 1994.
Sullivan, Mary Holt. Fort Smith, Ark., June 2, 3, 1991.

Swan, Dana. Telephone. Haverford, Pa., August 22, 1995.
Vertrees, Sue Carol. Telephone. Rineyville, Ky., May 6, 1992.
Walker, Edith. Campbellsville, Ky., May 18, 1991.
Walker, Maxine. Columbia, Ky., October 18, 1994.
White, Ernest Miller. Louisville, Ky., November, 13, 1989.
Winebrenner, Toni Shelton. Telephone. Palm Bay, Fla., November 7, 1996.
Young, Kay. Pulaski, Tenn., August 16, 1990.

Index

Notes

chickens - p. 88

Botanical drawing - 92 & 180 & 183 & 193 195, 204

A writer's life challenge - 92

Plum Thicket - 97

Character study - 98

Focus on writing - 99

Writing - 102

" 104

237

God expects us to adjust, submit our sin nature, to His righteousness through Christ.

The world expects us Christians to submit our righteousness in Christ to their own sinfulness.

12-31-16

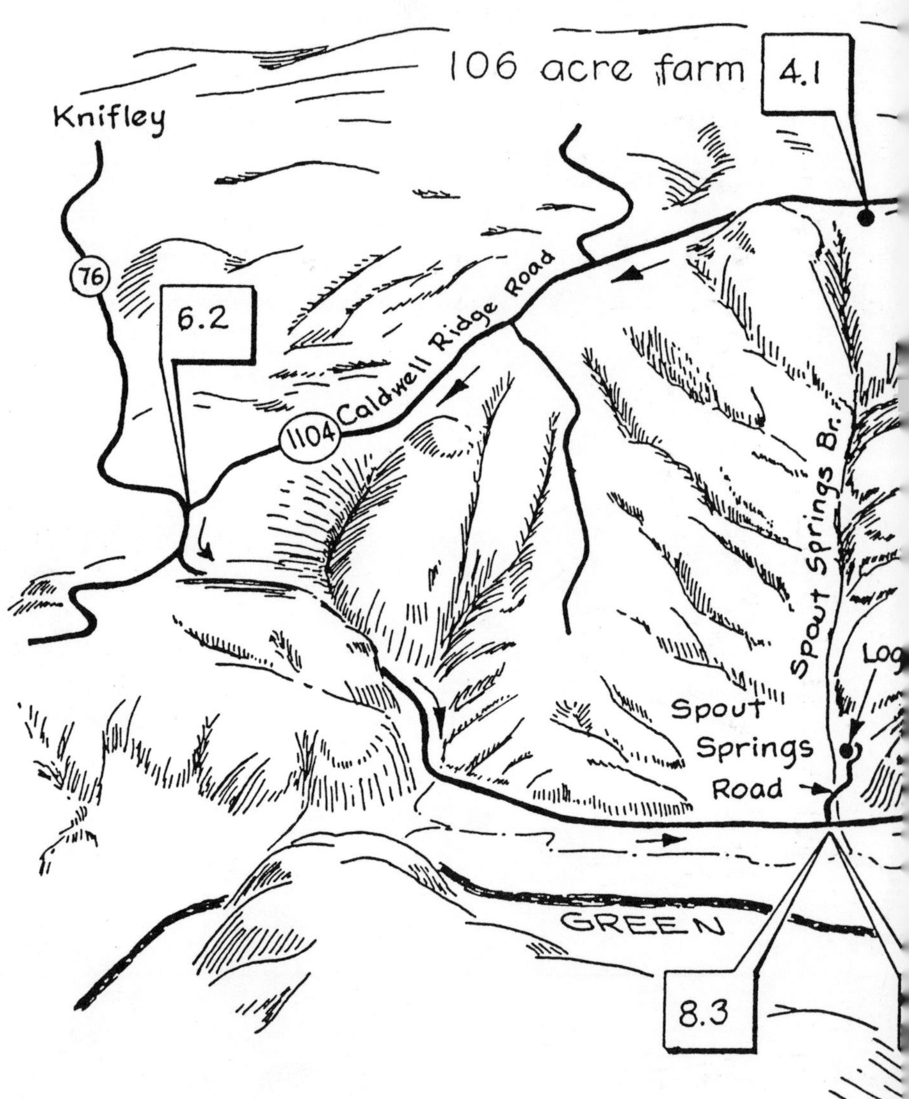
106 acre farm
4.1
Knifley
76
6.2
Caldwell Ridge Road
1104
Spout Springs Br.
Spout
Springs
Road
GREEN
8.3

Giles R